HACKSAW

The Jim Duggan Story

Hacksaw Jim Duggan
with Scott E. Williams

TRIUMPH
B O O K S

When it came time to dedicate this book, there was never a question: this is for my role models, my heroes, Celia Meadows Duggan and James Edward Duggan. My mom gave me my sense of family and sense of humor. My dad showed me throughout his life how to be a father. I have strived to be the parent that my parents were to me, not just by providing food and shelter but by offering love and understanding. In their spirit, I would also like to dedicate this book to my family: my wife, Debra, and our daughters, Celia and Rebecca.

This book is available in quantity at special discounts for your group or organization. For further information, contact:

Triumph Books LLC
814 North Franklin Street
Chicago, Illinois 60610
(800) 888-4741
Fax (312) 337-1807
www.triumphbooks.com

Printed in U.S.A.
ISBN: 978-1-62937-391-1
Design by Patricia Frey
Photos courtesy of the author unless otherwise indicated

CONTENTS

Chapter 1 Growing Up **1**

Chapter 2 College Days **9**

Chapter 3 My Life in Professional Football **15**

Chapter 4 My "Big" Break **21**

Chapter 5 Back in Georgia **31**

Chapter 6 Birth of a Hacksaw **41**

Chapter 7 Mid-South **49**

Chapter 8 Life with Dr. Death **69**

Chapter 9 Love Hits Me Like a 2x4 **77**

Chapter 10 The Sheik and I **99**

Chapter 11 (Prime) Time for a Comeback **113**

Chapter 12 A Rumble and a Giant Feud **127**

Chapter 13   Titusville   **137**

Chapter 14   The End of the Road   **149**

Chapter 15   WCW   **157**

Chapter 16   Mr. Saturday Night   **169**

Chapter 17   Fighting for My Life   **177**

Chapter 18   A Long Vacation   **191**

Chapter 19   Coming Back to the WW...E   **197**

Chapter 20   A Dark Day   **205**

Chapter 21   Family, Film Stars, and Community   **215**

Chapter 22   Hall(s) of Fame   **229**

Epilogue   **235**

CHAPTER 1

GROWING UP

IT ALL STARTED ON JANUARY 14, 1954, on a cold winter's night, in a little town in upstate New York. That night, James Edward Duggan Jr. joined a proud, working-class family that was headed by the two folks who would be my biggest influences and heroes—James and Celia Duggan.

My dad, James Edward Duggan Sr., had a career as a police officer that ultimately spanned 44 years. For the last 24 years of that career, he was the police chief of Glens Falls, New York, the town where I grew up.

Glens Falls was a very ethnic community—the French lived in the west, and the Italians were all up in the north end. The Irish, which included our family, lived in the east end of town near Saint Mary's Academy, where my dad had been a member of one of the school's first graduating classes. That was after the school relocated into a large building on Warren Street to accommodate growing student populations.

Ours was an industrial town, with a paper mill to the south of our home and a railroad to the north.

Dad worked two jobs, as a police officer and at a freight company, providing for his family and earning the money that would put my sisters through school, while Mom ran the house, with us kids. I was the fourth child in the family—I grew up with three older sisters, Mary Ann, Angel, and Sheila.

My mom, Celia, was born in Georgia and raised in Vero Beach, Florida. Later, she moved up to New York and married my dad. Believe it or not, it was a big scandal, because he was Catholic and she was Baptist.

1

Growing up was a great time—I often refer to it as "Mayberry," a place where our street had curbs, sidewalks, and trees, where we could play touch football and Red Rover. All the kids on both sides of Keenan Street, where my family lived, knew each other. It was just a great atmosphere, growing up. I know so many guys who had hard-luck stories from their childhoods, and some of them break my heart, but I had a great upbringing. We never had an awful lot, but we never were in need, or want, of anything. When one of us kids got a bike, it might be a used bike, but we never thought twice about it. I think we all knew, on some level, how hard our parents were working to make a home for us and to get us what we needed.

Even if there had been a problem in the neighborhood, my sisters were going to keep anything from ever hurting me. I still joke with them about it, how, since I was the youngest and the only boy, those girls carried me around like I was the Christ child—my feet never touched the ground! I was probably a little spoiled, to tell you the truth. Of course, they had a little fun with me, too. Our family had plenty of pictures of me as a small child, with my long hair, dressed up in the doll clothes my sisters had put on me.

We also had our share of pranksters in the neighborhood. On the far end of our block was an old abandoned place that kind of looked like the house from *The Addams Family*. The first time I was able to ride my tricycle all the way around the block, I got to the far end, when a gorilla jumped out of the bushes at me and let loose a really loud growl.

I screamed, "Aaaaahh!"

I started pedaling my little trike as hard as I could, screaming the whole way. Of course, there were at least 20 kids playing on our block at any given time, and they were out on my front porch when I rode up to the house, screaming, "It's a gorilla!"

Next thing you know, it was like a scene out of *Frankenstein*, with the whole neighborhood after this guy with pitchforks and torches. I ran into our house and all the way upstairs, where my dad was sleeping, screaming, "It's a gorilla! It's a gorilla!"

My mom came up, and Dad was trying to calm me down, but also asking me what happened.

"Were his clothes on?"

"Yeah, Dad," I said, "but it could be a circus gorilla."

They caught the guy, a young guy who lived down the road named Jim Beam (yes, just like the whiskey). My sisters read him the riot act.

"You go upstairs right now and apologize to him! You scared the devil out of him!"

I was in my room, with my feet dangling off the bed, and I had finally calmed down a little, when my door opened...and here came the gorilla!

"Aaaaahh!"

The guy pulled the mask off to show me he was just kidding around, saying, "Wait a minute! Wait a minute!"

I was just 13 or 14 when my dad became the police chief of Glens Falls. Of course, that meant that when I was a kid, I wasn't gonna be able to get away with anything. If I threw snowballs at someone, I could run and hide, but by the time I got to my house, the police cars would already be there, out in front.

"That's Duggan's kid, right there!"

They all knew me, so I was never able to get away with anything. Believe it or not, it wasn't really an issue, because I was a very, very straight kid, who didn't get into a lot of trouble. I was a Boy Scout, and I shoveled my neighbors' snowed-in driveways every winter.

That might be where some of the patriotic side of my wrestling persona comes from. I was always proud to be an American, and anyone who knows me can tell you I've always been a big John Wayne fan—always loved "The Duke." Of course, *The Quiet Man*, where John Wayne played an Irish-born boxer who returns home, was a big favorite in our Irish American household. For all I know, someone from my family might be in there—watch that movie, and you'll hear a song called "The Wild Colonial Boy," which was about an outlaw and contained the lyric, "And Jack Duggan was his name!"

Even though the Hacksaw Duggan that everyone knows looks like a far cry from that straight kid, the way my folks raised me has stayed with me.

To this day, I always try to be polite and courteous to folks, wherever I am. It's just the way I was raised.

Once, when I was 16 and had just gotten my driver's license, a Glens Falls cop stopped me for speeding. He told me he was taking me to the station, so I could talk to the captain.

I wanted to tell him, "But I already know the captain! Just give me the ticket!"

But I didn't. Of course, the officer and I knew each other. Glens Falls wasn't that big a town, and they only had 40 to 50 men on the force. I knew every one of them.

The officer took me to Captain Emerson, who told him to take me to Chief Duggan. We went into my dad's office, and my dad went *off!*

He barked, "Why'd you bring him here to me? Next time, give him a ticket, like you'd give anyone else a ticket!"

When the officer left, my dad turned to me and said, "Don't worry, I had to say all that for his benefit."

He knew these guys were trying to get one over on him, to see if he'd show favoritism to his son. He wasn't gonna let that happen, but as soon as they left, he changed right back into the supportive father I'd always been blessed with. He was comforting to me, because he saw I was devastated by the thought that I'd disappointed him.

My dad ran a tight ship—in his department, there were no sideburns below the ears and no mustaches over the lips. When the department was buying new cars and the officers asked for air conditioning, my dad said, "You know, we need air conditioning here about one month out of the year. Besides, ride around with your windows up, and you won't hear screams for help, you won't hear glass break."

As you might guess, he had a little heat with the union.

My sisters all graduated from Saint Mary's, and I went there until 10th grade. I played football, and when I wasn't playing, I was watching football pretty much every waking moment. I was a big Green Bay Packers fan, and loved Bart Starr, Jim Taylor, and Ray Nitschke.

But I gotta say, while I've had favorite players over the years, my biggest hero, my role model, was always my dad. I still remember him coming home, back when he was a detective, and he'd have this .38 snub nose, which I thought was really neat. To this day, I have a nice handgun collection, and I remember how my dad would talk about how important it was to be safe with any weapon. I started young, because I could basically get my ammunition for free, and Dad taught me how to shoot at the police firing range.

For me, football was big ever since I was a young kid. Back then, the practice field for the Saint Mary's football team was less than two miles from my house. Every day, the players would carry their cleats in their arms as they ran down to Maple Street and crossed the railroad tracks. All of us kids would wait for them and then carry their cleats and run with them the rest of the way. When I was little, that was a big deal for me, to be able to carry a player's cleats! Mrs. McKee, our next-door neighbor, would leave her garden hose running so the players could get a drink, if they needed one...but sometimes one coach would catch them and start yelling at them, "Hey! Get out of there! No one said you could drink!"

I was a big kid for my age, and I really loved football. My dad knew I might have a future, but Saint Mary's Academy was a very small school. Glens Falls High School was a major high school, and he pulled me out of Saint Mary's so that I would benefit from the bigger sports programs at Glens Falls High.

It really caused a big stir, because we all went to Saint Mary's Church, and I was going to be the first Duggan kid not to graduate from the academy there. My dad was a faithful Irish Catholic, and he and my mom had raised all us kids Irish Catholic. Dad was almost the perfect stereotype of the Irish cop, except that he didn't drink or smoke. He was a real straight shooter, and we were always at church, every single Sunday.

Playing at Glens Falls High meant getting more exposure and playing for a bigger team. There I met a football coach who would become one of my first mentors in athletics, Putt LaMay. He was a great coach, and when they built a new, fancy-dan stadium many years later in Glens Falls, they named it after him.

You'd never recognize me back then, because I was a real straight-arrow kid with very short hair, and when I first got to Glens Falls High, I stuck out like a sore thumb. At Saint Mary's, we had always worn uniforms, so I walked into Glens Falls High wearing a sports coat and tie. I got some funny looks!

All through school, I was never too hard to figure out. I had my family, my girlfriend (Tina Hopkins), and I played football, and if you didn't like it, we'd fight! Of course, it was a different time, and no one went to jail for that kind of thing back in the early 1970s.

My first year, I played football and then basketball in the fall, and in the spring, I ran for the track team. In my junior year, I joined the wrestling team. Everyone kept telling me how much bigger I was than anyone else in the school—at 16, I weighed 250 pounds. I had no idea about amateur wrestling technique, but we had a very good coach named Bob Carty. My first year, I won my section, but lost the first match of the state tournament. My senior year, I fared much better.

I ended up with 10 varsity letters—four in football, three in track, two in wrestling, and one in basketball.

Even though I played a lot of sports, I really focused on football, because I knew of the scholarship possibilities, and by this point, my dad was getting older. He was past the point where he could work all day as a cop, then work a shift at the freight yard, and then get by on a few hours of sleep before doing it all again. I knew that if I wasn't playing football, I'd probably be working in the paper mill.

I played many different positions, but my favorite was offensive line. I always thought of myself as the cavalry, as in, "They're trying to get the quarterback, but I'm gonna save him! Get off him!"

One of the hardest things about playing football for me was keeping my grades up enough to remain eligible. I just wasn't a great student; I struggled to keep a C average. A lot of that was that I just didn't like to study; it's not like I had a learning disability. But I did it. I stayed in school and stayed eligible the whole time.

And here's something you might find surprising about the ol' Hacksaw—I was in the chess club! I was actually pretty good, too, although I don't play as much now as I used to. Somewhere in one of my scrapbooks is a newspaper clipping about my signing with Southern Methodist University, with the headline "Chess-playing giant joins SMU." They had me photographed on one of those giant carpet chessboards with the big, life-sized pieces.

My senior year, my football team ended up playing an undefeated season and heading to Albany, to play Shaker High School, which was a giant, compared to our little school from upstate. And we won!

I guess it's my Irish blood, but I've always been an emotional guy—I laugh big when I laugh, I pray, I swear, and I cry when I'm sad. I wear my emotions on my sleeve, which is why I'm such a bad card player. As I left the stadium after that last, big game, the tears just started coming down.

My senior year was a good year in wrestling for me, too. I won conference in my weight class (unlimited, for guys who weighed more than 215—and, remember, I weighed about 250), and that year, I became the first guy from Glens Falls to win a state championship in *any* weight class. The finals were close—I won state by one point. It was a three-day tournament in Syracuse, and while my parents were there for the whole thing, I noticed that every day, as I kept winning, more and more folks from Glens Falls showed up.

I could hear them, in the stands, cheering for "Moose Duggan!"

To this day, if I'm out somewhere and hear, "Hey, Moose," I know it's someone from Glens Falls. It was just a nickname that stuck—when I signed to play college football at SMU, in Dallas, the Glens Falls paper's headline was "The Moose Is Loose in Texas."

CHAPTER 2

COLLEGE DAYS

BEING A "DOUBLE THREAT" IN FOOTBALL AND WRESTLING in 1972 really increased my value to colleges, and I got enough letters from schools that I made seven recruiting trips, which would be unheard of today because of changes to the NCAA rules about recruitment. I eventually settled on Southern Methodist.

SMU was actually my first recruiting trip. The school sent its offensive line coach, Bob Cuthbert, up to Glens Falls, where most folks had never seen anything like him. He was walking around this little town in upstate New York with a big Stetson hat and cowboy boots—he was a walking cliché of Texas.

Coach Cuthbert stayed a few days and watched me practice, and he and my mom hit it off right away. When I went to visit SMU, I had never even been on an airplane before, had never really been far from home, at all. It was like a whole new world.

When I landed in Dallas, I got off the plane wearing my trusty sports coat and tie. Cuthbert was waiting for me at the airport with the student who was going to be my host while I was there—a little SMU quarterback named Tully Blanchard. Unfortunately, the partying that would appeal to a lot of kids was not for the straight-arrow kid I was back then.

They told me, "We're gonna go out, get some beer, get some girls."

I said, "Well, I got my girlfriend at home, and I don't drink beer."

I could see them looking at me, like, "What the hell is going on with this guy?"

9

I guess it worked out—they dropped me off at the hotel and then went off to party without me!

By the time I was choosing a school, I had also visited Ohio State, Penn State, Kentucky, Syracuse, Rhode Island, the University of New Mexico, and Iowa State. The trips were designed to impress students, and I got to meet Woody Hayes at Ohio State and Joe Paterno at Penn State. The recruiters found me pretty easy to deal with, because just like at SMU, I wasn't looking to be taken out for a big, fancy-dan night out. All they had to do was drop me off at my room until it was time to go to the school for the big sales pitch.

At Ohio State, the offensive line coach took me onto the stadium field, had me standing right in the big "O" for "Ohio State."

"Okay," he said, getting louder and more worked up as he went. "It's the fourth quarter! There's a minute left, and we've got the ball!"

He kept firing situations at me as we ran down the field.

"It's third down and one, and we're going for it!"

By the time we got to the goal line, he had me all fired up!

He said, "It's fourth down! There's five seconds left to go for the national championship! We're gonna run the ball! We're gonna run it over you! *Are you gonna make the block?*"

I screamed at the top of my lungs, "Yes, sir, Coach! I'll make the block!"

I was hooked. When I got home, I told my parents I was going to Ohio State. My mom softly said, "Well, now wait a minute..."

She and my dad wanted me to consider SMU, because, as they put it, at Ohio State, I'd just be a number. SMU, on the other hand, *really* wanted me, and I knew that at a smaller school like SMU, I had a better chance of being able to start on the football team as a freshman. Just a couple of years earlier, the NCAA had changed the rules to allow freshmen to play. I knew going to Ohio State or Penn State would mean I wouldn't be able to play varsity right away. Instead, I'd be sitting on the bench for a year, maybe two.

On my signing date, I had people from Penn State, Kentucky, Ohio State, and SMU at our house. I felt really bad, because I really had liked Kentucky, and I hated turning anyone down. These were schools where people had treated me awfully nice, showing me around campus, being nice to my family, and I now had to tell all but one of them, "I'm really sorry, but I can't come."

The college reps were in the living room, and we called them into the kitchen, one by one, to tell them. I actually cried when we were turning down Kentucky.

"I'm so sorry," I said, with tears streaming down my face. "I feel really bad."

Penn State was a different story, because one of the coaches, John Nolan, had coached at Saint Mary's Academy, right there in Glens Falls. Nolan seemed really pissed, probably because he had figured his background at Saint Mary's meant he had me locked up. If anything, it might have worked against him, because I'd had him as a coach at Saint Mary's my freshman year and I didn't like him. Even at that age, I understood the difference between a good coach and a great coach. Putt LaMay had been a great coach. Nolan was a good coach, but he was also a bully, and I don't like bullies. Never have.

Remember the story about Mrs. McKee leaving her hose on for the Saint Mary's players? Nolan was the coach who would yell at them for taking a drink.

The Ohio State guy's reaction showed me that my parents were right—that school did not value me as an individual who could be an asset. He said, "Hey, it's okay—we'd win with you, and we'll win without you."

Now, I completely understand what my parents were saying, because my wife and I just went through the exact same thing with our older daughter, Celia. She was weighing scholarship offers from several different schools.

Any lingering doubts I might have had about my decision vanished the first time I walked into the SMU locker room as a player. The whole place was first-rate, with big wooden lockers, padded seats, and great facilities, way beyond anything I'd known at Glens Falls.

We played our conference games in the Cotton Bowl and nonconference games in Texas Stadium. I first walked onto those fields during my SMU recruiting trip, and it was like entering another world for this big kid from the little town in upstate New York. I still have the picture of me shaking Coach David Smith's hand, while the Texas Stadium scoreboard was lit up with "SMU welcomes Jim Duggan" in the background.

My family support stayed as strong as ever, even though geography separated us. My first big game in Texas, we played Texas Tech. My parents were there to see it, and knowing they were coming to see it had me so pumped up that I had maybe the best game I ever played. The newspaper headline in Dallas the next day read, "Duggan Shows Off for Folks."

Even though they lived on the opposite end of the country, my parents attended a lot of my games at SMU. Once, during a game against Texas A&M, I took a hit and ended up with a hip pointer, an injury that's a lot more painful than it sounds. It's basically a pelvic bruise caused by a hard impact to the hip bone.

I was in so much pain, but of course, I had that tough-guy mentality of "never be carried off the field," so I got up and tried to make it off the field under my own power. I made it as far as the sideline before I went down.

The doctors and trainers were working on me, cutting off my shoulder pads, when, all of a sudden, I heard a voice that kept getting louder...

"Jim! Jimmy! *Jimmy!*"

God bless her, my mom had come all the way down to see how I was.

I managed to gurgle out, "I'm okay, Mom. Please go away. I'm okay."

I went home to Glens Falls every summer and worked as a fireman. I enjoyed it enough that I probably would have ended up doing it for a living, had I not gone into wrestling. As much as I loved my dad, I knew I didn't want to be on the police force. I just couldn't see myself wearing those white police gloves and directing traffic around the town square.

I started off driving the fire chief's car, a big white station wagon with a siren on top. Glens Falls had two fire stations—the newer one was on Broad Street, a one-floor building that almost looked like something out of that old TV show *Car 54, Where Are You?* The other station, on Ridge

Street, had two stories and looked like a classic firehouse, with three poles, dorms, and a little living area upstairs.

I'm embarrassed to admit it now, but a few times, I had my girlfriend, Tina, call in false alarms just so I could drive the chief's car around town with that siren blaring! Tina, if you're reading this, it's okay—the statute of limitations ran out years ago. I'm *pretty* sure it did, anyway.

Later, I rode on the back of a pumper truck. I had to drag the hose to the hydrant, and then the truck would take off, so I had to get the hose hooked up to the hydrant, quick!

Once I was going by the fire station, not even on duty, when I saw the trucks taking off. I ran in and grabbed my gear. The fire was at a restaurant, a big building, and by the time we got there, it was fully ablaze.

Captain Jim Shine told me, "Kid, grab an inch-and-a-half line and hit that back door," so I grabbed the hose, ran around to the back, and kicked in the door. Everything in there was on fire, so I opened the hose and waited for the water to flow through from the pumper.

All of a sudden, the water came blasting out, and as soon as it did, between the steam and the smoke, I couldn't see *anything*. I had my head down, close to the nozzle, and I thought I was doing a hell of a job, spraying down the interior of the place, so I turned the hose to the ceiling.

Outside, the other firefighters were looking at the part of the building where I was, going, "Did a water main break? What's that water shooting up?"

The ceiling was gone! I was firing my hose straight up, into the air. I really thought I was doing a hell of a job, knocking that fire down.

Another time, I scared the hell out of a lady who had called after smelling smoke in her house.

The department always told us to grab something when we were coming off the truck, because we never knew what we'd need for any given emergency. When we reached the house, I grabbed a great big axe and jumped off the truck.

She took one look at this big kid, charging her house with an axe, and was probably more scared of what I might do to her fine china than of the smoke she smelled.

She yelled, "No, no! It's okay!"

Between growing up as a police chief's son and my time as a firefighter, I have a lot of respect for the guys who do those jobs, putting themselves on the line every day for the other folks in their communities. To this day, a lot of my friends are in law enforcement, and whenever I go into an arena, I'll go and talk to the cops there. There's a real sense that they're all a kind of extended family, which is only natural when you're trusting the guys around you with protecting your life.

My senior year, I had some injury problems, including a broken wrist I got playing against Wilson Whitley, a defensive tackle with the University of Houston. Whitley went into the College Football Hall of Fame in 2007, and during that game, more than 30 years earlier, he tore me up. The next day, the Dallas paper was not as flattering as it had been for my great performance against Texas Tech. This time, the story read, "Whitley goes through Duggan like a revolving door."

But even the injury couldn't end my streak; I played every game from the third game of my freshman season all the way through the end of my collegiate career.

I was also proud of winning SMU's Mike Kelsey Award, for "giving 110 percent effort." Kelsey had joined the SMU Ponys in 1959 as an outstanding freshman player. Sadly, he died in 1962 after suffering heat stroke during practice. But SMU remembers him to this day as a player who never gave less than all-out effort. SMU even put up a slogan over the passage coming out of the locker room, reminding players of the "110-percent Kelsey rule."

CHAPTER 3

MY LIFE IN PROFESSIONAL FOOTBALL

THE ATLANTA FALCONS HELD THEIR TRAINING CAMP at Furman University, in Greenville, South Carolina. The first time I went there, flying in from Albany, the plane stopped two or three times. I noticed that at every stop, bigger and bigger guys were getting on the plane.

Going to training camp was a dream come true. I had always dreamed of playing football, and here I was with the Atlanta Falcons. I didn't know my dream would be ending shortly.

Near the end of preseason training, I got hurt during a practice on an extra-point play. I was in a big pile of players, and I tore the ACL in my right knee. I went to a hospital in Atlanta, where I had knee surgery. After that, I was in a full leg cast for about six weeks. I stayed in Atlanta because I was eager to get back to active duty with the Falcons. As soon as I got the cast off I started rehabbing my knee, but it was too much, too soon, and the ligament just disintegrated. I just went down in a heap. I had to go back for a second surgery on that same knee.

When the knee recovered enough for me to move around, but not yet enough to return to active play with the Falcons, I went to Dallas and started working at a freight yard, which is a backbreaker of a job. I never minded hard work, but this was unreal, and to this day, I have a lot of respect for the guys who do that kind of work, because it is *tough*.

I knew that I did not want to make this dock my home, so I decided to give Fritz Von Erich a call.

I had met Fritz while I was on my initial recruiting trip to SMU; it was just a chance encounter. He had told me that with my size, I'd be a natural for pro wrestling. He asked me to think about it whenever I was done with football. I said, "Sure," but in the back of my mind, I was entirely focused on playing football in college and professionally.

Fritz (and more specifically, referee David Manning) trained me in the basic mechanics of wrestling, and Gary Hart, one of the top managers in the area, actually gave me my first pair of trunks, red and black. My first matches were in the old Sportatorium, this corrugated-tin building that was not exactly in one of the nicer parts of town.

Most wrestling fans know the tragic history of the Von Erichs; of his six kids, the only one to outlive Fritz was Kevin. I have no personal complaints about the Von Erichs, because they always treated me well, but there's no question that those boys (except for Jackie, who died in an accident when he was six) got the proverbial too much, too soon, of anything they wanted. I think that excess played a big role in their deaths. We used to drive around on their property, shooting off shotguns. It was a lot of fun, but each one of the kids had his own house at age 17, plus three or four cars. They were good-hearted people, but I think there was a lot of denial about the problems brought on by too much, too soon.

But while they were headlining, the Von Erich boys were so popular that when I tell people who weren't around to see it what it was like, they don't believe me. Kerry was just awesome—he had this tanned body with a physique like Hercules (I mean the Hercules of myth, not the guy I feuded with in Mid-South, although he was built, too). Bad guys would make fun of his "horse face," but that didn't keep girls from swarming him. The people in the Dallas area loved that entire clan, but there was something special about Kerry.

Toward the end of my time in Dallas, I got a call that hit me harder than any injury. My mom, just 65, had suffered a minor heart attack one that nowadays they could have detected and probably treated.

The first call from home, I was told that Mom had a minor attack but that the doctors thought she'd be okay. Later the same day, I got another call, telling me I needed to get home, right away. She'd had another attack, one much more serious.

I flew into Albany, the closest airport to Glens Falls, where my brother-in-law, Bill, met me. He told me I was too late—Mom had passed away. I was devastated, losing not only my biggest supporter, but someone I loved more than I can even describe. I couldn't completely process the news at first, because I couldn't imagine her not being around, when she'd always been such a huge part of my life. My sisters felt the same, as we'd all been very close. It was a dark time, not just for me, but for the entire family, but we got through it the way we'd always get through things, by pulling together.

I eventually headed back to Dallas, to resume wrestling training and work toward my return to football. It seemed to take forever for my knee to heal.

Once I left Dallas, I never came back to Fritz's group to wrestle, except for maybe an odd show here or there (like, in 1984–85, when he and Bill Watts shared some talent and co-promoted a little), but one thing I'll never forget is that distinctive Sportatorium aroma. It wasn't nasty, just this strange blend of smoke, beer, people, and sweat, plus something I can't quite identify (or maybe I just don't want to).

With my knee fully recovered, I went back to the Falcons, ready to play. Being a naïve kid, I didn't realize that I had become a liability to the team. As an offensive guard, I wasn't head and shoulders above anyone else, the way I had been in high school and college. The Falcons could replace me without missing a beat, and they were about to do just that.

I was in my room at training camp, when one of the assistant coaches knocked on the door and told me that our coach, Leeman Bennett, wanted to see me.

I was excited, thinking the coach was going to talk about the team's plans for me now that I was mobile again.

But then, the assistant coach said, "Bring your playbook."

Boom! It hit me like a hammer. I told the coach that I'd be right there, but I just sat at the foot of my bed for a few minutes, because I knew what "bring your playbook" meant. It meant I wouldn't be needing it anymore.

Being cut from the Falcons was one of the most devastating moments in my life. I had always thought I would be playing in the NFL for many, many years. I had always been good at it, and I think a person can't help but like something he or she is good at. And for me, being good at football got me recognition, which I enjoyed, and I enjoyed the competition. I always enjoyed that. If anything, I've been *too* competitive, my whole life.

And now, it was over. I couldn't believe it was happening to me. I had never planned on a life without football.

Furman University had a traffic circle, a little circular roadway, and I must have driven around that thing for hours after leaving camp. I was despondent. I didn't know whether to go back to Glens Falls, or to my little efficiency apartment in Atlanta, or back to Dallas, where most of my friends now were.

One more note about the Falcons, just one of life's weird coincidences. At training camp, my roommate was June Jones, then the backup quarterback. As of 2011, he is now head coach at SMU!

In the end, I went back to Dallas to resume my pro wrestling training. I had done two or three days of training with David Manning, a referee with Fritz's outfit, when I got a call from the Toronto Argonauts, a Canadian Football League team, saying they could use an offensive guard. I still don't know how they knew where I was. I guess it was kind of like the independent wrestling circuit—they just know where to find you.

I flew up to Toronto to meet with the coach, who in 1979 was Forrest Gregg. Coach Gregg was a football graduate of SMU and had coached for the Cleveland Browns, among others.

Playing Canadian football is very different from what Americans are used to seeing. They play under a three-down system, not four. I was on the punt team, and one time I was on the sideline, looking at the pretty cheerleaders, because I figured we had one more down before they needed me. Suddenly, the coach grabbed me and screamed, "Duggggggaaaaaannnnn!"

I'd forgotten that the punt had to happen on third down, because there *was* no fourth down!

Plus, as an American, I was on every special team there was—extra point, field goal, punt, punt return, kickoff, kickoff return, you name it. The reason was there was a limit on how many Americans could be on a team (a team could only have 15 Americans), and so they had to get the most out of each of us.

That same "American limit" ended up putting me off the team before I'd even finished my first season. Just days after I'd played my best Canadian game yet, against the Hamilton Tiger-Cats, I got called into the coach's office. I figured we were going to talk about extending my contract, since I'd just had such a strong performance.

Just like with the Falcons, I was wrong about why the coach wanted to see me. He told me that they were bringing in an American halfback to replace the Canadian halfback they had just lost, which would make 16 Americans on the team. The guard behind me on the depth chart was Canadian, and in practice, I was just barely beating him out, so they were going to give him my spot, bring in the American halfback, and then wish me well in my future endeavors.

This time, I had a little less uncertainty to deal with, because I knew after this that I had no more real future in football. I knew I wasn't cut out for being a coach, and my options for playing had just run out. That great game against the Hamilton Tiger-Cats ended up being the last football game I ever played.

I headed back to Glens Falls, trying to figure out my next move. Not long after, the World Wide Wrestling Federation came to town to put on a local show and changed my life forever.

CHAPTER 4

MY "BIG" BREAK

ARNOLD SKAALAND, ONE OF THE GUYS WHO RAN THE SHOWS for WWWF owner Vincent J. McMahon, was acquainted with my dad, and my dad told him I had wrestled a little for Fritz in Texas.

Skaaland told my dad to bring me down to the show. I had my pair of red-and-black trunks that Gary Hart had given me and a gold bathrobe, I was clean-shaven with my short haircut, and I came out for my hometown debut, in the Glens Falls Civic Center, against a guy named Moose Moroski.

I'll always remember Skaaland, not just as the guy who gave me my big break but as a true gentleman and quite a character. When Skaaland was running the arena shows, you'd find out who was winning your match by catching him backstage, where he'd be playing cards. He'd give a thumbs up or thumbs down, and pretty much left the particulars to the guys in the match.

The WWWF at that point was a regional promotion, based in the Northeast, not the worldwide powerhouse that WWE is today. Back then, it seemed like I was wrestling in the first or second match each night, against either Jose Estrada or Johnny Rodz. Boy, those guys hated wrestling me, because I had no idea what I was doing.

I also got in the ring with Angelo Mosca, a Canadian football player turned wrestler and a tough, tough guy. While I can honestly say I never got stretched (where a guy who knows legitimately painful holds clamps one on you and makes it hurt) in the wrestling business, Mosca was pretty rough on me. I didn't get it at first, but when I had a couple of years' experience,

I realized he was trying to send me a message about not working too stiff with guys like Rodz and Estrada, which I'd done simply because I didn't know what I was doing in the ring. At the time, I took my lumps from Mosca and thought, *Oh, the guy's just missing the mark*. But he wasn't, and although it took a couple of years, I ended up appreciating what Mosca was trying to teach me.

Rodz and Estrada didn't really teach me much, but that wasn't what they were there to do. They were just trying to survive working with the big green guy. Throughout my career, I never was much of a finesse guy. Once, a reporter asked me what my favorite move was, and I said, "Hmm, it's either the kick or the punch—I mean, that's pretty much it."

I did mix in power moves early on, and had the big spear and clothesline finishers, but you weren't coming to a Hacksaw Duggan match to see me apply a variety of complicated takedowns and variations on the figure-four leg lock. Later on, after I'd had my knee surgeries (two on each knee), my lack of mobility cut down even more on the number of moves I would do, but I was always primarily a brawler and power guy.

By 1980, when I was starting out in the WWWF, my wrestling experience was very limited. I had trained for a couple of months in Texas, and worked a few matches over the next couple of months. Aside from learning the mechanics of wrestling, the biggest impact on my life there had been a friend I had made, a wrestler named Gino Hernandez. Gino was a hell of a performer, and a very flamboyant personality. The other boys either loved him or hated him, but I took a liking to him right away. Gino had the world on a string. He was very handsome, and girls loved him.

He seemed to take a liking to me, as well. Gino even took me in when I was first starting out in Texas. Coming from a football background, where star players are kind of catered to, I didn't fully appreciate at the time how big a deal it was for a guy in Gino's position as a top guy to take a rookie like me and say, "Come and stay with me, and I'll show you the ropes."

My first match had been with Gino as a tag partner. His scheduled partner didn't show, and they asked me if I had my gear. I did. I also had a mustache, but no beard. I spent most of the match on the ring apron, twirling my mustache. Gino kept coming back to the corner and yelling, "Stop that!"

I couldn't help it. I was so nervous; in football, I was 50 yards away from the fans, and I had 10 other guys around me, plus shoulder pads and a helmet. Now, I was five feet away from these people, wearing short-shorts and patent leather boots. I felt naked! It was quite an adjustment.

Training for wrestling was different from training for competitive sports. Even now, I disagree with some trainers, including guys I always liked personally, like Bill DeMott, whom I worked with in WCW, and Steve Keirn, whom I've known for 30 years. These guys conduct classes, and they've got the students doing squats, running miles, doing 100 pushups at a time. You think Earthquake (John Tenta) could have done any of that? Kamala (James Harris)? Even Hulk Hogan? The big powerhouses in our business can't do that stuff, and that kind of training is driving away an entire segment of wrestlers, which adds to people's No. 1 complaint about today's wrestlers, which is that they're all cookie-cutter. They all have lean, muscular bodies, and they all have tattoos.

Promoters used to think in terms of variety, aiming to have a little something for everyone. Now, it's almost like watching a series of clones. And in the ring, they have the mechanics down pat—they can execute the moves down to a T—but the wrestlers have become the biggest marks of all. It's like they believe their own hype.

Let me take a step back and talk about the term "mark," which I hate. It's usually used to describe fans, but it's such a derogatory term, associated with someone who's being scammed. I never looked at it that way. I always felt I was giving a performance, and the fans were paying for that performance, just like the folks who go to see a play on Broadway. I never saw the fans as marks, and I'm sorry to use that term here.

Anyway, the wrestlers of today who concern me are the ones who come back to the locker room, and the other guys tell them, "Wow, that was a great match! Those moves were great!"

I'm usually sitting in the back, thinking, *Yeah, they were beautifully executed, and the crowd sat on their hands the whole time you were doing them.*

Meanwhile, I go out there and holler out a big "HO-OH!" Everyone in the place goes, "HO-OH!" And by doing that one shout, I've gotten the crowd more involved than I would have by doing bump after bump after bump, with none of the bumps making any sense in terms of the story of the match we're doing.

But in 1980, I was yet to discover the "HO-OH!" I was just a big kid in a gold bathrobe. And Gino Hernandez taking me and showing me around really was huge. Heck, even being let into the business was a big thing, and looking back, I think it shows that Fritz, David Manning, Gino, and everyone involved in training me and working with me early must have seen something in me, because wrestling back then was an incredibly tight-knit fraternity that was closed to almost everyone. Those guys weren't going to let just anyone into that brotherhood, and I know that sounds corny, but a brotherhood is exactly what it was.

It was a few years before I even appreciated the magnitude of what Fritz Von Erich did for me by bringing me into the business. I had never been a wrestling fan growing up; I had never even watched a match. I just had no conception of professional wrestling.

Whatever ideas my sisters might have had about pro wrestling probably all went out the window the first time I came home for a visit, after becoming "Hacksaw" Duggan, around 1982. I walked into the family home, with my bandana, beard, and long hair, and my sisters cried. They just couldn't believe what the straight-laced, short-haired kid they knew and loved had turned into. Of course, I was still me underneath this drastically different look, and they seemed to accept the outward changes a little more when they realized their kid brother was still in there, but it was an adjustment for them.

I can still hear them: "Jimmy, what have you *done*, Jimmy?"

I'd come home to support my dad, who was fighting stomach cancer. That tough old Irish cop beat the odds, but it was a fight. And when I first showed up and saw the reactions of people I'd grown up around to the "Hacksaw" look, it was one of only two times in my life that I became very self-conscious of how I looked.

It wasn't just the folks I'd known growing up, either. When I went to the hospital to see my pop, I saw police chiefs who had come from all over the state to show their support for my dad. Here was Jim Duggan Sr., a small-town police chief, and the clout and respect he had was amazing. He knew guys from all over, from the years he had spent working with the New York State Association of Chiefs of Police. It was great to see them supporting my pop, but I admit a few of them did give me some strange looks.

When I walked into the room to see my dad after he came out of surgery, a bunch of them were staring, and even though they didn't say anything, it was like I could read their minds: *"That's* Jim Duggan's son?"

It made sense—they knew Chief Jim Duggan Sr. as a man who ran a tight ship, a department where officers couldn't even have sideburns below their ears!

But my dad, God bless him, was always very supportive, even the first time he saw me with the long hair and the beard. He was never anything but 100 percent in my corner throughout my entire life, and that's a big part of the reason why he was and is my greatest hero, and the best friend I ever had.

I did a few arena shows as a preliminary guy, but the first thing of any real significance I did was to participate in Sgt. Slaughter's cobra clutch challenge. They were building up Sarge's finisher, the cobra clutch, as a deadly submission hold, and Slaughter went on TV to challenge any wrestler to try to escape the hold. I was one of the guys who went on TV and gave it a shot.

They'd set up a chair in the middle of the ring, and I sat down. Sarge came up behind me and put on the hold. I kicked and fought and eventually went dead.

While he was a vicious villain on wrestling shows, off camera, Sarge tried to teach me some things about wrestling. We got to be good friends, although we competed at everything. Once, we were driving to the next town when I saw a bowling alley.

I said, "That's it, Slaughter! We're gonna go bowlin'!"

We played two games, at a few bucks a game, and I beat him pretty good, so for the third game, the bet went way up. Sarge goes up for the first frame of the third game, and he was about to grab the ball with his left hand, like he had the first two games, but stopped, as if he had just remembered something important.

He smiled and said, "Oh, yeah! I'm *right*-handed!"

He drilled me. Yep, Sgt. Slaughter hustled me, in bowling.

Another guy I learned a lot from, about a year later, was Steve Keirn. Steve was a star in Georgia in 1981, wrestling on Superstation TBS, and was one of the first guys in Georgia to battle "Big" Jim Duggan, as I was known then.

Before the match, Steve told me, "Kid, whatever you do, don't give me a backdrop. I can't take a backdrop today." This green rookie looked at the veteran and said, "Yes, sir!"

I got out there and gave him all four of the moves I knew, and then I just froze for an instant, because I had no idea what to do next. I panicked and whipped him into the ropes, for, yes, a backdrop!

He kicked me so friggin' hard, he almost knocked my head off!

Steve and I still joke about it, and even though we're friends, all these years later, I'll goof around with him. When they had WrestleMania XXIV in Orlando in 2008, I saw Steve, as we were both in the upper decks of the stadium. The guardrail keeping folks from falling onto the lower deck was only chest-high, so when I saw Keirn talking to some young guy, I walked by and grabbed him, acting like I was going to throw him over.

He yelled, "Whoa!"

Then he saw it was me, and we laughed a little.

I thought it was pretty funny. Of course, my daughters were with me, and I had embarrassed them, but Keirn came up to me and said, "You got great timing, Duggan!"

"What do you mean?"

"You know what that guy was asking me? He was asking if he could marry my daughter!"

I said, "Well, hell, Steve, I was doing you a favor, then!"

I worked in Georgia (and a year later, in San Antonio) as a heel, which is what we call a villain in the wrestling business. Although I spent the majority of my career as the people's hero, I really didn't mind being a bad guy, especially once I understood the power the heel had over the people.

I mean, all the bad guy has to do is act annoyed by something a fan says, and by doing that, he pretty much guarantees that the entire crowd will be chanting it at him, which was what he really wanted in the first place. I also thought it was kind of funny that for a bad guy, the whole place can be booing him, and he just loves it. But for a good guy, or babyface, all it takes is for one fan to go, "Boo!," and it makes the babyface say, "Hey! Come on, buddy, I got feelings, too!"

Of course, there are always heel fans, and it's just something you have to be ready for.

But I'm getting ahead of myself. Come to think of it, even talking about Georgia is getting ahead of myself, because after a few months in the WWWF, Arnie Skaaland came to me and told me that he wanted to send me elsewhere, to gain some seasoning.

"Kid," he said, "you might have a future in this business, but you're going to need to come up with something better than 'Big' Jim, and that gold bathrobe has got to go!"

But Skaaland wasn't simply turning me loose; he had talked to a friend of his who was a big name in the business, Peter Maivia, who was willing to take me on with his promotion in Hawaii.

A tough Samoan, "High Chief" Peter Maivia had been a big star in the 1960s and 1970s, and he indirectly gave us one of the biggest stars ever, his grandson, Dwayne Johnson, better known as The Rock.

But when Skaaland told me where he was sending me, I wasn't thinking of Maivia's toughness, or even what I might learn there. All I could think was that I had won the friggin' lottery!

"Hawaii? Yes!"

I packed the little bags that were all I needed to carry what little I owned, and I got on a plane. When I got to Hawaii, someone from the promotion picked me up and took me to a little motel where I'd stay for my Hawaiian stint—the Chateau Blue, in downtown Honolulu.

Years later, I took my wife, Debra, there while we were vacationing on the island. We reached the spot where the motel had been, and she looked around and wouldn't even get out of the car.

It was a rough section of town, even back in 1980. There were pimps, prostitutes, mostly island people, and this little motel sat in the middle of it.

I hooked up with a couple of wrestlers there named Pete Austin and Mike Masters. Pete's gotten out of the business, but I still see Mike on the independents every now and then up in New York.

We all lived in this one-room motel apartment, and our coffee table was my hard suitcase. We made $40 a week, and my family would send us over peanut butter and crackers. More than once, we ate so much pineapple that our lips would burn.

In terms of working with a variety of guys, the great thing about Hawaii was that everybody loved the High Chief, and back then, Japan got some of the top American wrestlers to do regular tours. On the way back, they'd stop over in Hawaii and work big shows for Peter Maivia. So once a month, The Wild Samoans, then one of the top tag teams in the world, would come through, and every time they did, they'd take us lower-level guys out and buy us a steak! It was just about the only time we ever had meat!

Our other major source of sustenance was a Chinese buffet located near the motel. They hated us—three big wrestlers getting the most out of the words "all you can eat"!

Even though we were almost always broke, it was a fun time in my life. We worked on Waikiki, and played on one of the beaches where locals went, not tourists. We'd run on the beach to Waikiki, and I'd dyed my hair blond. I'm not saying I was a gorgeous-looking guy, but I was young, in shape, and we'd find girls from Iowa, or Missouri, looking for a good time on vacation.

Hawaii was also the place where I had my first exposure to marijuana. Maui-wowie! I also started drinking a little.

But you won't find many records of Jim Duggan wrestling there during this period. In Hawaii, I wrestled under a mask and was billed as The

Convict. I started out with a basic mask, but, like every young guy, I was trying to figure out a way to stand out. What I came up with was to put the initial "C" (for Convict, of course) on the sides. Of course, this led to fans mocking me with "Hey, Convict! Why'd you put ears on your mask?!"

I'd yell back, "They're not ears! It's 'C,' for 'Convict'!"

One night, we were wrestling in Pearl City, near Pearl Harbor, and Mike Masters and I met two girls and invited them to the show. They came and sat among that crowd of probably 250 fans. Aside from the girls, maybe 25 others in the crowd were not Samoans.

All the good guys, of course, were Samoans—Tama Tonga, Sivi Afi, and the rest. The heels were The Convict, Pete Austin, and the Hollies— basically, the other white guys. So the main event got going, and I was supposed to run down to ringside and trip Sivi Afi, causing the heel to jump on him for the 1-2-3.

Now, I had never before been in a wrestling riot in my life. But here came 200-plus Samoans, coming straight for me! The first guy ran up, and I reached back and whacked him silly, with a big fist. He flinched, growled at me, and kept coming. I just looked at my hands and thought, *Uh, these usually work!*

Suddenly, they were on me like fire ants. They had me by the ear, the arm, the leg, and they were beating the hell out of me. Last thing I remember, here comes this guy with a chair, and...

It was the only time I've ever been knocked out cold in my life.

Next thing I knew, I was in the dressing room. I was feeling sore as hell, but I probably didn't fully appreciate how bad they got me until the other guys helped me get my mask off. When it came off, everyone looked at my face and gasped.

After a few seconds of silence, I heard a couple of them say, "Oh my God, look at that!"

Apparently, after the guy clocked me with the chair, a circling mob of Samoans closed in and started putting the boots to me. One of the babyfaces, Tama Tonga (later better known as Haku in the WWF and Meng, in WCW), came out of the dressing room and dragged me back to safety.

The two girls we had invited, who had never been to a wrestling match before, thought it was all fake, so when they saw me afterward, with my faced all pulverized, they didn't know what to think!

But I learned a lesson that night—a very painful lesson, but a lesson, nonetheless. You don't fight the crowd; you fight your way *through* the crowd. Don't stop—keep going.

Not that we have wrestling riots anymore, but the "don't fight" mentality should be even clearer in this lawsuit-happy age. The joke is, you're a fake wrestler—until you punch somebody. Then they take you to court, and you're a trained killer!

In the end, as much as I had fun in Hawaii, at $40 a week, I was being starved out. Most guys who came in from the mainland lasted anywhere from a week to a few weeks. I stayed six months. And part of me hated to leave, because I was having a great time, even though I lived with two other wrestlers in a dingy motel room.

There's something very liberating about knowing that you could pick up and go, if you needed to, that feeling you have when you can toss everything you own into a single suitcase and say, "I quit!"

No responsibilities, lots of pretty girls, booze...and some drugs. That was when I started smoking a little weed—not saying I'm proud of it, but that's how it was.

But as much as I hated leaving all the fun of Hawaii, I couldn't afford to stay. I headed back to the East Coast to the WWWF, again working preliminary matches, and stayed there just long enough for them to see I hadn't learned much of anything! The company decided I could use a little more seasoning, and they sent me to Georgia.

CHAPTER 5

BACK IN GEORGIA

GEORGIA WAS THE HOME OF THE FIRST NATIONAL WRESTLING SHOW since the golden age of TV in the 1950s, and thanks to Ted Turner transforming local station WTCG into cable Superstation WTBS, the wrestlers on that station's *Georgia Championship Wrestling* were the only ones in 1981 to be seen nationwide.

The man running Georgia when I got there was Jim Barnett, a sharp guy and flamboyantly gay. Don't get me wrong—I have nothing against gay people, but Barnett was almost a cliché. He had the affected voice, the walk, everything you'd associate with a stereotype of a gay person in the early 1980s. I never really had much interaction with him, but it was that way for pretty much my entire career—I've never been an office guy, and I was never one of the guys kissing the promoter's or the booker's ass for a better spot, or whatever.

I wasn't a main event guy in Georgia, but at least I was doing better than the opening matches I had been doing for the WWWF, and was kind of in the middle of the pack. One of my first matches was a tag match, and it would be my first with the man who would probably go on to be both one of my best friends and the most frequent in-ring opponent of my career—Ted DiBiase. Teddy's partner was Tommy "Wildfire" Rich. Tommy at that point was one of the hottest stars in wrestling, but Teddy already had a reputation for being one of the smoothest guys in the ring of anyone in the business. So, Ted DiBiase and I started the match.

31

Even though I think he might be embellishing a little, I love the way DiBiase tells this story, so I'll stick to his version. As he said when he inducted me into the World Wrestling Entertainment Hall of Fame in 2011, he tied up with me, but I was as stiff as a board. The way DiBiase tells it, he looked at me and said, "Screw you," and walked over to tag his partner.

"He's all yours, Wildfire!"

Of course, we learned to work together, and Teddy and I would wrestle in San Antonio, Mid-South, and even in WrestleMania IV for the World Wrestling Federation.

In Georgia, though, Teddy and I didn't hang together too much. Teddy was in what I called the GQ mode, kind of like Ric Flair and Terry Taylor. These guys could be on the road for a month straight, and they'd still have pleats, crisp shirts and suits, and be perfectly groomed.

Meanwhile, I was walking around in sweatpants and T-shirts. Once, DiBiase and I were traveling together in his car, and I was smoking a joint. In his younger days, DiBiase was no stranger to having a few martinis, but he was *not* a pot smoker.

However, he was gracious enough to allow me to smoke in his car, and after I took a few puffs, he said, "Aw, what the hell—let me try that."

That turned out to be a bad idea. Wrestlers tend to haul ass down the freeways, and we'd managed to tear through about 100 miles in an hour and a half. But Teddy took two puffs, and it took us 45 minutes to make the last 10 miles of our trip!

But guys like The Freebirds, especially Terry Gordy (the big man who carried the team, in the ring), were right up my alley. Gordy and I hit it off right away. Terry had this van that reminded me of the Mystery Machine from *Scooby Doo*, and we'd head out on the road, drinking whiskey, day or night. We had some wild times!

Not long after I first got into the territory, I got to know some of the stars, like Buck Robley, Don Carson, and Bruiser Brody, plus Michael Hayes. Hayes was a great talker and had a lot of charisma, plus a cocky persona and flowing blond hair. He and Gordy had started The Freebirds tag team in 1979, when they were both teenagers, but Bill Watts in Mid-South added veteran

Buddy Roberts to the team when they went there in 1980, and they made an amazing combination.

By 1981, The Freebirds were one of the hottest acts in Georgia, and Hayes was assistant booker (in wrestling, the booker is the guy who decides who's going to win, what feuds and matches are going to happen, and who's going to be on top). Michael was always interested in that office stuff, how to make things run, to where even today he's one of the top writers for World Wrestling Entertainment. But in 1981, he was working under Robley, who himself was a very creative guy and someone I liked.

One night, I was supposed to meet a girl at a bar we went to a lot, but I didn't have a car. I went to Buck Robley and asked if I could borrow his car. He said, "Yeah, sure," and tossed me his keys.

Robley had this great big Lincoln Continental, and I drove it to the bar to pick up the young lady. We got back to the hotel for some drinks, and then got back into the car to leave. I started to back out slowly, but the car got to a point where it wouldn't move. I thought I was up against the curb. The engine revved, and my lady friend yelled, "You're against another car!"

I looked out and saw I had pretty much used Buck's car to push in the side of Michael Hayes' car. I just knew I was doomed; I had just crashed the booker's car into the assistant booker's car!

But I wasn't going to duck the responsibility; that's just not how I was raised. I went to Hayes' hotel room and knocked on the door.

The way Michael tells the story, he opened his door to find me standing there, with my bottom lip out like a sad little kid. I don't remember the lip being out, but I did tell him, "Uh, Michael...I, uh, wrecked your car."

He looked at me like I was nuts and said, "That's impossible! My car's in the parking lot!"

"Yeah," I said, "I know."

One thing about The Freebirds—they loved to pee on people. They thought that peeing on some unsuspecting guy in the shower was the funniest thing! At one point, they bought these little plastic water pistols and filled them with urine, so they could shoot piss at people. Archie Gouldie, a tough old guy who wrestled as The Mongolian Stomper, came into the area once, and I guess he had heard the stories about The Freebirds, because he told each one of them, "I will kill you if you piss on me, you understand? I will kill you! Look at me! *Kill...you!*"

I really believed he would have, to tell you the truth, and the 'Birds must have believed him, too, because *no one* ever peed on Archie Gouldie.

We ended up living at the Falcon Rest Motel, which was where I was when I met Gail Conway. She was a gorgeous girl and we hit it off right away, but she had a boyfriend named Vince (not *that* Vince). Her family liked him because he was a "respectable" guy who owned a repair business and lived in a house with a pool, and they didn't like me, with my long hair and bandana, living in a motel room with the only guy in a 50-mile radius crazier than I was—Terry Gordy.

Gordy and I actually broke the door at the motel so often that the landlady finally refused to get it fixed anymore.

But I left the motel to move in with Gail in her apartment. Vince used to drive by in his loud pickup truck, making sure we noticed him. One night, someone broke into her apartment, and the only thing that ended up missing was this .25-caliber automatic pistol that I had.

I was thinking, *Well, the only reason this guy would take the gun would be because he wants to get us into a situation where he has a gun, and I don't.*

To rectify this, I went out and bought a .357 Magnum with a six-inch barrel and a shoulder holster. I was walking around Georgia in August, where it's steaming hot, wearing a jacket to hide my holster. Guys would come up and say, "Hey, Duggan!"

I'd turn around, ready to draw: "Don't move, brother!"

My sister Angel, the prosecutor, found out what was going on and tried to talk me down.

"Jim," she said, "you're gonna end up in jail!"

I told her, "I'd rather be in jail than in the ground."

I was serious, too—I was convinced that Vince was planning to kill me. I even called the police to report the gun stolen, something my dad and his cop's mentality had taught me to do if something like that ever happened.

My dad's lessons and perspectives as a police officer have come back to save my butt, more than once.

Come November, I went with Gail to have Thanksgiving dinner with her family, and when I came back home, all four of the tires on my brand-new Trans Am had been slashed.

I said, "That son of a bitch!"

There wasn't a doubt in my mind—it was Vince.

It was time to end this, before Vince decided to end it himself. I went and got Gordy, who knew what was going on, and the two of us went to Stewart Avenue, a part of town where you expected to see Huggy Bear from *Starsky & Hutch* doing business. I mean, it was a rough section of town.

We went to this bar called D-4s, and there was Vince, sitting with Gail's brother, at the bar.

Vince hadn't spotted us, and I went to make a move on him, even though I knew this wasn't gonna be some squash job—Vince was a good-sized guy.

But Gordy grabbed me and said, "Wait a minute, Jim."

Back then, we drank our fair share of Jack Daniels, and Gordy convinced me this would be a good time for us to hang back for a few minutes, enjoy a little sippin' whiskey, and see what our friend Vince did.

After a few minutes, Vince got up from the bar and went into the bathroom. I followed him in, and we had some words. The talking didn't last too long before we got into a little fight.

Like I said, Vince was not a small guy, but I was a pro wrestler. I wouldn't try to go against him in the repair business, but fighting was, in a way, my business. I was glomming him pretty good, and in a few seconds, the blood was flowing.

Suddenly, Gordy grabbed me from behind and said, "That's it, Duggan, he's had enough!"

Vince, all glassy eyed, staggered about half a step toward me, probably just to keep from falling down at first, but he took a swing at me as he advanced. Gordy saw this and let me go.

"Oh, damn! He's fightin' back! Go get 'im, Jim!"

I got a few more shots in, when Ray Stevens walked into the bathroom. Stevens was one of the all-time greats in wrestling, but by 1981, he was in the latter days of his career and was working a few dates with us in Georgia. One thing about Ray—he had a reputation as an absolute wild man, going back more than 25 years, and he had not mellowed with age.

Ray knew next to nothing about the situation; all he knew was that a fellow wrestler was facing off with some jerk in a bar. Ray wanted to hurt the guy, and I almost had to start fighting Ray to keep him from really injuring Vince, because I knew I would have been held responsible for whatever happened. I got Stevens and Gordy out of there, and we split.

Of course, it all came back to bite me in the ass. Vince went to the hospital, and I got arrested. The police actually put out a warrant for me after Vince got to the hospital and swore out complaints against me and Terry Gordy. And Gordy never even touched him! But Vince claimed the two of us beat him up, and told a bunch of other lies. Was he kidding? I wanted Vince to myself—I think I would have fought *Gordy* to get a crack at him, especially every time I thought of what he did to my beloved Trans Am.

A couple of days after the fight, the cops showed up at the Falcon Rest Motel, but I wasn't there because I was staying with another wrestler up in north Georgia, while we worked a string of shows in that part of the state. I'm sure I wasn't on the top-10 most-wanted list, but they definitely were looking for me, and I was living on the lam!

Finally, the Georgia wrestling office got ahold of me and told me the cops had been calling the office, so they told me to go to the police station and turn myself in. Gordy and I went together, and even though we posted bond and got out of there pretty quickly, I'll never forget it, because it was the first time I had been arrested and been put through that whole process.

Back then, I kept a journal, and it ended up saving me. Vince and Gail quickly started having problems (surprise, surprise), and Gail called me the night before our scheduled hearing to tell me Vince was going to drop the charges. Gordy and I decided to celebrate this good news...by going out and having some whiskey!

We might have had too much fun, because the next day, we ended up running a few minutes late for court. When we got to the pretrial hearing, I addressed the court and said, "Your honor, this has all been settled..."

Vince stood up and interrupted, telling the judge that no, in fact, he wanted to move forward with the charges.

Fortunately, I still had my journal with a full accounting of the theft of my .25-caliber pistol, the slashing of my tires, and the cops who took those reports.

When the tires got slashed, I had told the cop, "The only reason this guy is doing this is, he wants me to beat him up so he can get charges on me."

That statement had also been part of the police report on the damage to my car, which was weeks before my actual fight with Vince, so the judge threw out the whole thing.

Aside from getting arrested, I really enjoyed my time in Georgia, but I knew it was time to go when they brought Ole Anderson in as booker in 1982. Ole was pretty successful as a tag-team wrestler and also made his mark as a booker, but he just wasn't the type of guy that I wanted to work with.

He was kind of like Bill Watts, in terms of being in your face, but without Watts' willingness to work with others and compromise at all. Ole was a shouter, he barked at everyone, and I just wasn't interested in that.

I met with Ole, and I knew right away it wasn't going to work. I had other offers, including one that I was very interested in—the Fullers, who ran a small territory that encompassed Alabama and the Florida panhandle, wanted me to go to work for them. I was kind of excited about the idea of living on the beach again.

So I gave Ole my notice and headed for Pensacola. The Fullers had some tough guys working for them, guys like Jos LeDuc, The Canadian Lumberjack. He played a madman on TV, but I always got along with big Jos. The thing about a lot of wrestlers is that their in-ring characters are different from who they really are. Even the best ones are just dialed-up versions of themselves. There are always exceptions—"Macho Man"

Randy Savage was as crazed and tightly wound outside the ring as he was inside—but most of us are much different from what people might expect from seeing us on TV. I mean, if you deal with me in my private life, you're seeing Jim. If I had "Hacksaw" with me all the time, I'd be in jail!

Jos LeDuc was also a quiet, polite guy away from the cameras and fans, and I enjoyed being around him.

When I went to Pensacola, Gail, who had left Vince again, came with me, but we stayed there only about six months.

The Fullers' territory was where I did the "Wildman" Duggan gimmick. If you ever see a picture of me in some old program where I have tangled hair, a scraggly beard, and a furry vest with chains across it, that's where it's from.

The first time I went to the ring as "Wildman" Duggan, I dropped down in the aisle and did a bear crawl to the ring; I quickly learned that was about the worst thing in the world to do right in front of a crowd of wrestling fans. If you're a bad guy, the worst thing you can do is put yourself at foot level, as I realized after about 30 fans just kicked the crap out of me.

It was also during this time that I made my first tour of Japan, where the fans made for a completely different experience. My first tour went for five weeks, and it was for New Japan Pro Wrestling, run by one of Japan's biggest wrestling stars ever, Antonio Inoki. I actually got to work with Inoki during that tour, and for a young American to be in with the top guy was kind of a big deal.

But I hated it—I *hated* Japan. The first week or two, it was great—the change in culture was interesting, and I was seeing a whole new world. But working for those large Japanese companies, I traveled every day, stuck on a bus, going to weird buildings with no hot water. The Japanese crowds, especially during my first tour, were very reserved. I'd be screaming at them, doing everything I could to get a reaction, and they would politely clap.

One good thing—I always said it was easy to spot your friends, the few times they came to shows there. You'd see a sea of black heads of hair, and the one that stuck out as different was the one guy in the crowd

I knew. If I wanted to, I could holler at him from the ring, "Hey, buddy! I'll meet you across the street at McDonald's! Get the McSquid sandwich—it's delicious!"

While I wasn't crazy about Japan, I loved Pensacola. The trips were short, I was getting a $500-a-week guarantee (which was great money for a little territory like that in 1982), and I was living on the beach. It was a good time in my life.

CHAPTER 6

BIRTH OF A HACKSAW

ONE DAY, I GOT A PHONE CALL FROM BRUISER BRODY, who apparently had seen something in me when we were in Georgia together. He wanted me to head back to Texas to work for Joe Blanchard's Southwest Championship Wrestling, a territory based in San Antonio.

He said, "Hey, you wanna learn how to work, get over here and work with me."

I didn't immediately recognize the magnitude of what he was saying, or how big an opportunity working with Brody was. What I did know was that I had it made in Pensacola, making a good guarantee and living on the beach, but Brody talked me into giving notice and heading to Texas to see if I could learn enough to make a bigger name for myself.

From early on, I had the basic mechanics down—I knew how to hit the ropes, how to land when taking a bump, how to execute the moves. But my understanding of the business and why things work, that didn't come until much later.

Part of that was because I had been a competitive athlete, and going into a business like wrestling, where everything's a work, or part of the show, was a serious adjustment. I struggled with that, which was probably a big part of the reason I was an underneath guy for so long, even though I had the physical tools most promoters wanted.

For example, if I got beat in a match, I'd pop right back up after the three-count instead of selling for my opponent, because in my competitive athlete's mind, I was thinking, *I could beat this son of a bitch*, and I wanted to show people that. But that's not pro wrestling; wrestling's about telling a story and convincing people to buy tickets to see how it turns out. And sometimes, that means my part of the story is going to involve putting someone over whom I knew I could take in an actual fight. That was the biggest adjustment, because the pro wrestling mind-set is the opposite of the competitive athlete's.

When it finally came to me, it was like the doors had been opened wide. It was not a progression. All of a sudden, it was like the lightbulb went on. It just hit me, like, "Wait a minute! If I do it *this* way..."

And a lot of the lessons that led to that change in thinking boiled down to what I learned from Frank Goodish, aka Bruiser Brody. Brody was not a teacher in the sense that he would sit me down and have me take notes on his lectures or anything like that. He led by example, and he would watch us young guys work and tell us what we should work on. When we had good matches, he would also take the time to say, "Wow, that was pretty impressive."

Brody was a giant of a man. He was around 6'4", 300-plus pounds, with almost zero body fat. His thighs were huge; I'd never seen anything like them. And he used that size—Brody was a very intimidating man, very loud, very boisterous, and he dragged his chain (the one he brought to the ring with him) everywhere.

In fact, it was that chain that inspired my 2x4, indirectly, at least. Brody was talking to me about gimmicks and said, "If you're gonna bring a gimmick to the ring, forget the sequined robes. Make it something you can use."

He wasn't just talking about using it on my opponents; he also meant that I might need something to defend myself against crazed fans. He used the chain because it legitimately could do some damage. A few times, I used a piece of lumber as a foreign object, something I did more and more, especially in my Mid-South days, until it just became part of my getup in the World Wrestling Federation and everywhere else. But it was Bruiser Brody who got me thinking in that direction.

Ironically, I think Brody's intimidating nature was one of the reasons that Jose Gonzalez, the guy who killed Brody in Puerto Rico in July of

1988, got away with it. He was able to convince a jury that Brody was dangerous to him and he was defending himself when he stabbed Brody to death in a locker room. It was a miscarriage of justice, but that guy used Brody's own intimidating persona against him.

Brody could definitely be a handful. One night, he had gotten into a beef with the office, and we were supposed to wrestle in San Antonio. We went out there, and he hit me, and I went down, selling it. He clamped a headlock on me, and I swear we sat in that headlock for at least 15 minutes.

The crowd started booing like crazy, but Brody wasn't fazed. At one point, still holding that headlock, he leaned into my ear and whispered, "I'm showing you how to work with the office, Jim."

We sat there for however long it was and then *boom!* We went right to the finish.

I never found out exactly what was going on that night with Brody and the front office, but he stayed after that, so he obviously got things worked out.

And from what I understand, that was not the only time Brody pulled that stunt when he had a beef with a promoter. He did something similar, also in San Antonio, in a match with Mark Lewin in 1986 or so. Back then, getting paid fairly in wrestling was almost unheard of, and a lot of guys had to fight to get even close to what they should have gotten, so Brody would occasionally send a message: "I may go to the ring as scheduled, but you can't make me work."

Brody also taught me little tricks to create suspense and get the fans going, like when you throw a guy out of the ring,

Brody also helped me come up with the ring name I would use for the rest of my career. Starting out as "Crazy" Jim Duggan, I was a bad guy in San Antonio, as I had been in Georgia. I sputtered through my whole interview, because I didn't know how to do one and had never really gotten to do it in the WWWF or in Georgia. One thing I did that picked up a little heat came from when I first arrived, and the announcers called me "Dugan" (pronounced DOO-gan, as opposed to DUG-GAN).

I got on the mic and said, angrily, "My name's not Dugan—it's Duggan! D-U-G-G-A-N! Two Gs!"

That was my whole promo!

Pretty soon, the fans were chanting "cock-eyed Dugan" at me, and I'd stand there with my hands on my ears, screaming, "Stop it!"

Later, when I was in Mid-South, Bill Watts (who owned the company and regularly acted as one of its TV announcers) would explain to TV viewers that in my football days, I was on special teams and would cut through the other team's wedges like a hacksaw.

But...

The real story is, after being "Big," "The Convict," and "Wildman," I was looking for a name that would work, and one night in San Antonio, I found one, thanks to Brody and Buck Robley. The three of us were sitting around, drinking and batting around names. Finally, one of us (I forget which one) said, "What about 'Hacksaw'?"

As soon as I heard it out loud, I knew it was a name that would work for me. And for 30 years, it *has* worked for me, even though I get the occasional smartass fan question, like, "Why are you 'Hacksaw' when you carry a 2x4 to the ring? Shouldn't you be '2x4 Duggan'?"

Brody was not the only wild character on San Antonio TV, though. I teamed early with Mike "Hippie" Boyette, who was never dull. The wrestling business was full of strange guys, but even by wrestling standards, Boyette was out there.

Once, Boyette announced on TV that he was going to bring in a concrete block and break it with his head! He gave his promo and reared back...

Boom!

The concrete block looked good as new, but Boyette was staggering around. He went for a second shot anyway...

Boom!

Now, he had blood pouring from his head, and he was getting mad. This time, he hit it even harder...

Boom!

He ended up needing help to get off the interview set. He didn't even know where he was by the end of that "demonstration."

Manny Fernandez was another unpredictable character. He and I went to a strip joint one night. After we'd been there for a while, I had to go to the bathroom, and when I came back out, Manny was in a fight with some guy. For some reason, the stripper up on stage decided to jump on Manny, so he turned and popped her.

Maybe it's just the way my dad raised me, but one thing I've never had patience for is a man putting his hands on a woman, so I was horrified.

I certainly wasn't thrilled with Manny, but I knew we needed to get out of there. We took off, and since we had gotten out of there before any cops showed up, we thought that was the end of it.

About a week later, I was out again with Manny. This time we were with Tully Blanchard, son of promoter Joe Blanchard, and the hotshot quarterback I had met a few years earlier on my SMU recruiting trip. It was about 2:00 AM. Tully had just gotten this beautiful white Cadillac, and we were all piled inside. The bars in Texas close at 2:00, so we decided to go to Shoney's for some breakfast. At one of the other tables was the stripper from the fight a week earlier, along with her boyfriend. Apparently, she spotted us as we were leaving, because this guy was coming out of the restaurant and toward us in the parking lot.

He walked up and said, "Hey, Manny."

Next thing we knew, he had made three or four quick jabs, and Manny was just gushing blood from the side and the arm. The guy had a knife!

Manny was squirting pretty good, and as he propped himself up on Tully's Cadillac, he was screaming for Tully to take him to a hospital.

Tully looked with horror at his new, white Cadillac (now with red smears) and told Manny, in a very deliberate tone, "Don't worry, the ambulance is on its way. It's coming."

The next day, we were taping TV, and when I got to the arena, there was Tully's brand-new Cadillac, the same lovely shade of white, except for an area near the front bumper, where it looked like someone had started to paint the car red!

I never had an incident that bad, but after a show in Corpus Christi, a coastal town in southern Texas, I was out with another wrestler, a burly, rough-looking character named "Bruiser" Bob Sweetan. After we worked the show, I wanted to hit a convenience store, pick up a few provisions, and get out of town.

We pulled in and got out of my Trans Am (the same one that bastard Vince had cut the tires on), went into the store for a few things, and came out, when another driver damn near ran me over before I'd made it 20 feet! I spun around and threw my Gatorade bottle, and it hit the side of the guy's car.

Two guys bailed out of the car as I got into the Trans Am and started it up. One of the guys from the car reached into my open window and punched me in the face! That was enough for me—I got out and dropped the guy who'd punched me. The other guy, who had this big Afro, was dancing around like he thought he was Muhammad Ali. I just snatched him by his hair and pulled him to me. Just as I was blasting him in the face, I was lit up by the big, bright spotlight from a police car.

I let the guy go and sprinted for my car, but stopped almost instantly when I heard, "Halt!"

Okay, I thought, *you got me*.

They took me to jail and kept me overnight. The one thing about it that really pissed me off was that they wouldn't let me keep my glasses. At first, I was ready to fight—seriously, I was yelling that these guys were *not* going to get my glasses. Then a cop I knew, someone I was on friendly terms with, took me aside and said, "Jim, it's not worth it. You're not gonna win this one. Just give me the glasses."

That made sense; I calmed right down—"Yes, thank you, officer, for pointing that out to me."

I handed over the glasses.

The next morning, they let me out, and the case never ended up going to court or anything. But I had another unpleasant surprise waiting for me—Sweetan had taken my car and driven back to San Antonio, where we all lived, hundreds of miles away!

I finally caught a ride back to San Antonio and caught up to Sweetan, and you'd better believe I chewed his ass out. He apologized, and that was that. But Sweetan was a real piece of work, which became clear after I knew him for a few months. I didn't realize it by the time of the Corpus Christi trip—if I had, I'd never have had him in my car at all, much less all the way to Corpus Christi and back—but he turned out to be a real piece of garbage, in my opinion. He was just a mean guy and a bully, and I've never had any patience for bullies.

On the total opposite end of the spectrum was Tito Santana, a guy who I'd also end up working with or alongside later, in both Mid-South and the WWF. I always liked Tito, whose real name is Merced Solis.

In Southwest, I met another guy who would become a good friend—a smaller wrestler named Ricky Morton. Ricky was teamed up with Ken Lucas, a guy who kind of reminded me of Tito, because both of them were true gentlemen who always handled themselves professionally.

One of my regular travel partners was "Killer" Tim Brooks, who at one point let me use his driver's license to go to K-Mart and buy a .22-caliber rifle. And the guys at the store accepted it as my I.D.! Tim was something like 5'10", while I was 6'3", and the weight on the license was around 210 pounds, while I was at least 275 at that point.

Once I had that gun, we'd be out making road trips through Texas and do a little rabbit hunting as we went. Texas had rabbits that could only be called "Jumbo Jacks," not regular jackrabbits. We'd kill time on the way home by spotting jackrabbits and pulling over so we could try to get them with a couple of shots from that rifle, usually without even getting out of the car. I know now that we were lucky not to be sent to jail for doing that, but we had to occupy ourselves somehow on those long, dull trips through the middle of nowhere. Plus I was pretty wild back then, a lot more than I am these days, brother.

One time, I was with Wayne Farris (later known as The Honky Tonk Man), and we had stopped, because we'd spotted a rabbit. I fired off a couple of shots, and one of the casings bounced off the ceiling of the car and landed inside the back of my pants!

I sat there for about half a second, and then I felt this white-hot burning down my butt. For those of you who aren't gun people, when a gun fires and ejects a shell casing, that casing is *really* hot. I damn near jumped through the roof of the car. I was yelling so much that Wayne thought I'd shot myself.

We used a spotlight at night for finding rabbits, and at some point we started using one with a red tint. This made it a natural for the kind of goofy pranks wrestlers always play on each other. If I was in a car coming up on a vehicle we recognized as another wrestler's, we'd break out the spotlight and click it on and off, so the guy would see the blinking red light and think the cops had gotten him.

More than once, a guy pulled over only for me and whomever I was riding with to drive by, laughing at him on the side of the road. And more than once, I could hear, "Very funny, Duggan!"

Manny Fernandez was often one of San Antonio's top heroes, but in real life, I had some problems with him. I already mentioned how I saw him get rough with a woman in public, and on another occasion, after I'd been in Southwest for a while, he dislocated my shoulder during a match. We were doing a spot where he took me down with an armdrag, but he held on longer and more tightly than he was supposed to and just drove me into the mat. He later swore it was an accident, but looking back on it, I really think he did it on purpose.

But that kind of thing is just part of wrestling. A wrestling locker room is a tough barnyard, and there are a lot of big roosters in each one. A lot of profiling went on—back then, since it was such a closed business, if you were a new guy coming in, you were a potential threat to everyone who was already there.

When Buck Robley left San Antonio, I was sorry to see him go, because he had helped me a lot in figuring out how to develop my own persona in wrestling. However, not long after he left, I got a call from him, with a job offer to come and wrestle in the promotion where he was now booking—a little region called Mid-South Wrestling.

CHAPTER 7

MID-SOUTH

BUCK ROBLEY ENDED UP NOT STAYING AS MID-SOUTH BOOKER for very long after I got there, and I'm not sure why. I do know that the company's owner was a forceful personality, and whoever was calling themselves booker, all the final decisions came down to one man— Mid-South Wrestling owner (and longtime wrestler) "Cowboy" Bill Watts.

As much as the "protect the business" mentality had been a part of every promotion where I had worked up to this point, "Cowboy" Bill Watts took it to another level.

Kayfabe—which refers to the portrayal of everything involved in a wrestling show as real and not predetermined—was very, very powerful. In Mid-South, heels and babyfaces could not ride together, or even be seen in public together, because Watts' TV shows were selling the idea that we were in serious grudges that fans would have to pay to see resolved in the arenas.

Watts also thought it was important that Mid-South wrestlers be thought of as the toughest guys around, so if a wrestler got into a bar fight and lost, the wrestler would be fired.

He could also be brutal to some of the guys who approached Mid-South about breaking into the business. Some of these kids had no business trying to get into wrestling, but I also saw some kids who had some athletic skill and were respectful to the wrestling business. But even when they came in, they got treated rough, maybe a little too rough.

I remember one kid who had some amateur wrestling background and contacted Mid-South about trying out to be trained, so Watts put him in the ring with Steve "Dr. Death" Williams. Now, wrestlers generally are tough guys, but Doc was on another level. He was a four-time All-American in wrestling, a two-time All-American in football at the University of Oklahoma, and was even tougher than he was strong. Just to give you an idea, Doc caught an elbow wrong during a TV taping match in June of 1985. He went to a doctor in Shreveport, Louisiana, where we taped TV, and had 108 stitches put in around his eye. Doc drove a few hundred miles to Tulsa, where he wrestled a match that same night.

So Doc and this kid who wanted to try out rolled around on the mat for eight minutes or so, and the guy was just sucking wind, with his tongue hanging out. Then, Watts went into the ring and told the kid, "Okay, put a headlock on me. Let's see what you can do," and the kid did what Watts told him to do. Watts suplexed the kid onto his head and just stretched the hell out of him. The kid ended up leaving the building in an ambulance.

It was brutal, and while I understand the idea of wanting to make sure that people think of wrestling as a tough sport and not something that just anyone can do, I really think he took advantage of that kid. I like Bill, and I consider Bill a friend of mine—we never had a problem and always had respect for each other—but on that occasion, I think he went too far.

A lot of people had problems with Watts, because he was very opinionated, very vocal, and very strong willed, and he was not someone who was ever going to sugarcoat anything to spare your feelings. But we always got along, because he enjoyed athletes, guys who had that competitive fire. If you look back at his top stars, I think a lot of the guys he featured heavily fit into that mold. The Junkyard Dog, Steve Williams, and myself all had strong athletic backgrounds. Watts liked jocks, and he liked legitimate tough guys, because he knew guys like us would always go out and give it everything we had.

And while I might not be crazy about how Watts treated that one kid, I understand his mentality—it was to protect his business. In every bar in every town, there was at least one tough guy who figured he could take a wrestler, and there were a lot of challenges thrown out. And a lot of us were cocky, too, which didn't help—we weren't *looking* for fights, but for a lot of us, it was easy to find them.

I remember one fight in 1983, I think, where Terry Allen, aka Magnum T.A., and I were supposed to meet up at a bar with a couple of wrestlers new to Mid-South, have a drink with them, and kind of welcome them to the area. But we ended up getting challenged, and we took it out to the parking lot. By the time the new guys were pulling into the bar parking lot, there were half a dozen guys laid out, Magnum was busted open, and I was screaming at a guy while hanging off the hood of his car.

I can just picture two young wrestlers coming in for their first night, seeing that as they pulled in, and thinking, *What in the hell have we gotten ourselves into?*

Another time, in 1984, I was at a bar one night, sitting at a table, when I got hit with a piece of ice from somewhere in the crowded barroom. I was determined not to sell a piece of ice, but pretty soon...*thunk*. I got hit again. *Thunk*. And again.

By then, I decided to do something about it, so I got up to see what was going on. I looked over at the next table, and there was Steve Williams, some girl, and then on the other side of her, Hercules Hernandez. Herc and I were feuding at the time, so we weren't going to be sitting and drinking together in public, but I thought, "It's gotta be them!"

I whizzed a piece of ice back at them, but my aim was off, and I missed both of them, hitting the girl in the middle square in the chest! She saw me and got up to come after me, but she had reared back with her drink as she was coming, totally telegraphing her intention to toss it at me. When she threw it, I sidestepped and it missed me. Then, she started swinging at me. Now, there are two sides to this story—I say I picked up a chair and held her off with it, but Hercules for years claimed I pinned her to the floor with the chair. Either way, I kept her away from me.

Her boyfriend (or maybe just some guy trying to be chivalrous—who knows?) came up and socked me, and I turned and socked him back with a pretty good shot. He fell back, landing near Hercules. Now, maybe the guy was a fan and knew I was feuding with Herc and Doc at the time, so he thought this would work—he looked up at Herc and said, "Let's get him!"

Herc took his big fist and just blasted the guy! Now, the whole place was erupting, and it was a full-out barroom brawl. People were coming from all over, and a lot of them were piling up around Doc. Doc had his fist drawn back, and he was throwing these five-inch punches, just dropping people. Herc looked like a big windmill, with his giant arms swinging around, and bodies were flying everywhere.

The band stopped playing, and the lights came up. Herc ripped his shirt off and practically started cutting a promo while surrounded by piles of wounded drunks. Herc and Doc were fighting half the bar on their way out, as Terry Taylor came walking in. Poor Terry was horrified at the carnage!

We got out of there, and Doc and Herc piled into Doc's van to do likewise, but the last of the bar people came running out and started putting the boots to the van. They'd go a few feet and then stop and get out, which made everyone run away, then get back in and people would start kicking the van again—it seemed like it took them forever just to get out of the parking lot. And of course, as soon as they did, here came the cops. They got Hercules for drunk driving, and we all ended up with papers served on us—it was a mess.

And God bless him, to the day Doc died, he said, "Duggan, I promise, we did *not* throw that ice!"

Oops!

Ted DiBiase was on fire as a heel at that time, and he and I combined as The Rat Pack, maybe the most hated team in the area since The Freebirds had set the territory on fire in 1980, with a feud against Mid-South's top hero, the Junkyard Dog.

Teaming up with DiBiase as The Rat Pack was probably my first major career break. Teddy had been a clean-cut, clean-wrestling hero since his debut in the late 1970s, but in Mid-South he cut loose as a villain, turning on his (real-life) longtime friend, the Junkyard Dog. Dog, whose real name was Sylvester Ritter, was phenomenally popular, and when DiBiase turned on him, he became the most hated man in the area. The way Teddy turned on JYD also set up a great gimmick for Teddy—he had "injured his hand" in a previous match and had to wear a "protective glove" over the damaged hand. JYD had become North American champ, which meant he inherited previous champ Bob Roop's contract, including a defense against his good friend, DiBiase. They wrestled clean for a few minutes, but at a key point in this hero-versus-hero match, DiBiase appeared to put a foreign object into the glove and knocked out JYD with it.

As his feud with JYD went on, he brought me in as a partner to battle JYD and various other Mid-South heroes.

Ted and I complemented each other, because he was a smooth, technical wrestler whose experience let him carry the match, and then I would come in for some explosive brawling. We were quite a combination, if I do say so myself. And Bill Watts saw that the combination would work; Watts had a great mind for the business and had the personality for it, where he could lay out the angles and know how to pace them, because he knew how to make people react the way he wanted them to.

I always liked Ted and considered him a friend, but he and I were not hanging out a lot together away from the ring. That was really because Teddy was a very *GQ* kind of guy. He'd rather have hung out in fancy places, while I was out with Terry Gordy or Steve Williams at some smoky hole in the wall where my head nearly hit the ceiling every time I stood up.

Part of The Rat Pack's image was that we always had some ingenious plan to cheat the heroes, and one of the most clever came in the fall of 1982, when The Rat Pack challenged JYD and his partner, Mr. Olympia, to a Mid-South tag-team title match. Dog and Olympia were the champs, but DiBiase raised the stakes by making it a no-disqualification match (meaning anything goes) and stipulating that the loser of the fall would have to leave Mid-South for 90 days.

The match was set for the Mid-South TV tapings at the Irish McNeill's Boys Club, in Shreveport, Louisiana, where, coincidentally, the Louisiana State Fair was underway (the Boys Club was adjacent to the fairgrounds).

The day of the match, two unexpected things happened. First, a gorilla was at ringside for the entire show, handing out balloons to the kids in the audience, apparently to promote the fair. Second, Bill Watts announced that Hacksaw Duggan could not be found and even speculated that I could very well be in jail somewhere, given my wild nature.

Rather than forfeit the match, DiBiase brought in Matt Borne, a journeyman villain from Oregon, as his replacement partner. Watts played on what I'm sure the fans suspected: that DiBiase was willing to throw his new partner to the wolves. If Borne lost, it was no big deal, because he didn't work for Mid-South anyway. Whatever was going to happen, the one certainty in the fans' minds was that JYD would not be losing. He was the most popular man in the area, even more beloved in Louisiana than any member of the New Orleans Saints football team. Seriously—the guy was practically a folk hero to those fans.

Thirty years later, that angle remains something that people who saw it never forget, and a big part of that was how we all executed it. Even before the show started, I was outside the arena, in the gorilla suit, waving at folks and making gorilla noises while a fair worker encouraged the wrestling fans to stick around for the fair.

Even though they'd seen me for a few months by now, the audience really had no clue it was me under that gorilla mask. I spent the show cheering for the babyfaces, leading the crowd in chants for their heroes, until my big moment.

That moment came when DiBiase tossed Dog out of the ring during the tag match. I walked over and helped JYD to his feet, brushing him off. When he turned around to go back into the ring...*boom!* I hit him in the back of the head and pulled the mask off. The people started shrieking, "It's Doo-gan! It's cock-eyed Doo-gan!" The fans sat in stunned silence as Borne capitalized on my sneak attack for the three-count—The Dog would be forced to leave Mid-South, and no one could believe it!

After the match, the three of us gave an interview and talked about how brilliant our plan was. We didn't even get a lot of boos—the fans were still so shocked about The Dog being gone that they were damn near silent, although the crowds we saw in the arenas after that aired were *plenty* hot at us!

The Dog got his revenge, though, by coming back as the masked Stagger Lee. The idea was, it was obviously him, but we couldn't prove it without unmasking him, so he had outsmarted The Rat Pack. What a great gimmick!

And as much as we feuded on wrestling shows, in real life, JYD was a great guy, a generous man with a heart of gold. But that feud established The Rat Pack as a dangerous group, with DiBiase and Borne as a tag team, and with me as an out-of-control enforcer.

Behind the scenes, Borne was more trouble than he was worth, and we ended up having a problem that would apparently boil inside him for decades. It started in late 1982 as we were heading into Baton Rouge, spending the night there before a show the following evening. Borne had a girlfriend, and while we were all in a bar, they got into an argument, and the next thing I know, he's slapping around this poor girl.

As I mentioned earlier, if there is one thing in this world guaranteed to piss me off more than anything else, it's a guy hitting a female. Whether it's Lex Luger hitting Elizabeth shortly before she died in 2003, or Steve Austin hitting his wife, Debra, for a big guy to hit a woman who's much smaller and not nearly as strong as he is says a lot about that guy's personality.

Anyway, I got the girl away from him and got her out to my car. Next thing I know, Borne's out there spitting on my car, but I wasn't stopping to deal with him. I just wanted to get her out of there safely.

The next night, we were at the arena for the show. Borne came up to me in the hallway and started arguing with me, and he finally tried to get me with a leg-dive takedown. I pushed him down and put the boots to him.

Ernie Ladd jumped in and broke it up. Ladd was 6'9", a monster of a man, and a great athlete. He'd played pro football before getting into wrestling, and he was Watts' booker at that time. Ernie was a good man, but he was not someone you wanted to test physically, so when he wanted to break up a fight, it was getting broken up.

I went back to the dressing room, where DiBiase was getting dressed for his match. Borne slammed open the door and snarled at me, "Duggan... it's not over!"

Well, back then, if it wasn't over, then it was on! I charged him again, and this time, we were inside the dressing room, out of sight of Ernie Ladd or any other would-be peacemaker, and DiBiase wasn't about to jump in to take up for Matt Borne. I worked Borne over pretty good, and thought that was it.

And for about 27 years, that *was* it. Since then, I had seen him hundreds of times, as himself and as Doink the Clown (a gimmick he took on in the WWF in 1993). In all that time, while we were never going to be pals, we had always been congenial to each other.

In 2010, I was working a wrestling convention and show in White Plains, New York, and Matt Borne was on the card.

Borne came up to me the night of the show like we were long-lost buddies and said, "Hey, Hacksaw, you're looking good! Can I get you some water?"

"No thanks, Matt—I'm good."

"You need a lift after the show?"

"Nah, I have a ride to the airport, but thanks, anyway."

Then he told me we were working against each other that night. I said that was cool with me.

"Okay," he said, "I'll hit you with a chair, and then you hit me with the 2x4..."

"Matt," I said, "there are 100 people out there. I'll go out there and go, 'HO-OH,' and do the USA chant, you hold your ears, we'll do a few spots, hit the clothesline, and we're out of there."

He suddenly got really mad and started cussing at me—"Goddamn son of a bitch!"

I went out for the match, and we did a sequence where he got a shot in on me, and I was down on all fours, selling it. All of a sudden, here he came with a live kick—I mean, he went all out—and I managed to figure out what he was doing about half a second before he connected, just quick enough to get my hand up to partially block it. Still, the impact knocked my hand into my nose, which started dripping blood. If I hadn't gotten the hand up, he would have kicked my teeth out of my mouth. The whole thing just caught me off guard.

Now, in wrestling, if someone accidentally or even carelessly hits you too hard, that's called a potato. But this was no potato, because he followed it up with some hard punches. One of them gave me a big egg, growing out of the back of my head, and there wasn't much I could do from down on the ground.

But I got back up onto my feet, and I was ready to go. I mean, I was 56 years old—way past the age when I'd be looking to fight anyone, but I *knew* I could beat Matt Borne's ass!

He bailed out of the ring and grabbed a chair. Well, hell, I rolled out and grabbed my handy 2x4, ready to carry out the chair-board exchange he'd proposed backstage, but in a way he'd never forget.

We were in wrestling's version of a Mexican standoff, so I told the referee, "You tell him to go back to the dressing room, and we'll finish it there. I don't need to embarrass him in front of people, and we're not gonna do it on camera, but if he wants a fight, let's do it in the dressing room!"

I went down to the dressing area, but when I laid down my 2x4, I put it within reach, because I knew Matt often carried a box-cutter, and I knew no matter what, he was going to have some kind of weapon. Matt Borne was not going to try me on, empty-handed. I was pumped up and ready to go.

Just then, Butterbean, the boxer who's been involved with wrestling shows on several occasions and was part of the convention, came up to me and said, "Hey, Hacksaw! How ya doin'?"

"Get away from me!"

He said, "C'mon, Hack, I never lose my temper like this—it's no good!"

I said, "'Bean, I'm trying to defend myself!"

I felt bad later, because he was just a friendly guy. I actually got his number and called him after all this, to apologize and tell him the whole story, so he'd know why I was so cross.

Anyway, I waited for what seemed like hours (but was probably about 20 minutes) when the referee came down and said, "Hacksaw, he's not coming."

I learned later that Borne had taken his bag, with all his ring gear and all the gimmicks he was selling at the convention, and put it in his car before the match had started. After our match, Borne left the ring, went out a fire exit, got into his car, and left, which told me he had premeditated and planned the whole thing. He thought he would knock my teeth out, leave me lying, and make his escape.

But even now, I can't stay too angry about it. I mean, the last I heard, he was living out of the back of his car. After he left the WWF in the 1990s, he'd work indie shows in the clown outfit, and everyone used to call him "Krusty the Klown," because he'd have his trunk open, cigarette hanging out of the corner of his mouth, in his filthy clown suit. How could I hold a grudge against someone that pathetic? It would be a waste of energy.

The weird thing was, after White Plains, he tried to keep it going. He'd get on the Internet and challenge me. Folks would ask me about it, and I'd just say, "I'm not even gonna comment on Matt Borne."

To be honest, I thought about not even mentioning Borne, or any of this stuff, in this book, but the more I thought about it, the more I realized that you folks reading this deserve the whole story, not just the comfortable parts of it. But even this does one thing I wouldn't ever want to do, and that's elevate Matt, because let's face it—this will be the most publicity he's gotten in a long, long time. I mean, outside his little New England wrestling area (and nothing against that area—I know a lot of good people there), no one even remembers him.

My problem with Matt Borne was nothing—heck, people say the Iron Sheik bust in 1987 (which we'll get into) was the worst thing that happened to me, but even that was nothing compared to a wreck I was in shortly after I started in Mid-South in 1982. What I'm about to tell you is something I seldom talk about, and it was the worst thing that ever happened to me in my life.

I had met a young lady named Vickie Voda, and we had moved in together in the first house I ever bought in Louisiana. We were very close, and one weekend, I had a double-shot booked, and she was coming with me. The first night was in Jackson, Mississippi, and I don't even remember the second town, because I never made it there.

I still had my Trans Am, and I want to say one thing: I'll talk a lot later about the crazy, fast driving we used to do, but I want to be clear that in this crash, my speed was not a factor, and the police reports (with about a dozen witnesses) back that up. I'm more than willing to take responsibility for my mistakes, but this happened because of another driver's carelessness, and I don't know if I can ever forgive the guy, even if I knew who he was. Actually, it might be better for everyone that I don't know who he is.

Anyway, we were driving along a levee when a car coming toward me from the opposite lane tried to cut a left turn right in front of me. When he realized he couldn't make it, he just stopped, and doing that turned him into a roadblock.

I went onto the shoulder of the road to avoid hitting him, but the shoulder gave way, and the car flipped twice before landing on the roof. Vickie was thrown from the car.

Luckily for me, the roof of the Trans Am crushed down onto me when we rolled over, and when it did, my bucket seat broke, so I ended up lying flat as the car rolled over.

I never really lost consciousness the whole time, and I remember being upside down in a field by the side of the road. The other driver who had caused the whole thing by trying to make that turn got out, saw what happened, and left.

For a minute, I realized that Vickie wasn't sitting in the car with me, and I thought she must not have been with me at all. But when I spotted her shoe, what had just happened finally hit me.

Some other drivers came upon us within a few minutes, and they got out to see if they could help. A few people looked for Vickie after I told them she must be out there, somewhere. I tried to help search, but I was so banged up, I could barely move.

One of them found her in some bushes. I crawled over to her, and she was still alive. I lost track of time, but the ambulance arrived and took both of us. We rode together, and I remember asking the medic riding in the back with us, "How is she?"

He said, "Not good."

We got to the hospital in Jackson, where they examined her quickly and decided she would have to be treated in a nearby hospital that had a bigger trauma center, because of the extent of her injuries. I got emergency treatment, but then the hospital discharged me, because I had no health insurance. I was on a gurney, in horrible pain, and I asked if I could at least get a shot for my pain.

The doctor just shook his head and said, "Sorry, you're discharged."

Just a couple of minutes later, two guys came in and told me Vickie had passed away. They had taken her in another ambulance to the bigger trauma center, but she passed not long after they pulled out.

I was sad, furious, and miserable, all at once, and I had no way of letting it out. I remember I took out my wallet and bit down on it as hard as I could. I left teeth marks in it that never faded, because biting down on it as hard as I could was the only way I could keep from screaming.

If I could change anything in my life, this would be it. To this day, I feel sorry for what happened and will never forget Vickie. Back then, we did not wear seatbelts, but to this day, every time I buckle my seatbelt I think of Vickie and her family. I am so sorry that she was even with me that day.

Grizzly Smith picked me up and took me to his house, because he lived in the area. Grizzly took care of me for a while, and when I could move around a little, he brought me back to the house I had shared with Vickie.

Remember how I said earlier there were only two times I was self-conscious about how I looked, the first time being when my dad was in the hospital? The other time was Vickie's funeral. Making things worse, I was still broken up, and I don't mean just emotionally. My ribs were still compacted, and I could barely walk.

Ricky Ferrara was a short guy who had been a wrestler, but not a very successful one. He was a stout guy and had a lot of power, but his height worked against him. By 1982, Bill Watts had him working as a referee in Mid-South, and he struck a lot of people as a sour little guy, a guy who always had a thousand little complaints. But Ricky Ferrara was also someone who truly cared, who really reached out to me and became a good friend to me during this period, one of the most difficult times of my life. Ricky helped carry me to the funeral, and I remember everyone looking at me, all her well-to-do relatives, and I could hear the muttering: "Vickie died with *that* guy?"

After the funeral, I just lay around my house. I didn't want to see anyone. I wouldn't even bathe or answer the phone. But Ricky kept coming by the house, every day, often multiple times a day. He'd knock on the door, he'd ring the bell, and he'd repeat the process a few times. Then, he'd go back to his car, he'd smoke a cigarette, then he'd come back and knock, ring the bell—this little guy wasn't giving up. I think he'd have smoked his way through a carton, one at a time, if he had to.

Finally, I opened the door and let him in. He spent a lot of time with me, and I don't know how I would have pulled out of the misery that wreck put me in had it not been for Ricky Ferrara.

And for someone who was known to be a sour little guy, Ricky Ferrara made me laugh. He used to have this little old blue Toyota, and when I was a heel, we used to ride together to the New Orleans shows. When we got into town, if I saw any kids standing around, I'd roll down the window and yell, "Hey! None of you little bastards better throw rocks at this car!"

Next thing you know...*Ping! Ping! Ping!* Those kids usually had good aim!

I'd hear Ferrara growl, in his French accent, "Duggan, shut up!"

But he always liked me, as much as I aggravated him. I think, in all the years I knew him, the only two people outside his family he seemed to like were me and my future wife, Debra.

I'd ask him, "Hey, Ricky, how about the pope?"

"Ah, that lousy pope..."

I mean, he didn't like *anybody*. Ted DiBiase loved to play pranks on him, just to see him get worked up. DiBiase would get those loaded cigarettes, like tiny firecrackers, so they'd pop when someone lit up. DiBiase would take one and put it in Ricky's pack. Ricky would be sitting there smoking, when, *pop!*

"Gah, DiBiase, you bastard!"

Man, he got agitated with DiBiase!

He later opened up a gym in Pineville, and it was in his gym that I got in my 505-pound bench press, which was my personal best. I owe Ricky a lot, to say the least.

If being part of The Rat Pack was my first major break, then splitting away from DiBiase and becoming a good guy was quite possibly the biggest break of my career.

The angle was simple, but it spun me off into a new direction as an American patriot and gave me an instant, personal issue with DiBiase. Here was the angle: after booting Borne out of The Rat Pack, I took offense at DiBiase's joining up with anti-American manager Skandor Akbar, particularly since Akbar had previously managed the Iranian known as the Iron Sheik. I went on TV and announced I was parting ways with DiBiase, but he and I both said we would not fight each other and that he would stay out of my new feud with Akbar and his hired guns. Of course, this obviously meant that the first chance he got, which turned out to be during a match between me and Kendo Nagasaki (managed by Akbar), DiBiase nailed me with his loaded glove and joined Nagasaki and Akbar in beating me down. From that point, the feud was on.

The ironic thing was that when I made my Mid-South debut in 1982, it was as a bounty hunter looking to collect the money Akbar had placed on the head of "Captain Redneck" Dick Murdoch. But after a week or so, Akbar was never again in my corner, and people forgot our brief association.

And, obviously, it worked out great for me, because I've been carrying the American flag ever since. From the very first time I went out there as a good guy, leading the "U-S-A!" chants and showing my love for my country, it just felt right. And maybe it was the John Wayne fan in me, but I never enjoyed anything in wrestling as much as showing my patriotism and feeling the love that the people have for this great country. And that's for real.

And I think the fans can tell when it's for real. A lot of guys have done the "U-S-A!" thing, like when the WWF tried to put that gimmick on Lex Luger in 1993. They gave him an incredible push—interview segments, his own bus tour, patriotic music, red-white-and-blue trunks—the "total package," if you'll pardon the expression. People would actually come up to me and ask if I was mad that he was doing my gimmick. I always had the same answer.

"The difference is, that's not Lex," I'd say. "That's the WWF, trying to manufacture a personality. And the people know that—they know the difference."

Now, Lex's previous gimmick—"The Narcissist"—he did great with that, because that was him. To be honest, I did see Lex's patriotic gimmick and push as a sign that it was probably time for me to move on, and it probably did play into my decision to leave the WWF in 1993.

But I don't care if we're talking about Lex, or Kurt Angle, or anyone else—I don't think anyone does the "U-S-A!" thing better than I do, and that's because people can relate to me, and they know that with me, it's a genuine feeling. It's truly from the heart, and something I am legitimately, extremely proud to do; my success has come from people seeing that it is real. My dad was a proud American, and it was something he instilled in all his kids, even through the 1960s, with all the political unrest in the country.

Anyway, the timing was right for me to turn back in 1983, because at that point, the fans were kind of turning me babyface anyway. Those Mid-South fans liked hard-nosed tough guys, and I could feel that there were a lot of them who liked my wild, brawling style in the ring. Obviously, Bill Watts saw the same thing, and he was right—once again, he showed that he knew exactly what his fans would respond to.

But I do have to make one confession, and I'm revealing this to the fans for the first time—I loved Skandor Akbar. In real life, his name was Jim Wheba, a guy from Texas, and he was as proud an American as anyone, even though he played his villainous role very well.

One of the most memorable moments of our feud—which went on and off for three years—occurred on May 4, 1985. I was wrestling Kamala, in Jackson, Mississippi, when Akbar came in and threw a fireball at me. I'd never had fire thrown at me before, and this was a huge fireball. I had no idea how big it would be, but I trusted Akbar, and he threw a fistful of fire. It singed my beard, and could actually have hurt me bad, if I hadn't closed my eyes. It did singe off my eyebrows.

We turned it into this great bit where I was injured and might never be able to return. We did this bedside interview, with me looking all burned. We took iodine and cigarette ashes and rubbed them into my skin, and we shaved half my beard. When that interview aired, it got over huge. Now, this was back in the days of "no work, no pay," but this was such a strong angle that Watts paid me a few weeks to sit at home, just to sell the injury. It worked out, because I lived in the woods of Louisiana, like a hermit, away from people. When I wasn't on the road, I tended to go to the gym and back home, and that was it.

Akbar was also a great teacher, and I learned a lot from working with him. Mostly, what I learned from him was how to do a proper interview. He knew how to get his points across, how to emphasize the important aspects of the upcoming match and still get his shots in, to make sure he was as hated as ever. And he had a real style to the way he talked. He would always refer to my "big, bell-pepper nose" and always referred to New Orleans as the "Crescent City."

It took me a while to realize it, but doing an interview was a vital part of the business, and like everything else in wrestling, it was a learned trade; you didn't just all of a sudden walk out on camera and start talking. For Bill Watts, you weren't going to do just one generic interview—you were going to do one for every city you were going to, and you had to get across the story of the match. If we were having a coal miner's glove match, I would wear the glove during my interview to show off the metal studs on the knuckles. And Watts ran a tight ship—if you didn't get your points across well enough, he'd have you do the interview over. And over. And over. And over. And...well, you get the idea.

And Akbar's main charge, Kamala, was a guy who didn't do interviews, because it was part of his gimmick as a Ugandan savage, but he didn't need to. He was huge, and actually pretty athletic. Away from the ring, he was James Harris, who's still a friend of mine all these years later. I always liked working with him. James invented the spot I called the "weeble-wobble, but you don't fall down." His opponent would nail him once, and he'd stagger; nail him again, and he'd teeter even more; and finally, the other guy would give him a big shot, and James would go down. When he did, the place would pop huge, every time. I still use that spot with young guys who have size.

A lot of people don't know this, but James is also a wonderful singer—seriously, he has a great voice. And he was one of the most even-tempered wrestlers I ever knew. In the 30 years I've known him, I've only seen him go off twice. Once was in Europe when we were all in the WWF in the early 1990s. We were on the bus, and Brian Knobbs and Jerry Sags—The Nasty Boys—had one of those portable VCR units, and they were watching *Blazing Saddles* over and over. If you've never seen it, it's a funny movie, but it does have a lot of racial epithets, including the n-word, and everyone on the bus could hear it. After about three full viewings, James finally turned around and yelled, "That's enough of that!"

And you had better believe The Nasty Boys turned it off, immediately.

The only other time I saw James that angry was in 2010, when we were both working one of those Insane Clown Posse wrestling shows. He and I worked a match at 4:00 AM, because the shows were part of these all-day festivals. It was the first time in 32 years of wrestling that I ever stood in a wrestling ring as the sun was coming up. We were there all day and all night, and James ended up going off because all the delays in getting us out of there caused him to miss his flight. But James is a true gentleman.

After The Rat Pack split, my popularity soared, although on at least one occasion, some fans still held a grudge, or maybe someone just decided to show how tough they were.

One night, we were working in Monroe, Louisiana, and I was against DiBiase, substituting for JYD. We actually had a pretty good match, and after 15 to 20 minutes, we were both bloody and panting. Back then, Mid-South had only a rope surrounding the ringside area to serve as a barricade between the fans and the wrestlers. On this night, the fans were gradually pushing the barricade closer to the ring, and when I was outside the ring, a fan clipped me with his fist. I reached back to get the guy, who couldn't have been but 18 or 19, but his old man sitting next to him got a good shot on me. I hit the guy twice, and down he went.

The guy sued me, Mid-South Wrestling, and the arena management. I remember thinking, *Wait a minute—this guy punched me first!*

I even had a police officer, who had been my escort to the ring that night, as a witness, so I decided to go to court. The father hadn't done me any real damage, but he could have, and I don't care how tough you are—it hurts to get punched in the face.

I had done damage to him, which in court he described as his right front orbital lobe being strained after being pushed in. They had to operate through the roof of his mouth to fix it.

It took so long to get to court that when it did, it was seven years later, and I was living in Florida, working for the World Wrestling Federation. Debra and I flew into Louisiana for the trial, and paid for hotel and a rental car. I still remember sitting in court; my suit was too tight, and my tie was never straight.

The guy got on the stand and said, "I don't know what happened—the guy just hit me."

The arena and Mid-South owner Bill Watts settled out of court. I should have, too, but I was young, dumb, and naïve, and thought I should go to court because I had the right to defend myself.

The judge said I used excessive force in defending myself and awarded the guy some money. Then, I did the dumbest of dumb things—I appealed. When it was all over, I had flushed a boatload of money down the drain. Live and learn.

The matches with DiBiase and me were brutal, even when no fans got involved. We were getting juiced every night (caused by cutting our foreheads with tiny razor blades, a little bit of blood mixing with sweat to look like a gusher, a practice I always hated and never did unless absolutely necessary). After a few weeks of matches with each other, our heads had turned into hamburger from bleeding every night.

We finally went to Ernie Ladd, who was the booker at the time, and asked if we could do without the blood when possible, to give our heads a little time to recover. Teddy pleaded our case.

"Ernie, it's a Sunday afternoon, we don't have a big crowd here, and we still have another show tonight," he said. "Can we just take it easy on our heads?"

Ernie said that was fine, so we went out and had our match. Our first spot was a little give and take, ending when I, as the babyface, popped Teddy and gave him a big bump, which the crowd always reacted well to. This time, when I did it, I misjudged and popped Teddy on the nose, and you would have thought I'd cut his throat, because he was just gushing blood.

Teddy put his hand up to his face, looked at the blood, and then just glared at me.

I was muttering, "Oh, man, Teddy, I'm so sorry."

I was serious about my dislike for the blade. I thought it was desecrating my body to intentionally cut myself. The pain wasn't a big deal, but I've never been into self-mutilation: I'm not a piercing guy, and I've never been a tattoo guy. DiBiase used to joke that it looked like I was arm-wrestling myself with the blade, with one of my arms knowing we needed to get some blood and the other arm fighting off the blade.

One night, we had a pretty heated match, and at the designated spot, I went down and bladed myself. I came back up and Teddy said, "It's not enough!"

We did some brawling, and I went back down and cut myself again. I got up, and he said, "Jim, it's still not coming out!"

So I repeated the process until I looked down and saw blood all over my boots. I was pouring blood; DiBiase was just screwing with me! There was blood everywhere, and DiBiase was looking at me, holding back from laughing his ass off, still going, "More, Jim! You need more color!"

CHAPTER 8

LIFE WITH DR. DEATH

I MET STEVE WILLIAMS IN 1982, when he came into Mid-South from the University of Oklahoma. Doc had been an All-American in wrestling and football there, and both Bill Watts and Jim Ross were big OU guys.

Here's how tough a guy Steve Williams was. His wrestling nickname, Dr. Death? He got tagged with that in *eighth grade*.

We would end up becoming best friends, but initially, Doc and I didn't get along, which I chalk up to that competitive athlete's instinct. Especially in those days of wrestling, walking into a new locker room was like stepping into a snake pit of tough guys. Everybody was sizing each other up, and when Doc arrived, I was one of the big dogs, so we eyeballed each other for a long time. But once we got to know each other, we realized we had a lot in common, and our friendship really took off from there.

Doc and I ended up being roommates and sharing a house in Ball, a little town in central Louisiana. What a name for a town. It even turned into a joke, when we'd ask a young lady, "So, would you like to come to Ball?"

As you might imagine, I got slapped, more than once.

But Doc was the best roommate anyone could have asked for, and a perfect fit for me. He was extremely neat and was actually an excellent cook. I, on the other hand, was extremely messy and can't even boil water.

Doc and I had some close calls on the road. Mid-South was notorious for the travel—every one of us went up and down these lousy, two-lane roads through Louisiana, Arkansas, Texas, Mississippi, and Oklahoma. The travel was a grind, and the wrestlers tried to make it a little more tolerable by riding in style—Magnum T.A. had a Mustang GT, Butch Reed had a Camaro, JYD had a Mercedes, DiBiase had a Z-28. It was like race car city, especially late at night, coming down the little stretches of interstate we'd come across between country roads. Everybody flew by, even on those two-lane roads, and a lot of guys had accidents. Buddy Landell once rear-ended Butch Reed.

Sometimes, though, conditions were too dangerous to drive in at all. One night in 1983, I was driving out of Little Rock and had to be in New Orleans (a few hundred miles away) the next night for another show. I had just bought a brand-new Lincoln Town Car. It was cardinal red, just a gorgeous vehicle.

It was a snowy, rainy, icy night. I figured I would ride out that night, instead of getting a room and heading out in the morning, which could have meant cutting it too close to showtime in the event of an accident or even a bad traffic jam.

The Junkyard Dog had ridden out to Little Rock with me, but he wasn't coming with me to New Orleans, at least not that night.

"I'm not doing it, Jim," he said. "The weather's just too bad."

"Oh, come on, Dog—it'll be all right."

JYD wouldn't budge. But Magnum T.A. said he'd ride with me. Magnum was a good kid, and we'd worked together a lot, so I was glad for the company.

We jumped into the Lincoln and got going. Doc and a girlfriend of his were following us over the one and only main road that went from Little Rock to Shreveport, which we had to go through to get to our final stop.

We were probably going too fast for the weather conditions, and we came around a corner right before this long bridge. When we made the corner, we hit a patch of black ice. I was trying to regain control of the car, spinning the wheel one way, then the other, while Magnum kept repeating, "Just make the bridge...just make the bridge."

He was right, too, because if we made the bridge, we'd hit one of the guardrails and bounce off. It would be rough, but at least we'd be stopped. But if we went off the road before the bridge, we were going into the water, and since this was a body of water controlled by a levee, that meant a long way down before hitting the water.

We made it to the bridge and hit the guardrail on the right-hand side—*boom!* Now, we were totally out of control—*boom!* The car hit the left-hand side. As we bounced from side to side, Magnum and I kept talking to each other: "I'm okay, you okay?" "Yeah, I'm okay. You okay?" "Yeah, I'm okay, you okay?" "Yeah..."

We kept bouncing from side to side until we hit the left side of this north-south bridge that we had entered from the north. My Lincoln was on the south end, and thankfully Doc was far enough behind us that he was able to pull over after we came to a stop.

Doc's young lady stayed in the car, and he walked over to see if we needed help. Physically, we were okay, but as the three of us stood on the side of the road, looking at my previously beautiful Lincoln, I was in total denial.

I think it was Magnum who asked, "Um, so you figure it's totaled?"

"Nah," I could hear myself say, "It's brand new. They're...they're good cars."

The car was still jutting out into the road at the edge of the bridge, though, so the three of us realized we should try to stop traffic before someone ran into the wreck and really got hurt. I turned around and started walking north up the bridge when out of the fog and ice, I heard the big booming horn of an 18-wheeler, coming from the south.

Doc and Magnum were in the road, waving their arms and yelling, "Stop! Stop! Stop!"

But the truck couldn't stop, because of the ice on the road, and they both got out of the way just in time. The driver couldn't get it locked down, and the 18-wheeler hit the Lincoln, broadside, but the truck still didn't stop. It went up over the wreckage of my car and almost rolled all the way over the Lincoln before falling and crashing onto its side.

I was on the bridge, and I could see the truck crashing its way down the bridge, so I started running as fast as I could, because it was coming right at me. I could hear the scream and scrape of the metal getting closer and closer.

I was almost to the north end of the bridge when I knew time had run out—that truck would have smashed me, and I wouldn't even have slowed it down. At the last minute, I jumped over the railing on the left side of the bridge and hit the bank of the river. I rolled all the way down into the river as the 18-wheeler crashed on past me. The Lincoln's wheels, the front axle, went off the right edge of the bridge at the same time.

My glasses were gone, I had lost a boot, and my hands and feet were in that freezing water. I could barely breathe, but I do remember thinking, *Thank God Doc parked where he did*, because if he had pulled off to the other side of the road, at that same spot, his girl would have gotten wiped out, because that was where the truck was sliding.

Meanwhile, Doc and Magnum were up top, running as fast as they could across the bridge and screaming, "Duggan! Duggan!"

I managed to blurt out, "I-I-I-I-'m down here!"

They were both kind of shocked, because as they later told me, they were both convinced I was dead, either from going off the bridge or getting hit by the wreckage.

I made my way up the riverbank, far enough up that Magnum could grab me and pull me up over the bridge railing. I looked and saw the 18-wheeler, folded on its side, and now we had another problem—this was a tanker truck, and whatever it was hauling was now pouring out onto the frozen roadway. I felt responsible, so I ran over to the cab of the truck. It was still on its side, passenger side up, and the driver was in there, strapped in place by his seatbelt. He looked like he was in shock.

I was yelling, "You all right? You okay?"

He said, "Why, yes, I'm fine," so calmly it was kind of scary.

I grabbed the driver, managed to undo his seatbelt, and pulled him out of the truck cab. Meanwhile, Doc and Magnum had gone back south to warn any other drivers that might be coming through. The truck driver was sitting on the guardrail like nothing had happened, while I had my head in my hands, going, "Oh my God, I can't believe this! I totaled my new car, we got a jackknifed 18-wheeler...what else can go wrong?"

At precisely that moment, I could hear the engine roar of another 18-wheeler, off in the distance. I tore my shirt off and started waving it like a flag, screaming, "Stop! Stop!"

That one hit the brakes and glided a little on the ice, but managed to stop, as did the next few vehicles to come along. Pretty soon, the cops were there, getting everyone's statements and processing the scene.

Turned out that tanker truck had been carrying hot asphalt, and when it tipped over, all that asphalt fell onto the road. So, not only did I wreck my new car and an 18-wheeler, I closed the main highway between Little Rock and Shreveport for about two days. I made the newspapers!

I ended up having to go to the little police station, but not before an Arkansas state trooper and a local cop had a good, long argument about whose jurisdiction it was. Finally the state trooper told me I was under arrest and told the local cop to take me to his police station. The local cop, who hadn't given me a second glance before now, got me into his car and looked over at me. He turned away, but then turned his head back to me and said, "Wait...Hacksaw Duggan?"

So we were heading back to his station, talking wrestling the whole way—this guy was a real fan. We reached the station, and the local officer called the district attorney and explained what happened but stressed how it had been an accident, and the D.A. said, "Eh, just let him go."

I ended up getting a ticket for driving too fast for the conditions on the road.

Doc, his girlfriend, and Magnum had followed us to the station in Doc's little car, and the four of us rode out of there, with me driving. It was now coming up on daylight, so we were all exhausted, but I was without my glasses and missing a boot.

Doc and Magnum made the show, but I just couldn't make the trip after all that had happened. It ended up being one of the only days I ever took off while working for Mid-South.

As 1983 came to an end, my stint as a babyface was really catching on, and Mid-South was about to get an influx of talent that would make 1984 a huge year for the company. This, despite the fact that Vince McMahon's World Wrestling Federation was expanding from its northeastern base and waging war against the regional offices as he tried to become a nationwide wrestling promotion.

Not that we were short on talent in 1983—look at any of those Mid-South cards and you'll see lists of names, guys who either were or would become some of the biggest names in pro wrestling.

Magnum T.A. had been a great friend and tag partner for me, and I enjoyed watching him develop his confidence and become a real star. Magnum really came into his own during a feud with Johnny Walker, better known as the masked Mr. Wrestling II. "Two," as he was called, was a character and I liked him personally, but he hated working with me. Like when I was in Georgia with DiBiase and Tommy Rich, Two found me a little stiff.

Once, Two and I were wrestling and I popped him pretty good—I didn't mean to, but I didn't know what I was doing, and I was a little unprofessional and careless. As soon as I popped him, I just cringed, because I knew I'd nailed him way too hard—plus, I had at least 60 pounds and four inches on him. As I looked at him, there was this little red spot on his white mask, and the dot got bigger...and bigger...until pretty soon, half his mask was blood-red.

I actually saw him at an NWA Legends Convention in 2009. I told him that it had gone full circle for me. I was now the veteran getting the crap knocked out of me by young kids with no idea what they're doing in the ring. We got a good laugh out of that.

Of course, Wrestling II was no cake walk, either. His finisher was a big running knee lift, but what most folks don't realize is that it wasn't the knee to the gut that hurt—it was the slap to the back he did to get a good popping sound and sell the move. Man, that used to sting! But he always put up with me, and even when I popped him that time, he made sure I knew later there were no hard feelings. He was a good guy.

Another one of the young guys I enjoyed working with was Barry Darsow, who had a great gimmick for getting heat in an area like Mid-South, where patriotism got over huge. "Krusher" Darsow became "Krusher" Khrushchev in order to learn Soviet training techniques from Nikolai Volkoff, but by doing that, he swore allegiance to the USSR, and he got a lot of heat as a traitor to the United States.

I was wrestling him in late 1983 when Nikolai came down with my coal miner's glove, which they had "stolen" from me earlier. Nikolai nailed me with the glove, and I started coughing up blood. People were horrified, and these Mid-South fans were not cream puffs.

Now, I know there are stories about blood capsules, but we weren't using any special effects stuff like that in Mid-South. What Bill Watts had me do was stick a hypodermic needle in my arm to draw blood, inject the blood into a condom, tie it into a knot, and give the rubber to the referee. When Nikolai hit me, I went down, and the ref slipped me the rubber. I put the rubber in my mouth, and then Darsow held me up while Nikolai hit me "in the throat." At that point, I bit the rubber, and the blood splattered everywhere. They carried me out, and the people thought I'd been beaten half to death.

What none of the fans knew was that this was an angle designed to "injure" me for a few months to build up big return matches with both Darsow and Volkoff. Watts worked out a deal with Dusty Rhodes, who was booking and wrestling as the top babyface down in Florida, to send me down there while they sold the injury in Mid-South. Between cable and the Internet, you could never pull that off today, but wrestling was so regional then that I was able to go into Florida as a heel for the couple of months I was out of Mid-South.

CHAPTER 9

LOVE HITS ME LIKE A 2X4

THE STORYLINE IN FLORIDA WAS THAT KEVIN SULLIVAN, who was playing a cult leader character that brainwashed people, possessed me and sent me into battle against Dusty Rhodes. We did these "first-blood" matches, where the winner was the first one to make his opponent bleed. The finish was great—the referee would go down, and while he was "out," Dusty would bust me open, but Sullivan would come up with that tough-skin stuff and some Vaseline to close the cut. Then, we'd hit Dusty, and he'd juice just in time for the referee to "wake up" and see it, awarding me the match.

Those fans went nuts. "But he was bleeding first!"

Being a heel again was kind of fun, if I'm being honest. I was living with this gorgeous lady named Geneva, who I think was Ronnie Garvin's ex-wife, as my landlady—she had this huge house with this little efficiency apartment and a pool. I met a very petite stripper named Terri, and I gotta say, those were some wild times. One time, Terri and this other girl were fighting, and the other girl (who was a lot bigger) was beating her up pretty good. I tried to pull the bigger girl off Terri, and she said she was going to get some friends, come back, and kill us both.

Now, I don't like to judge people, but this broad struck me as the type who, if she said she was going to kill you, she meant it. I had my pistol, and I put it on top of the front wheel of my car and waited outside in case anything went down. Nothing did, but that was just the kind of craziness going on there.

77

A few years later, when I was in the WWF and we were on tour through Florida, I was coming to the ring when I heard this loud, shrieking, "Jim! Jim!"

I turned around, and there was Terri, with two little kids clinging to her. I just stood there, in horror, thinking, *Oh, no.*

If you're reading this, and you have memories of seeing me in Tampa around 1987, and my match was lousy, I apologize, but I was a little distracted. I saw her after the show and she introduced me to her husband, a great guy whom she had gotten with right after I left for Mid-South. I was glad to see that she had found herself a genuinely nice fellow...and that I wasn't going to be explaining how I was a daddy!

When Bill Watts called me to say it was time to come back to Mid-South, I kind of waffled—"Gee, Bill, Tampa's really great!" But he talked me into it and I went back. It's a good thing I did, because as it turned out, that was where I would find my one true love.

Right after I left for Florida, at the end of 1983, Watts and Memphis promoter Jerry Jarrett had put together a talent trade that ended up bringing Terry Taylor, The Rock & Roll Express, and The Midnight Express, with manager Jim Cornette, to Mid-South.

Terry Taylor was from Vero Beach, where my mom grew up, so he automatically became my family's favorite wrestler. He was a smart, good-looking guy who was very likable, but he put his foot in his mouth more than anyone else I ever saw. A lot of times, he was just being honest, but I think lack of diplomacy has caused him to shoot himself in the foot more than once. He and I have remained friends, and he was a real student of the business; he even kept notebooks of finishes and kept up with what was going on.

But the popularity of The Rock & Roll Express, Ricky Morton and Robert Gibson, was just amazing, and they were good guys, too. We've remained friends to this day.

They had a unique look, as they were smaller than most wrestlers, but they were really quick and exciting to watch. They wore these full-length tights with bandanas tied onto them at various spots. One night, they were in a match when Robert went up to the top rope. Unfortunately for him, one of his bandanas had gotten caught in the rope, so when he did his dive, it caught and caused him to face-plant onto the mat.

The new talent led to business shooting up, but what also helped was the creativity of a Memphis booker who came along named Bill Dundee. I got along pretty well with Dundee, a New Zealand native and longtime wrestler—although at 5'4" he did have a bit of a Napoleon complex and would say things like, "I'm bigger than all of you if I stand on my wallet."

He was a character. But still, he and I never had any major problems.

One night, we were in the hotel bar in Bossier City, Louisiana, while a player from the Dallas Cowboys was there and buying drinks for everyone. The first couple of rounds, I thought it was a really nice thing for him to do, but he kept buying shots! We had to spend most of the next day in the studio, cutting our TV promos for our arena matches. Back then, we had to do separate promos for every city, every match, one after the other. It was always a long day, a lot more tiring than it sounds, and it was not something you wanted to be doing with a hangover.

A couple of the wrestlers thanked the football player and tried to get out of there, explaining that we all had a big day of TV in the morning. Next thing you know, this guy was telling all of us "phony wrestlers" how we were sissies and how he could drink anyone under the table, because, by God, he was a Dallas Cowboys football player.

Well, I didn't want to be rude to the guy, but I also didn't want to get plastered, and I was getting sick of his lip, so I started dumping out my drinks onto the floor.

I got into Dundee's ear and told him that drinking too much the night before we had to cut all the promos was just looking for trouble, and I spread the message to some of the other wrestlers, too. They spread it to more guys, and by the end of the night, the Cowboys player had spent hundreds of dollars, he was completely plowed, and the floor of the bar was soaking wet.

The lights came on at midnight when the bar closed, and that football star stood up, wobbled for a second, looked around, and then puked his guts out. This barroom full of wrestlers broke out into applause, giving him an ovation.

Another night, Terry and I were in Alexandria, Louisiana, at the Sheraton bar, and this guy started arguing with me in the bathroom. I don't even remember what it was about, but it got to the point I figured we were done talking. Unfortunately, when I went to hit him, I slipped on the pee-soaked floor and took a bump right there. The guy put a couple of boots to me while I was down and ran out the door.

I came out of the bathroom with my knees swollen up and my glasses crooked, covered in pee, thinking, *I don't imagine I'll do that again.*

The clean-cut, wholesome-looking Terry Taylor stared at me like I was an alien from outer space.

A star from the Mid-Atlantic territory spent a couple of months in Mid-South in 1984, and although he didn't make a huge impression on the main event scene, he made perhaps the biggest difference in my life out of every wrestler I ever worked with.

Jay Youngblood was the son of Ricky Romero, a talented journeyman who probably attained his biggest success in the 1960s in the Amarillo territory owned by the Funk family. Jay adopted a Native American gimmick, complete with the headdress and war dance, and did pretty well for himself, especially in tag-team wrestling. On Thanksgiving night in 1983, Jay and partner Ricky Steamboat beat the Brisco Brothers in one of the feature matches of the first Starrcade, a Crockett Promotions show that was shown on closed-circuit TV throughout arenas in the Mid-Atlantic territory where Steamboat and Youngblood were the most popular tag team they'd seen in a long time.

In 1984, Jay and Steamboat kind of went their separate ways, and that summer, Jay ended up coming to Louisiana to wrestle for Bill Watts' Mid-South Wrestling.

Jay told me that he knew this girl who would be perfect for me. Her name was Debra Haynes.

DEBRA SAYS:
I was living in Charlotte, North Carolina, at the time, and Jim was in Louisiana. I had known Jay and his family for years. I used to babysit his little girl. A few months after he left the Carolinas to go wrestle down south, he called one day and said, "Debra, I've met the perfect guy for you."

Friends had tried to fix me up before, so I said, "Yeah, right."

It was funny that he would have even thought of Debra and me, because when Jay first got into the area, both Dr. Death and myself, we didn't like him. He just rubbed us the wrong way—he was a cocky young guy, the kind of guy who was good looking and knew it. Doc and I were ex-jocks who didn't have a whole lot of patience for anyone we considered a "pretty boy."

But we did some traveling together, and Jay won us over. He was funny, and he really was a nice guy, even if he *was* very self-confident.

So, one night, we were driving back home from a show in Biloxi, Mississippi, and he was telling me about Debra. He then told me something that has kind of haunted me for years: "I'll introduce you, the two of you are going to fall in love, and then I'll never see either one of you again."

Not too long after that, he introduced us. We did fall in love, and we never did see him again.

DEBRA SAYS:
I remember it being the end of summer in 1985, about a year after Jim and I met. We were in the car with Bill Watts, and we got to talking. He asked us how we met, and we told him about Jay Youngblood introducing us.

A few days later, on one of Jim's rare days off, Jim and I got a call at home. It was Bill Watts, and he was calling because of some news he had just received.

"I'm sorry to have to tell you this, but I thought you two would want to know. Jay Youngblood passed away. He was on a tour of Australia, and it looks like he had a heart attack."

I still get chills thinking about Jay, and that phone call, to this day.

In 1984, Debra was still living in the Carolinas, and Doc and I were still roommates at our house in Ball. When Jay gave me her phone number, I called, and we talked for a good long while. We called back and forth, the next few weeks, and after dozens of conversations, I felt like I probably knew her as well as I knew anyone. Something just clicked. I can't even tell you what it was, but we just hit it off, and I think we both knew there was something here.

I invited her to come down to Louisiana, and so she flew into Alexandria. I met her at the airport, and I still remember the little blue-and-white dress she wore. She stayed for two or three days, and we planned another visit.

DEBRA SAYS:
We kept planning trips for get-togethers, and the trips kept getting longer and longer. He and Doc even started taking me on some of their shorter road trips, and my only complaint was that sitting in the backseat, I couldn't even look through the windshield to tell where we were, because these two massive guys took up the entire front!

Jim and Doc even figured out ways to get little mini-workouts in. We'd be on a two-lane highway, and those two would get out when we got to a diner somewhere. We'd order food for the three of us, and then the two of them would go running down the highway—however long it took for the food to be ready, that was how long they had to run. I'd pick up the food and then get in the car and pick them up.

I always used to joke that Debra brought a little more stuff every time she came down, and before I knew it, she had more stuff in that house than me or Doc!

82

Before much longer, Debra moved in, and we ended up living together about four and a half years before we finally got married.

When The Rock & Roll Express moved on, around 1995, The Fantastics had a tough act to follow. But Bobby Fulton and Tommy Rogers worked hard and did a good job winning over the people.

They also took their lumps on the road. Sometimes, the long road trips were great bull sessions between the guys. But one time, a carload of us were driving late at night when a couple of us had to take a leak. You have to understand, these were country areas, and it's not like there was a rest stop every five miles. If you had to go, you just pulled over and went into the weeds, so that's what we did. When we were done, we got back into the car and took off once we heard the car door shut. We resumed the conversation and had gotten about 10 miles down the road when I said, "Well, hell, Bobby must be laying down and...shit! He ain't even in the car!"

We turned the car around and found him, but he was not happy.

Those guys used to catch hell—we'd be in the car in Louisiana, and we'd see a sign that said, "Fresh shrimp ahead," and I'd go, "Hey, it's The Fantastics!"

But they didn't just take it. They'd usually come back with something like, "Yeah, we saw a sign a mile back that said 'big-mouth bass,' and there was Duggan!"

But while things were really good in Mid-South during this period, big changes were happening in wrestling. Vince McMahon's WWF had been in the Northeast region for decades, but when he bought the promotion from his dad (Vincent J. McMahon, who had been in charge when I started there in 1980), he had the idea to go national. With cable TV becoming more popular, it was easier than ever to have wrestlers featured on a nationwide show, and Vince wanted it to be his wrestlers and his show.

He went after local TV slots and the top talent in every territory. Mid-South was no different, and Junkyard Dog defected in August of 1984.

Bill Watts wasn't concerned, though. After McMahon's first WrestleMania in March of 1985 (with Hulk Hogan and Mr. T in the main event against Roddy Piper and Paul Orndorff), I remember Watts saying that McMahon would never follow WrestleMania, that it was a onetime shot. And because Watts' shows outdrew the WWF anytime McMahon tried to run a show in our area, I can see where Watts would think that. But it sure didn't play out that way.

For me, JYD leaving was like getting a promotion, because I now had the main spot as the top good guy, and business stayed strong. As big as JYD was, a hot territory (which Mid-South was) was always bigger than any one talent.

The same was true a few years later when I was in the WWF and negotiating a new contract with Vince McMahon. At one point during our meeting, I said, "If you don't need me here, I don't need to be here."

He said, "Jim, we don't *need* anybody here."

Watts was kind of the same way, and his territory stayed strong, right up to the end. The oil crunch of 1986 really hurt him, just as he was trying to go national, and that's what did him in, but that's a whole other story. All I can tell you is, as early as 1983, I was earning a $3,000-per-week guarantee (more, if business was good enough to get me a bump), which was great money for that time period.

In late 1984, my biggest in-ring feud ever resumed, when Ted DiBiase returned to the Mid-South area. Our 1983 feud had ended when I beat him in a series of "loser leaves" matches, and he spent about a year wrestling on WTBS for World Championship Wrestling (formerly Georgia Championship). However, earlier in 1984, the WWF had taken over the WTBS slot from the Georgia/WCW group (another sign of McMahon's company taking on the other promotions and trying to go national), and booker/owner Ole Anderson was able to get back on the Superstation, but only at the crack of dawn on Saturday mornings. His territory was drying up, and DiBiase realized he'd be better off coming back to Mid-South.

His debut was pretty memorable television, if I do say so myself. For weeks, Steve Williams (who was now wrestling as a villain) had been bringing a football helmet to the ring, evoking his OU football days, and slugging people with it to gain illegal advantages during his matches. Finally, to end this abuse, I challenged him to a helmet match; we'd put a helmet on a pole, and whoever got it first could use it.

However, when it came time for the match, Doc was in the ring but I was nowhere to be found. Finally, Ted DiBiase came out and gave Doc my old SMU helmet, explaining that he had beaten me up and taken it after I'd tried to jump him in the parking lot.

Later, Mid-South officials found me in a bloody heap, but they explained that I demanded to come onto TV and speak to the people, and I gave a promo that I'm still pretty proud of. As two officials supported me, one under each arm, I said I got blasted from behind by Ted DiBiase and two masked thugs. They had mugged me and stolen the helmet, but I was ready to fight Doc and bring him to justice for all the abuse he'd been doling out to people. Of course, the officials said I was in no condition to go, and they had me taken to a hospital—and all of this laid the groundwork for the next leg of my feud with DiBiase.

And now, here's the rest of the story.

I was out in the back of the Irish McNeill's Boys Club, where we did the Mid-South TV tapings, waiting for them to come get me for my big promo. I rolled around in the mud and tore my shirt—I had one hell of a fight with myself. I got a great big blade, and I was waiting and waiting for the right time to cut myself. Finally, referee Pee Wee Anderson came out and said, "Go ahead and get the juice, and we'll bring you in."

I said, "Cool," and I hit it, cutting myself three or four times, and I was so worked up and sweaty from the fight I had with myself that the blood was coming down pretty good.

Pee Wee poked his head back out the door and said, "Did you get it?"

I said, "Yeah!"

He said, "Okay, great—I'll be right back."

I was like, "You'll be right back? It's coming now!"

I was sitting there when I heard someone walk up—it was a cop with his flashlight. He saw me and went straight to his radio—"We got a man down! Man down!"

I jumped up and told him, "No, sir, officer, it's okay! I'm all right!"

He said, "No, you don't realize how bad you're hurt."

The cop called for an ambulance, but then Pee Wee came out, and they dragged me back in to the TV studio area. I was draped over the barricade, doing my promo, and it ended up being better than anything we could have planned, because in the background, you could hear the siren of the ambulance they'd called for me getting closer and closer.

It's a good thing the promo was the only thing I was supposed to do, because they hauled me right out of there in an ambulance. They were checking my blood pressure, and when I tried to tell the medic I was okay, he looked at my crossed eyes and said, "Oh my God—he's going into shock! Look at his eyes!"

The real reason I didn't want to go to the hospital was that Shreveport was a big party town, and the last thing I wanted was to kill all night at the hospital. I would have been happy getting tape wrapped around my head and going out with the guys, looking like I had walked right out of *Spirit of '76*. I ended up not going to the hospital—they checked me in the ambulance and decided that if I said I was okay, I wasn't hurt badly enough for them to keep me.

The DiBiase feud culminated in another deal that was a lot of fun—the best-dressed man in Mid-South contest. Teddy was and is a dapper guy, while I'm just fine in T-shirt and jeans. But he had repeatedly insulted me for having no class, so I challenged him to see who the fans thought looked better in a tux.

The best part was Teddy looked so much sharper than I did. His shirt was crisp, he had pleats in his pants, and not a button was out of place. I came out with my shirt half untucked and my tie crooked, but the crowd was going to pop more for me, no matter what. He demanded we do it over, so the next week, they did it by measuring sound levels so that even boos would register as sound, and they got electronic sound monitors to measure our reactions. I got a great ovation, and when they announced Teddy, those fans sat on their hands. I mean, it wasn't total silence, but it was a pretty quiet group, because they didn't want their jeers to count in the villainous DiBiase's favor.

So once more, I was declared the winner, and DiBiase was furious. He'd been carrying a baseball bat "for protection" because I was such an uncouth brawler, and he carried it out to the TV truck in the parking lot, where the monitoring equipment was being kept. After losing an argument with TV show director Joel Watts, DiBiase turned to come back into the building, when he stopped and looked at the vehicle parked next to the TV truck. Anyone watching knew what was coming next, but it still got him a lot of heat.

He pointed and said, "Isn't that Jim Duggan's car?"

Seconds later, he was bashing in my windshield with the bat, until I ran him off. Poor Teddy—he was trying to break out the windshield, but the way they're made, they just crack and don't shatter on people, so he actually was starting to blow up from the effort!

It led to some big rematches, including one in Houston that people still talk to me about at conventions and other appearances. It was a street fight (which basically meant no disqualification and no rules), with us wearing tuxedos, with taped fists, in a steel cage, with the coal miner's glove on top of a 10-foot pole, and the loser had to leave town for 30 days. It was every stipulation match there was, all rolled into one. Well, DiBiase had a tour of Japan scheduled for the next few weeks, so guess who left town for 30 days?

Ted DiBiase versus Hacksaw Duggan was such a perfect feud, not only because of the issue of the friendship and the betrayal, but also because of our styles. I had one interview line that summed it up so well that I used it many times over the years.

"You know," I'd say, "Ted DiBiase may be the best pure wrestler in the world...but he can't fight worth a lick! And when he gets in the ring with Hacksaw Duggan, there ain't gonna be no go-behinds, no takeovers, no fancy-dan suplexes. It's gonna be a fight!"

In reality, the biggest fights usually were against the fans, especially for the heels.

You hear people say things like, "You see that old man whack that wrestler with the cane?"

Yeah, it's real funny, unless you're the guy getting hit with the cane—it hurts, old guy or not. And a lot of times, fans would throw stuff, and the thing was, they'd never hit the heel they were throwing at—I was working once when a battery whizzed right by my head and hit a lady in the front row.

Two of the roughest towns were Houston and Oklahoma City, because the arenas in both cities served mixed drinks, not just beer, at the concession stands. One night, back when I was still a heel teaming with DiBiase, we were in Oklahoma City the night after they'd had a rodeo, and dirt was piled up on one end of the arena floor. Back then, all the heels had to stay through the end of the show, especially if Watts was doing a hot finish, because we were essentially our own security. We walked to our cars together and sometimes helped each other back to the locker room. I was waiting in the wings with a few other guys, while Ted DiBiase battled JYD in the main event. Ted loaded the glove and hit Dog with it to pin him, which triggered a riot. Riots in those days were pretty common, and we often came to each other's aid.

Unfortunately, the heel at the front of the pack was King Kong Bundy, a 450-pounder who was about as wide as he was tall, and he wasn't setting any land-speed records, especially coming down the incline of the stairs in the aisle we were taking to get to ringside. We were all backed up behind him as he slowly descended one step at a time.

DiBiase also partnered up with my old pal Steve "Dr. Death" Williams, even though Doc and I couldn't be too friendly in public, since he had turned on me in the summer of 1984 to set up a wrestling feud. I used to have a lot of fun working with Doc. We did this one spot where one of us would catch the other in a schoolboy (like a cradle move that pins your opponent's shoulders to the mat), and then the other guy would reverse the cradle, to where the first guy was now getting pinned. But we kept reversing it and reversing it until we rolled right out of the ring! We'd be rolling around until we got under the ring where no one could see us. Then, we both laid on our backs and just started kicking our legs up, pounding the hell out of the ring from underneath it. The ring would be bouncing up and down, and we had a laugh when we heard fans at ringside shouting, "They're killing each other under there!"

During this stretch, between late 1984 and early 1985, my old friend Terry Gordy came in and worked a few shots for Mid-South, as Watts and World Class (the old Dallas promotion, where I'd started out) were sharing talent. Fortunately, Debra often went out with us, both as designated driver and to keep the two of us from getting into too much trouble.

DEBRA SAYS:
I wasn't much of a drinker, so I drove, and it's probably a good thing I did. One night, we went to a bar and were in the parking lot, standing there, when Jim and Gordy decided that we all loved each other very much, so we had a big group hug, right against the trunk of the car.

I was trying to tell them, "Guys, we're falling, we're falling!"

We fell against the trunk, and then ended up in a pile on the ground. And I was on the bottom of the pile!

I was wearing white hose, which got shredded, and my legs were even scuffed and bleeding a little. And then we went into the bar.

About 10 to 15 minutes later, inside the bar, Jim came to me, looking enraged, and said, "Who did that to you?"

I reminded him about our spill in the parking lot, and I had to go into detail, since he didn't immediately remember it, even though it had just happened.

We decided to go, but when we got to the parking lot, there was this little-bitty car, a Volkswagen bug, parked directly behind us. Jim and Terry literally bounced the car partially out of our way, lifting, pushing it, and dropping it a little at a time.

"Guys..."

I was telling them to stop, but they kept at it.

"Guys, look..."

They weren't listening.

They finally lifted the car and moved it. We got in the car, and it was only then that Jim and Terry realized what I'd been trying to tell them—we were able to pull right out just by going forward. The bug might have been parked behind us, but our path forward was totally clear.

I fussed at them, "Why'd you two beat up that poor little car?"

They looked at me, like two little kids who got caught playing too rough during recess. They both said the same thing: "Oops."

Debra actually got involved in one of my Mid-South feuds, when I brought her onto television to "show how a real lady behaves."

At the time, in fall of 1985, Dick Slater was in as booker and as one of the area's top heels. Slater was a good hand in the ring and a tough guy, but in Mid-South, part of his gimmick was his valet, Dark Journey. This young lady interfered heavily in his matches, and it wasn't long before Bill Watts had the idea of pitting Slater and Dark Journey against one of his top heroes and another female. But at the time, I was also feuding with "Mad Dog" Buzz Sawyer, and Slater was also feuding with my sometime tag partner, "Hacksaw" Butch Reed. I had worked some with Sawyer in Florida in 1984, and he was just one of those guys I never got along with. There wasn't anything specific that happened; it was just two guys who rubbed each other the wrong way.

The angle set up at the TV tapings (held in the Irish McNeill's Boys' Club in Shreveport, Louisiana) started when Debra and I were doing an interview in the ring. Slater came down with Dark Journey, and we argued back and forth.

In an effort to protect me, Debra ended up jumping on Sawyer's back, and he drove her back into the corner. One thing that kind of pissed me off, for real, was that he made no effort to protect her on that move.

DEBRA SAYS:
That jerk almost broke my ribs. He almost knocked me out.
The only way I even know what happened is I watched it later
on TV.

Meanwhile, I'm slugging it out with Slater, and when Sawyer comes
back at me, I turn and pop him one. As he goes back, he drops an elbow on
Debra, this young woman who's never been in the ring before in her life.
The angle was, as the villain, Sawyer would deny that he elbowed her on
purpose, but would give this real phony, insincere apology, designed to set
up our grudge matches.

Dark Journey pulled out a steel rod hidden in a box of flowers and
blasted me, and I went coast to coast with a blade, ending up with about as
much blood as I ever got. So I was selling it, but as all the other babyfaces
came out to make the save, I crawled over to Debra. The key to the visual
was, Debra was wearing all white and had platinum blonde hair, and I was
busted open, so the blood on her white outfit really stood out. The last
thing the TV viewers saw was me cradling Debra in my arms, drenched in
blood, screaming, "Sawyer! Superdome! Superdome!"

This all led up to a big match on Thanksgiving night in 1985 at the
Superdome. Mid-South was running a deal with Crockett Promotions, the
group that had taken what was once Georgia's spot on cable station WTBS,
where we would hold a couple of live Mid-South matches for the Superdome
fans and then broadcast a closed-circuit feed of 1985's Starrcade event.

Our live main event was Slater and Sawyer against Hacksaws Duggan
and Reed, with Debra in our corner and Dark Journey in theirs. It was a
brutal match—Reed and me, Sawyer and Slater, we were just beating the
dog (no pun intended) out of each other, and it ended up with Debra and
Dark Journey going at it, although that did not go as planned.

DEBRA SAYS:
Dark Journey interfered a lot, and when she jumped into the
ring, I jumped in to go after her. I had a button-up shirt on, and

when we started grappling, she grabbed my shirt and it came completely open! At least I had a belt on, and the shirt was tucked in, so I was able to pull it back shut, but I mean...it was too late.

That was when I learned never to wear a button-up shirt to the ring.

Yeah, she popped right out, and got the biggest crowd reaction of the night! Debra got going pretty good, too, though. After the match was over and we got to the back, Debra had her fists clenched, and she had clumps of Dark Journey's hair in her hands.

DEBRA SAYS:
I swear, I don't remember even touching her hair.

We actually had managed to have Thanksgiving dinner with some friends in New Orleans, but they were unavailable a month later when we were working Christmas night there. It was something my own kids would experience with me in later years, but that was just how the business went—not a lot of family time during the holidays.

Debra went with me again, and the only place open to eat on Christmas was Waffle House. So that was our Christmas in 1985.

Not long after, I had a match in Baton Rouge with Slater in which I almost killed him, completely by accident. We were doing a finish where we would brawl, and he would leave the ring and run to the dressing room, thereby losing by countout. I got so caught up in the excitement that I grabbed the ringside mic as he was headed down the aisle, and I yelled, "Let's get him, everyone!"

I knew it was a mistake the second the words came out of my mouth. Dozens of crazed Cajun fans swarmed into the aisles after Slater. He made his getaway, and later, in the dressing room, he hollered, "Duggan, what were you thinking?"

I had to apologize; it was just one of those times my enthusiasm took over my brain. I did learn a lesson that night about thinking about what I said to the fans.

For all the travel we did on those godawful two-lane roads, some of the worst scares happened close to home. One time, Debra was driving, and we were in a little town outside Baton Rouge in kind of a suburban area. I was sleeping in the passenger seat, and Debra was going straight through an intersection, because she had a green light.

This kid in a Corvette coming from the side had a red light, but he blew right through it, and Debra ended up clipping the tail end of the Corvette, which spun around and hit another car that was stopped on the other side of the intersection.

I hit my head on the window, which busted me open (or as they say in wrestling, "I got a little juice!"), but if I hadn't been wearing my seatbelt, I'd have shot completely through the windshield. I was definitely awake then!

Since it was one of those little towns where everyone knows everyone, people were coming by to see the wrecked Corvette of the kid (he was about 19) who had run the light. Someone walked by and said, "Oh, his dad's gonna be so mad."

I looked up and said, "His dad? What about me? That [I pointed at the wreck of what had been my Toronado] is my car!"

It was unbelievable—everyone there knew who the Corvette driver was.

I have always tried to keep my temper in check, but it was really starting to snowball and I was just getting madder and madder. Debra and I were lucky to be alive, and all these people could talk about was the smashed Corvette and this "poor kid's" dad. It took everything I had to keep my mouth shut while the cops cleared the intersection.

DEBRA SAYS:

I saw the Corvette out of the corner of my eye, but I really didn't think he was going to blow through the red light. By the time I realized he wasn't going to stop, it was too late.

I was only doing about 45 mph. I almost avoided hitting him, too, by slamming on the brakes, but I still caught the end of his car, which spun him around.

Later, I was sitting on the guardrail, and Jim came up and asked if I was okay. I said I was, but I was shaken up, and I wanted to know when we'd be able to go home.

Jim looked at me for a second and said, "Home? Debra, we still have a show to do in New Orleans."

One of the people on the right-hand side of the crash site had seen what happened, and they recognized Jim, so when he said he needed to get to Baton Rouge to rent a car, they offered to take him in their pickup truck.

There was just one catch—first, we had to go to their house and meet their parents. We ended up going 40 miles out of the way, each direction, to say hi to their folks. So we went to Baton Rouge to rent the car, to New Orleans for the show, then all the way back. When we passed by the gas station near where the wreck had been, our poor car was just a mess—it was completely totaled.

The weird thing was, for all the mishaps I had, I was able to avoid tons more thanks to my experiences driving in bad conditions. More than once, I was able to drive (slowly, but safely) through patches of icy roads, past and around pileups of vehicles, and make it through without a problem. And I could do that because I had learned over the years (and thousands of miles) when to brake, how not to brake too much, plus when and which way to pull the steering wheel to keep from losing control on a wet or icy road.

A lot of times we had to drive fast, because we'd have shows two nights in a row in towns hundreds of miles apart. Once, I had Debra with me, and we were coming through Beaumont, Texas, just east of Houston. It was so foggy we could hardly see anything at all, when all of a sudden, a herd of cows stood on the road right in my path.

DEBRA SAYS:
I'd never seen anything like the way he drove through that, and the only way I can describe it is that the car was like Pac-Man, with Jim zigging and zagging, and he managed to avoid every single one of those animals.

But I noticed there had been several sets of headlights behind us, and one by one, they disappeared. And there was no place for those poor people to turn, so it wasn't like they just pulled off the road.

We stopped at the very first gas station we got to after that, because Jim and I were both worried enough about folks driving along that road that we wanted to call the cops and let them know about the unsafe conditions, but I still wonder about those poor people with the disappearing headlights.

Even though the travel was a grind, the Mid-South days were a lot of fun. We did thousands of miles a week, mostly on two-lane roads in the middle of nowhere, but we often traveled four to a car, and that gave us time to come up with ideas for our own angles and bits. And for a guy who was such a forceful boss, Bill Watts was actually receptive to the guys who had ideas.

Around March of 1986, Watts saw the trend was definitely going toward national TV, and he tried to take Mid-South nationwide, changing the name to the Universal Wrestling Federation.

Around that time, Jake "The Snake" Roberts started calling me, telling me I needed to move up to the WWF, as he had done a month before.

"You really need to get up here," he said. "The payoffs are great, and the houses are big."

Those calls got me thinking, but I was doing okay, so I stuck it out with Watts for a while.

One of his big early events was the May 29, 1986, tournament in Houston to crown the UWF heavyweight champion. I was a top seed, as I went down in history as the final North American champion (Mid-South's top singles title). In the finals, I met new heel and old friend Terry Gordy, as The Freebirds were among the new talent Watts brought in.

Before our final match, One Man Gang (another new arrival) showed up with Skandor Akbar to challenge me. We brawled out of the ring, and Gang ran my head into the corner post of the ring. Unfortunately, Gang was blinder than a bat, and I was blinder than Gang. Back then, there were bolts sticking out of the corner posts where the ropes and turnbuckle connected to the ring. On this post, the bolt was sticking out, and neither of us saw it, so when he ran me into the post, that bolt went right into my head.

It cracked my skull, and they took me back to the dressing room. Paul Boesch was one of the first promoters to have a nurse stationed backstage, and we all knew her as "Bad Breath Sally," because she had the worst breath of anyone I ever met.

She was trying to treat me, and I knew I had to get back out there quick to face Gordy, but I was *pissed*. I was cussing everyone in sight. My head was squirting pretty good, and Sally took an Ace bandage and wrapped it around my head.

I stomped around the dressing room and back toward the ring, still pissed, and the bandage started riding up on my head to the point where, as DiBiase later put it, "Duggan looked like a Conehead out there!"

It must have been a weird moment, because I was stomping around, screaming and cussing, but the sight of "Conehead" Duggan had everyone else in the dressing room trying to keep from giggling, even though they knew I was really hurt.

Meanwhile, Gordy had no idea how badly I was injured. In Houston, the heel and babyface locker rooms were on opposite sides of the Sam Houston Coliseum, and Gordy was in the other dressing room.

I kind of remember going back to the ring, but the building was spinning around and around, and that whole match is kind of a blur. I do remember a spot where Gordy was in the ring and I was on the floor, and he reached down to grab me up by my hair and drag me in. He later said that when part of my scalp came loose and gave Gordy a quick peek at my skull, it was "like peeling a banana." He had blood all over his hands and just kind of recoiled back, yelling, "Aw, shit!"

I went to a hospital after the match that night (in which Gordy became the first UWF champ), but I had that old-school mentality and felt the show had to go on, so the next night I was in the next town, ready to go. This went on for a few nights until my head swelled up so bad I could hardly move, not because I was getting full of myself, but from blood poisoning. Even my ears swelled up.

Gang felt awful about it, but I knew he didn't do it on purpose. Some guys were careless with their opponents in the ring, but Gang was never like that. Accidents happen, and when you got two big guys out there, flying around, people were going to get injured.

In fact, injury was the reason I changed from using the spear as a finisher to the "Old Glory" kneedrop and flying clothesline. This was right around the time I first went into the WWF, and right around the time I had one of my arthroscopic knee surgeries to repair damage caused by doing the flying spear. Hulk Hogan was the one who said to me, "Why are you killing yourself flying through the air like that, when you could get just as big a pop using a running clothesline? Maybe you jump a little on the clothesline, but you still wouldn't be flying like that, because *that's* where you're gonna get hurt."

After a few months of life in the new UWF, I decided that my best option for making a living was with the WWF, so I called Vince in the fall of 1986. Vince always got accused of swiping guys from the other promotions, but I'd bet a lot of those guys were the ones who made first contact with Vince, even though I'm friends with a lot of guys who say, "Yeah, Vince called me..."

He didn't call me—I called Vince; well, I called his office. Vince didn't take my call, but he did return it. We set up a meeting, and I liked what I heard about the opportunity to make some money.

At the time, Debra and I were living in Pineville, Louisiana, and I had to talk with her about it, because the WWF travel schedule was even more notorious than what Bill Watts' guys were used to.

I gave Bill Watts my notice, worked out my last dates for him, and I was WWF-bound!

CHAPTER 10

THE SHEIK AND I

I HAD THOUGHT I WAS A PRETTY BIG DEAL IN MID-SOUTH. Hell, I had headlined shows at the Superdome. But when I saw Hulk Hogan headlining WWF shows that were drawing tens of thousands of people every night, I thought, *Wow. This is a whole different level.*

One thing I believed then and still believe now is that Madison Square Garden in New York City was the top of the mountain; no matter what kind of performer you were—singer, comic, wrestler—if you could draw a crowd to Madison Square Garden, you had made it. And in our business, the WWF had become the dominant force, so being near the top there meant I had made it.

From the moment I debuted for the World Wrestling Federation in early 1987, I was getting a really strong push, building me up as a strong patriot going against the evil foreigners Nikolai Volkoff and the Iron Sheik. In one of our early brawls, I even bled a little on WWF TV, which was almost unheard of at that time.

As a WWF character, Nikolai Volkoff was a proud, anti-American Communist from the Soviet Union, the (now-defunct) Communist superpower that was the U.S.A.'s foe in the Cold War. Of course, in real life, Volkoff was from Yugoslavia and was one of the most kind-hearted, generous gentlemen in the business. He was someone who truly loved the freedom that the U.S.A. stands for, but he played his "Evil Commie" role well. As part of his gimmick, Volkoff would insist on singing the Soviet national anthem before his matches; this was something he'd started doing in Mid-South back in 1984 when he and I feuded in Bill Watts' territory. It always got him a lot of heat with the fans, and he'd been doing it in the WWF for more than two years by the time I arrived. Funny thing—I don't think it was ever the exact same song twice.

Anyway, as a proud American, I was always finding ways to interfere with his singing his Communist anthem; one time, I cut the microphone as he was singing. Think about that—if you tried that today, OSHA would be all over you.

I would cut strong, patriotic promos, where I'd say that no one was going to sing the anthem of an anti-American country while Hacksaw Duggan was around. Probably the strongest was at WrestleMania III, the WWF's legendary 1987 mega-event in Michigan's Pontiac Silverdome, where I snatched the mic before Volkoff and the Iron Sheik (Khosrow Vaziri, an Iranian athlete who was a strong amateur wrestler before defecting to the U.S.A. in the 1970s) had their tag match against The Killer Bees, Brian Blair and Jim Brunzell. I got a huge cheer when I said Volkoff wouldn't be singing his Russian anthem, "because this is the land of the free and the home of the brave," which is actually kind of funny, if you think about it.

Before the show started, I looked out in awe of that incredible crowd, billed as 93,000 people. Of course, I was out there without my glasses, so all I could tell, at first, was that the first three rows looked full.

I ended up running in on the match, blasting the Sheik and Volkoff with my trusty 2x4, as that record crowd in the Silverdome cheered me. Being in front of a crowd that huge was awesome, and I got chills after I cleared the ring and had that huge crowd chanting "U-S-A! U-S-A!" along with me. It was an incredible moment, the thrill of a lifetime, and anyone watching could tell that with the buildup the WWF had given me to that point, they had some big things planned for me.

I was also excited about the planned program with Volkoff because I was comfortable working with him—we'd had a series of matches in Mid-South three years earlier, and I had a lot of respect for him as a gentleman, like I said earlier, but also as one hell of an athlete. He was incredibly powerful—in his heyday, he had a chest that you could have rested a can of soda on top of.

Nikolai and I had something in common, too—we both had problems with Manny Fernandez. Manny, as you might recall, "accidentally" dislocated my shoulder in a match in San Antonio. Well, Volkoff had a problem with him, too, a couple of years earlier, during a match in Florida. Manny potatoed him once too often, and Nikolai hit Manny so many times and so quickly that Manny couldn't even fall down. Every time Manny would start to go down one way, Nikolai would hit him so hard that he changed his trajectory.

Nikolai was an incredibly nice man, but he was also an incredibly strong man and a genuine tough guy—he knew how to box, and he knew how to fight. But I never had a problem with Nikolai, because he was a genuinely good guy, and to this day, every time I see him, he asks how my sister Sheila's doing.

Anyway, we continued the feud with either Nikolai and the Iron Sheik against myself, or both of them against me and a partner, for the next several weeks. Our series was really taking off.

On May 26, 1987, we flew into Newark, New Jersey, for a show that night in Asbury Park. I was in the baggage claim area, waiting for my gear to come out on the conveyer belt, when the Iron Sheik walked up to me and said, "Eh, Hacksaw, maybe I ride with you? I don't have credit card [to get a rental car]."

Now, I was new to the company, and I didn't want to be rude to a guy who'd been there forever, but I was also over 18, so I want to make very clear that I take full responsibility for my own decisions here. I know this whole thing has become an infamous story in wrestling, and I am here to tell you folks reading this the whole story, for the first time. But please know that while I am including all the details, I make no excuses.

Maybe I should have had reservations about being seen giving a ride to someone I was feuding against so heavily, but the kayfabe mentality that the old-schoolers had was dying out, and the sense of it was not as strong in the WWF as it had been with Bill Watts' Mid-South territory. To be honest, as a newcomer, I was actually kind of excited that the Iron Sheik wanted to ride with me.

We were headed up the turnpike (it was just about 50 miles from the airport to where we were working that night, in Asbury Park), and Sheik said, "Well, maybe we stop and have a beer, Hacksaw."

I had never been much of a beer drinker—I would drink vodka or whiskey when I was out drinking, but that was about it—and I told Sheik I didn't feel much like having a beer.

But he kept asking—this guy really wanted to have a beer—so we stopped at a convenience store and picked up a six-pack of Saint Pauli Girl beer.

I had about five or six doobies rolled up in a plastic baggie and stashed under the driver's seat. I was smoking one as we headed down the Garden State Parkway toward Asbury Park. Sheik was drinking one of the beers and asked me if I wanted one, and I said, "Sure, what the hell."

I really didn't think anything of having an open container of beer in the car, even though somewhere in the back of my mind I knew it was probably against the law in New Jersey. I was just so used to the attitude that people had in Louisiana, where things were totally different—heck, in Louisiana, along the major roadways, we had drive-thru daiquiri huts.

So I wasn't even worrying about concealing my beer when I drove right by a New Jersey state trooper, but a few seconds later, I noticed that the trooper had pulled onto the roadway and was right behind us. I still didn't appreciate how serious the situation was when he hit his lights and pulled us over.

The trooper walked up to the car and said, "License and registration."

I handed them over, and he asked me to get out of the car and walk around to the back of it.

When I got there, he said, "Sir, I smelled something in there, and I'm going to search the vehicle. Do you have anything in the car you want to tell me about?"

I didn't know what to think, because while I don't know that the cops in Louisiana would have let me go after finding marijuana in my car, I can say that the patrol officers there were willing to cut me breaks from time to time, not just because they knew me as some famous wrestler, but because a lot of them knew me personally. Officers who patrolled their communities used to have some discretion in dealing with people there, because they often knew the people who lived there better than any judge or other public official.

Of course, cops can't cut you a break today even if they wanted to, because everything's being recorded, whether it's one of those dashboard video cameras, recordings of their radio transmissions, or a thousand other ways of electronically monitoring everything those officers do. Plus, just like a lot of people in every walk of life, some cops now have a different attitude. We live in an era of gossip Internet sites and reality TV, where people with no talent whatsoever can get famous anyway, and cops are only human—it's natural that some of them would love the opportunity to bust someone who's been on TV, because there would naturally be some publicity attached to that.

But getting back to May 26, 1987, once the trooper told me he was going to search the car, I knew I should just tell him the truth, so I said, "Yes, sir, there's a small amount of marijuana under the driver's seat."

If he appreciated my honesty, he wasn't letting on, because he firmly said, "Hands on the hood, feet back, and spread 'em."

I did what he said, but I also said, "Officer, we don't want any trouble. We're just passing through town, professional wrestlers on our way to a show."

I thought explaining myself would help, but the next thing I knew, he was radioing for backup, and within minutes, there was a swarm of patrol cars around our car. These state officers were pretty intimidating guys in their crisp khaki uniforms, sunglasses, patent-leather boots, and those belts that held everything from handcuffs to mace to nightsticks.

But I definitely cannot say that they mistreated me. They even double-cuffed me, which meant that they used two pairs of handcuffs—one of each cuff around one of my wrists, and then the other half of each pair of handcuffs cuffed to each other. This was not something they had to do, but it was very decent of them to do it that way; I was a big guy, and using one pair of handcuffs to restrain me as they would a normal-sized person would have been extremely uncomfortable for me.

Then, the troopers pulled the Sheik out of the car. He had one of those little man-purse things, and they opened it up. A vial of white powder (which later tested positive as being cocaine) fell out when they set his little bag down on the car, and they arrested him on the spot. They put us in separate cars and drove us to the New Jersey State Police depot.

I ended up being charged with an open-container violation, for the beer that the first officer had seen me with, and a misdemeanor charge of possession of marijuana. But when they got us to their station, they did a full inventory and search, and the Sheik's little purse-thing had two grams of cocaine in it, which was a felony amount.

I can't lie to you—in wrestling, the boys all talk about each other, and everyone has at least a pretty good idea what everyone else is up to. Even though I hadn't seen it, I figured the Sheik probably had some cocaine on him when I agreed to let him ride with me. Like I said, it was poor judgment, and I make no excuses for it.

But after they found that cocaine, the search was on. They rooted through every pocket of every article of clothing and looked at every slip of paper. And that meant a lot of slips of paper—as wrestlers, we always had to keep every receipt of every expense. And those officers shook out every receipt we had, shaking each slip of paper like they were expecting to shake loose even more cocaine.

They went through everything we had. The last things they went through were our wallets. They went through mine and didn't find anything of interest, but when they opened up the Sheik's wallet—*boom!* Another gram of cocaine fell out.

The way the cops looked at it, he had three grams in separate containers, which (to them) justified charging the Sheik with possession with intent to distribute, a more serious charge than simple possession of the exact same amount. I already felt awful about having been caught with something so stupid, but I was practically an angel with my little beer and five joints compared to my traveling companion. I signed an appearance bond and was released, but the Sheik had to appear before a judge for an arraignment.

Of course, I was still the Sheik's ride to the show in Asbury Park that night, so I couldn't just leave him there. I had a paperback book I was reading, and I'd made my way through half the damn thing when the Sheik finally came out of the courtroom hours later.

The cops had left our car in an off-road area near where we'd been stopped, so a patrol unit took us back to the car, and Sheik and I resumed our drive to Asbury Park, where he and I were wrestling each other in a grudge match as one of that night's main events.

Okay, so there's not much question about what the dumbest thing I did that day was, right? But the second-dumbest thing of the day was probably that when I got to the Asbury Park show that night, I didn't tell anyone—not any of the backstage brass, no one—what had happened. I actually thought that the whole incident would fly under the radar. Brilliant move, right?

My first call that evening was to Debra. I told her, "Honey, we got busted today, but I don't think anybody knows."

Debra took the news pretty well, mainly because she was looking at it the way I was looking at it—I had gotten a misdemeanor arrest for a little pot, not exactly the crime of the century. But neither one of us had looked at the bigger picture.

That picture became clear the next morning, when Debra called me at the hotel where I was staying and said, "Jim, everybody knows! The phone's been ringing off the hook here! All your friends have called to check on you, and it's all over the news."

Another thing I regret about this mess is that I didn't call my dad about it. He was still the chief of police in Glens Falls, so he went into work that morning and got ambushed by media people asking about what had happened. Here he was, one of the most respected police chiefs in that part of the country, and he had to hear questions about his son involved in a cocaine case. Even though it wasn't mine, I was kind of found guilty by association. I still feel awful about putting my dad in that situation, all because I hadn't really appreciated the magnitude of it.

But he handled himself as professionally as ever. He only had one comment for any reporter asking about my arrest: "My son's over 21."

We ended up being the main story on the back cover of that morning's *New York Daily News*, with a headline that read, "Boozing Bozos," with a picture of the Sheik and a picture of me. In all the news stories about it over the next few days, the main words that jumped out at readers were *cocaine*, *professional wrestlers*, and *marijuana*.

And, of course, they all made a big deal out of the fact that the guy I'd been busted with was my "hated rival," the man I was wrestling against that same night.

That morning, May 27, my first call after hearing from Debra was the call I should have made the day before—I called my pop. God bless him, he was never anything but 100 percent supportive.

"Jim," he said, "did you get arrested for cocaine?"

I said, "No, sir, Dad, I got arrested for marijuana."

He raised his voice a little, and he said, "I knew sooner or later you were gonna get arrested for that shit!"

But I think he just needed to get that out of his system, because from then on, every single word he said to me about it was totally supportive. And it wasn't just him—my whole family rallied around me, and I will never be able to thank them enough for how much they took up for me, both publicly and privately, with people who had known me personally.

After I finished talking with my dad, the next call was to Vince McMahon. Now, I know a lot of people in the wrestling business have laid out horror stories about working with Vince, but he treated me pretty fairly, and as much of a workaholic as he's always been, he was actually fairly approachable back in 1987.

Still, having to call Vince McMahon was not something people looked forward to, even under the best of circumstances. I was dreading the conversation even as I dialed his office number.

Usually, calling Vince at the office meant sitting on hold for five minutes, listening to that awful Muzak that companies pipe over their phone lines while you wait. However, when I called his office that morning and told the receptionist, "Hi, it's Jim Duggan for Vince McMahon," it was almost instantaneous, like, *click-click*, "Jim?"

And I will remember verbatim what he said next until the day I die: "Jim, what have you *done* to us?"

"Vince," I said, "I'm ashamed."

He said, "Turn in your tickets, and go home!"

Boom! He had hung up the phone.

Back then, the wrestlers had stacks of paper tickets that we used to get from town to town when we were on tour. Telling me to return mine had the same effect as that coach telling me to turn in my playbook—it meant they were done with me. I was devastated.

I found out later that pretty much the same thing happened to Iron Sheik—Vince fired him on the spot.

What happened next is a story that very few people know about. After returning my WWF tickets, I now had to find a flight back home to Louisiana. I booked a ticket to get me home, but then my flight got postponed. I had nothing else to do but wait, so I went to a bar a few blocks from the airport and I got smashed. When it was time to go, I made yet another terrible decision in a series of them—I actually drove myself back to the airport. Almost immediately after I pulled out of the bar, a police car pulled behind me and followed me all the way to the airport. Especially after what had gone down the day before, I was scared out of my mind.

I remember trying to concentrate on driving so as not to get pulled over, but I kept thinking, *How stupid can one man be?*

I think the fear of that situation actually might have sobered me up a bit, because I made it back to the airport without a problem and flew back home. My wife picked me up at the airport, and there wasn't a whole lot of conversation along the way.

Over the next couple of weeks, my family really took the brunt of the publicity and a lot of the embarrassment. I went back home to Louisiana, because my pop and my sisters felt like the best thing I could do was to be out of the spotlight for a while and hopefully let things die down.

I felt like a heel the whole time, even though keeping a low profile was something my pop had recommended. He was doing interviews with our local news station (Glens Falls received the Albany affiliates) in front of the house where I'd grown up. The two local newspapers dredged up every nasty detail on me they could find, and my family in Glens Falls really went through hell with those media people. Meanwhile, I was in Louisiana, holed up in my house in the woods.

I followed another piece of advice from my pop while I was there—I didn't read the paper, and I didn't watch TV. Fortunately, I wasn't facing the kind of media onslaught my poor family was facing in New York—in Louisiana, it really wasn't that big of a story.

I did spend some time feeling angry—feeling sorry for myself, if I'm being honest. I would sit on the porch and drink a lot of whiskey, and if any rabbits hopped by my house, I'd use my rifle to blow them in two. I was a very different guy back then; these days, the most interaction I have with wildlife is feeding the ducks that waddle around the pond near our home in South Carolina.

A few weeks went by, and while I was hunkered down in Louisiana, my old buddy Jake "The Snake" Roberts was pleading my case to Vince McMahon every chance he got. Jake has had his share of problems over the years, but he was almost always a good friend to me. In 1987, he also was one of the most popular wrestlers in the WWF, so he had a little more pull with Vince than a lot of guys. He called me a couple of times, first to let me know he was going to bat for me.

From what I learned later, Jake would tell Vince, "Look, Duggan just got caught by circumstance, no different than if he'd been in a car wreck. You know the Sheik was gonna get into trouble at some point."

Jake really tried, but Vince was pretty firm against bringing me back. A few days after Jake's initial calls, Jake called again to tell me about a big speech Vince had given the boys.

At a TV taping in Buffalo, just a few days after I'd gotten fired, Vince called a meeting of all the wrestlers and pounded on the podium as he said, "This job is bigger than a six-pack and a blowjob! Duggan and Sheik will never, ever work for the WWF again!"

I listened as Jake told me what Vince had said, and after a couple of silent seconds, Jake said out loud what I'd been thinking: "Jim, brother, you're screwed. You're done."

At that point, I went on a serious bender. I was tearing it up with whiskey and drugs, because I was really in a dark place. A week or so went by, and I got to thinking, *Well, I gotta go to work, somehow, somewhere.*

I actually called the NWA, which by 1987 wasn't really the international union of promoters that it had been when I broke into the business. It was Jim Crockett Promotions, the TBS-anchored company that was Vince McMahon's closest competition. I still had memories of Crockett that were less than fond, but Dusty Rhodes, whom I'd worked with before and gotten along with, was booking the area. I called Dusty and lined up a job interview in Atlanta, but within a day or two of making that call, I got another call, this time from Bruce Pritchard.

Bruce had worked as an assistant to Houston promoter Paul Boesch, and Boesch switched his allegiance to the WWF in April of 1987 when Bill Watts sold Mid-South Sports to Crockett. When Boesch made his move, his staff, including Bruce, went with him. For Bruce, it ended up being a big move, as Bruce Pritchard ended up working for Vince for more than 25 years.

At this point, Bruce wasn't very high up the food chain, but he was working hard at the WWF offices in Connecticut in what today is called "talent relations."

"Just keep your head down," Bruce said, "and lay low. We're going to bring you back."

So I kept my head down and I laid low, just like he said. At the end of August, I got a call from the WWF—not with an offer to come back full time, but to let me know Paul Boesch himself had insisted on bringing me into a show in Houston that was very personal to him. It was to be held on August 28, 1987, and that night in the Sam Houston Coliseum was going to be Boesch's retirement show, his final night as the official promoter of Houston Wrestling.

Paul Boesch had been a local institution in Houston dating back to the 1940s when *Houston Wrestling* first aired, making it one of the first televised wrestling shows in the country. In fact, here's something you might not have known—Boesch did play-by-play for the first Houston matches to be broadcast, which made him the first sportscaster in the history of Houston television.

Boesch had wrestled around the country in the 1930s before joining the U.S. Army during World War II. He was a decorated combat veteran when he returned to civilian life, and to wrestling, at the end of the war. He even wrote a book about his wartime experiences, called *A Forest in Hell*. Boesch was the assistant promoter in Houston for decades until he took over in 1967, following the death of promoter Morris Sigel. Wrestlers everywhere were used to unfairly low payoffs, but Paul was also known as the last of the good payoff men—when you wrestled in Houston, you knew you were going to get at least something approaching what you deserved.

Paul was a good man, and I would have been proud to work that show under any circumstances, but it especially meant a lot to me that he would go out of his way to have me booked on that show when he knew I'd had a rough time.

I was booked against my old pal, Ted DiBiase, in a match that the program for that night billed as a "feud-settler."

DiBiase had gone to work for the WWF in May of 1987, just after Bill Watts ended up getting out of the business by selling his UWF to Crockett Promotions. It was funny, because in my last weeks with the UWF, Teddy always said, "Man, I can't go to the WWF! You guys all have gimmicks—Hacksaw, JYD, Jake the Snake—I'm just plain old Ted DiBiase."

Of course, he ended up with the best gimmick of them all, as "The Million Dollar Man."

We all thought he had won the lottery, because as The Million Dollar Man, he had to live the gimmick—he had a valet, Virgil (a wrestler named Mike Jones), and was getting chauffeured in a limousine. Teddy would be staying in some four-star hotel each night, while we were in the Super 8. He flew first-class, while we crammed into coach.

Virgil even carried his bags in public. Ted would say, "C'mon, Virgil, it's not gonna look right—you gotta carry the bags."

I always thought Teddy was the perfect Million Dollar Man, because that was kind of an extension of his own *GQ* self, and he carried it off perfectly.

The night of the Boesch show, my match with DiBiase was going great... until my hamstring blew out. It came out of nowhere—Teddy and I had done this spot thousands of times, where he'd go for a kick, then I'd catch the foot, spin him around, and give him an atomic drop. But on this night, I missed the foot and jerked down too far as I tried to grab it, and my hamstring blew.

Teddy knew right away something was wrong, but we worked through a few more minutes before ending the match. I was determined not to just give up, in part out of respect for Paul Boesch but even more because this was my first night back, and I wanted to have a good match to prove my worth.

I hobbled to the back where Jay Strongbow, one of the WWF's backstage agents, was standing next to Vince McMahon. Strongbow said, "Vince, you gotta give the kid some credit for gutting it out!"

I think seeing that I would always go all out for him might have factored into Vince's decision to bring me back. But he's also a master tactician, and if he sees a possible use for you, he'll bring you in. Look at his history—he's brought in and brought back guys who have had very public problems with him (Bret Hart) and who have been his mortal business enemies (Eric Bischoff).

I got out of the arena that night as quickly as possible, because I didn't want to be perceived as being injured or weak.

Meanwhile, the legal case against me kind of went away. I got a form of probation where, if I stayed out of trouble (no arrests or anything like that) for three months, they would remove the marijuana conviction from my record. I completed my term of probation, and that was that—I was clean.

Unfortunately, as I look back over my career, I don't think I ever, ever fully recovered from that fall. Even though I had a good, strong career, it probably held me back from getting to that next level, the world-championship main event level.

But I was established and popular enough that I had survived an ordeal that a lot of guys would not have survived. A lot of guys would have crumbled having to deal with all of that, and I came close to going under a couple of times. I mean, it was scary, humiliating, and overwhelming, all at once—talk about going from the penthouse to the outhouse! In one, dumbass move, I devastated the family that I loved and admired, and I derailed my career, just as I approached what was going to be an all-time peak for me.

I'll tell you something else—it's been 24 years since this happened, and I have never again touched a Saint Pauli Girl beer!

CHAPTER 11

(PRIME) TIME FOR A COMEBACK

SOON AFTER I CAME BACK, the WWF put me on *Prime Time Wrestling*, the Monday night show that predated *Monday Night Raw* on the USA Network. They liked the way I did my interviews, how I kept them lively, and they felt like I could flow with the chatter that they did between matches.

The *Prime Time* formula was simple—the co-hosts would sit in a studio and introduce matches from around the country, with some talk in between. Some of the lineups over the years featured various combinations of Vince McMahon, Bobby Heenan, Curt Hennig, Gorilla Monsoon, and Roddy Piper, among others.

Whoever had the idea to make me a temporary co-host created a little friction between myself and Hillbilly Jim. Hillbilly was always a friend of mine, but we were both babyfaces, our gimmicks were pretty similar, and he was another one of the *Prime Time* co-hosts. When the WWF put us on the show together, it created a situation where we were constantly trying to take attention from each other.

Hillbilly and I would talk over each other, lean over into each other's camera shots, and just generally mess with each other a bit.

I thought it was just another form of friendly competition, or at least semifriendly, like the games of one-upsmanship wrestlers frequently got into when they were competing for the same spots. But one night, I walked into a locker room to find my "friend" Hillbilly Jim in the middle of a pretty passionate speech to the other boys who were in there.

"You know that Vince lied to all of us," Hillbilly said. "He said he wouldn't hire Duggan or Sheik back, and there's Duggan's stuff, sitting right there!"

I walked in and said, "Hey, Hillbilly, can I talk to you in the shower?"

He followed me in, and I said, "Hey, Hillbilly, shut up!"

He looked down and said, "Aw, what? I didn't mean nothin' by it."

Uh-huh.

One thing I did like about doing *Prime Time* was being around guys like Curt Hennig and Bobby Heenan, two of the funniest people I ever met. Bobby used to sneak vodka into the water bottle he was drinking from on camera, and he thought it was hilarious to leave his mic on when he went to the bathroom between segments. We'd all be sitting there, waiting for Bobby to come back so we could tape the next bit, and suddenly, we'd all hear *pppppppppssssssssshhhhhh!*

Trust me when I say there were a lot of outtakes, funny things that no one will probably ever see.

A lot of the guys were out of control, but a lot of people make the wrong comparisons with wrestlers. We're not like a sports team; we're more like a rock band. It was a different city every night, in front of a lot of people, and we were very visible and recognizable.

Growing up, I couldn't get a girl for anything. I had one girlfriend in high school, and one college sweetheart. But after I became a wrestler, all of a sudden I was on TV and people were paying attention to me. My first exposure to that was in 1980 when I'd been part of the WWWF. Sometimes, we'd be having such a good time that other things would slip our minds.

One night, Jake Roberts and I went out partying in Detroit in the middle of January. Jake was one of my favorite traveling partners, and a good friend. I know he's had problems, but he was always someone who stuck with me. After we turned in that night, we woke up in the morning to find about six inches of snow outside. We went out to the car to get some stuff, and when we opened the trunk, I don't know which was stiffer—my 2x4, or Jake's python, Damien, frozen solid.

Jake worked with an animal handler, because as you might imagine from the previous story, Jake went through a lot of snakes. The animal guy's name was Albert, and he was a strange dude. He had a houseful of snakes, bugs, spiders, and lizards.

A couple of years later, in 1991, Jake became a villain and attacked "Macho Man" Randy Savage with a cobra as part of a new feud for the shows. One night right before this, we were all playing cards in the locker room, and Albert came in to announce he had found Jake a cobra. He had de-venomized it, which we would not learn until later, but the thing would still bite you.

He dumped this 10-foot cobra onto the floor, and it started to rise up, like in the movies, with its hood flared out around its head. We were all backing up and away from this thing, but Albert was just saying, "Don't worry!"

Albert tried to distract the snake with one hand while grabbing at it with the other, but the snake darted toward him and bit him right on the web of the hand.

Here's something I learned about cobras that day—when they bite, they don't strike like a rattlesnake; they bite and hold on! Albert had this snake on his hand, screaming in pain, and the whole dressing room suddenly looked like a battle royal—we were all heading for the door!

Andre the Giant, who did *not* like snakes, pretty much crushed everyone as he made his way out of the room.

A lot of those tough guys were scared to death of snakes. One of my best buddies was the Junkyard Dog, and more than once when he was on the toilet, I'd take off my belt and slide it under the stall. You'd be amazed how much a belt looks like a snake slithering around when you give it a good push.

I got to where the snakes didn't bug me too much, mainly because I got used to them traveling with Jake. Sometimes I really felt for Jake, too, because his walk to the ring was like the Bataan Death March. I mean, we were working nearly every night, doing double-shots on the weekends, and every time he walked to the ring, he had to carry 100 pounds of python in a bag, slung over his shoulder, every step of the way.

Meanwhile, I'd be backstage, saying, "Hey, could somebody find me a 2x4, please? Hey, thanks, buddy."

Once, we were driving to a show down south. We were flying down the road in a rented Lincoln, with Damien the python (the fourth, sixth, ninth—who knows?) in his bag in the backseat. The snake was pushing to get out of the bag like they always were—it was really a pretty horrible life for the snake, if you think about it.

A lot of guys didn't like Jake, for whatever reason, and they'd take it out on the snake. As a heel move in the ring, they'd put the boots to the snake, but they were really kicking the thing. You won't see Vince having guys bringing a snake in a bag to the ring today—he'd have PETA all over him.

Anyway, we were cruising right along when I looked in the rearview mirror and saw this great big python head looking over my shoulder.

And I know you're probably reading this, going, "Oh, come on, Hacksaw, they're not poisonous! Don't be such a baby."

Well, yeah, but they bite! And this is a 100-pound snake biting your ass, you know? You think a bug bite's bad? This thing's mouth looked like it could swallow a softball.

I yelped and hit the brakes. We went sliding into the parking lot of a Stuckey's. There were all these families in these old-fashioned rocking chairs they had outside, watching two burly men with long hair bring their car to a screeching halt, get out, and start fighting with a python. We got the thing back into its bag and took off.

To this day, I bet there's some guy in Alabama telling his friends, "I'm tellin' you, you'll never believe what I saw! These two guys had a snake..."

Another time, we wrestled at a show at the Rosemont Horizon in Chicago. Jake was in the main event, and I was in the match right before. After the show, we were heading out when we saw a crowd. At the back of the arena, there were people jammed in just trying to see the guys. There was this bank of eight double doors between us and the parking lot.

I waited for Jake's match to finish and for him to take a shower. We figured it would be cleared out by then, so we grabbed our bags and headed out of the locker room. There were hundreds of people still there, and they were just rabid. We spun around back into the locker room and pulled the door closed.

We'd spotted the limo that was taking us from the arena parked on the far side of the crowd, so I said, "Okay, Jake, on three, we'll make a break for it!"

One...two...three!

Jake bolted out, and I shut the door behind him, staying inside the locker room. I could hear Jake just getting mobbed! A few minutes later, I went out a door on the far side, ducked down, crept past everyone, and got to the limo, while I could hear Jake shouting, "Duggan, you bastard!"

Of course, weeks later, giving me just enough time to think he forgot about it, he got me back. We walked into a Roy Rogers restaurant at a shopping plaza off the New Jersey Turnpike, and a lot of people were inside. These people were starting to realize who we were, and Jake got his food first, then got to the exit door before turning around quickly and shouting, "That's right, folks, Hacksaw Jim Duggan is right here, and he's signing autographs!"

He might have gotten recognized, too, but he bolted, making sure I got all the attention. I always said that Jake was one of the most fun guys to party with, but he was the last guy you wanted driving your getaway car.

We had some adventures in the air as well as on the road, and some of these were no fun at all. Once, around 1989, we were flying from Las Vegas into Phoenix, Arizona—me, Jake, and Jake's wife, Cheryl, sitting together in one row. Longtime fans might remember her from Jake's 1988 feud with Rick Rude, where the story was that Rude was trying (and failing) to seduce Cheryl, building up to a series of matches with Jake and Rude.

Anyway, we were flying out on America West on a midnight flight, and a midnight flight out of Vegas meant pretty much every passenger on the plane was drunk.

That made it even worse when we got into the air and hit the worst turbulence I have ever experienced in my life. I've flown literally millions of miles, and I never came across worse turbulence than what we had on this flight. It hit while the flight attendants were serving drinks, and it was so bad that the flight attendant went down and the cart fell on top of her.

She wasn't the only one getting hurt—the overhead compartments were popping open, and people's carry-on baggage was flying out and hitting folks in their seats. The plane was shaking like it was about to come apart.

Usually, heavy turbulence only lasts a few minutes, but this went on forever. The three girls sitting behind us, who were totally drunk, started screaming at the tops of their lungs, "Oh God, help us! God, help us, please! We're gonna die! Oh, Jesus, oh no!"

Of course, that just added to the anxiety level, and we were already nervous enough—Cheryl dug grooves into Jake's arm with her nails. She and Jake were white as ghosts, and I doubt I looked any better.

The one thing I kept telling myself was, "These things don't crash right out of the air, man. They crash during takeoff and landing, but very seldom do they just crash in midflight. We're not gonna crash. We're not gonna crash. We're not gonna crash."

Finally, we got through it and landed safely in Phoenix. The captain came on the intercom and apologized for the rough flight, told everyone where to report if there were any injuries, and so on.

We got to the arena and did the show in Phoenix. The next day, though, I was walking to my flight out of Phoenix, and the closer I got, the more apprehensive I got about getting on the plane. I was scared to death. I finally forced myself to get on board, because I knew if I didn't, I'd never be able to get on a plane again.

And when that flight went fine, I felt a little better about flying. To this day, I really think if I hadn't gotten on that plane out of Phoenix, I might have been out of the business, because I might never have gotten on another plane.

Jake changed once he discovered the crack pipe. I'm not proud of it, and I make no excuses—we all messed around with drugs and booze. But crack was just a different animal, something I would never touch.

One time, not long after I'd come back to the WWF after being fired for getting busted with the Iron Sheik, Jake and I were in a cab when Jake said to the driver, "Hey, man, I need to find a little rock."

And he wasn't talking about the capital of Arkansas.

The cabbie said he knew just where to go. Next thing I know, we're in deep in the heart of the hood, where Jake and I both stuck out like sore thumbs.

"Jake," I said, "Jesus! Come on, man, I just came back to the company."

We pulled up in front of a crack house, and Jake ran inside. Out in the car, I was just picturing a camera crew and a bunch of undercover cops busting everyone in a three-block radius. But I wasn't just scared—I was starting to get pissed off.

After a few minutes, I said, "Screw this." I got out, slammed the door, and started walking down the street.

I'm a tolerant guy, but I admit, I was getting pretty nervous when the voices started coming out of the shadows.

"Hey, white boy! Whatchoo doin' down here, white boy?"

I walked a little faster and started muttering, "I'm gonna kill you, Jake!"

I made it a few blocks before the cab pulled up, with Jake inside, and we went on our way.

The crack cocaine eventually caused Jake and I to drift apart. He was pretty open about his using, and he always struggled with it, which I guess he still does to some degree to this day. I don't understand his mentality of doing it when he knows it's going to be a problem, but he's a good guy, beneath all his problems, and I hope he's okay.

At one point, shortly after I had come back to the WWF, the company had practically its own air force—six King Air planes, which were top-of-the-line turbo propeller airplanes. We used them a lot, especially when we had three days of double-shots in a row, which was whenever there was a three-day weekend because of a holiday. We'd do six shows in three days: wrestling in the afternoon in Washington, D.C., taking a car to the airport, hopping onto a King Air, flying to New York, driving to Madison Square Garden, and wrestling there. That was one day. The next day, we'd repeat the process, going from Hartford, Connecticut, to Boston, then the next day it would be from there to Maine.

These King Air planes would only fit five or six guys, and on one of these flights, I was with Junkyard Dog, Koko B. Ware, and Hulk Hogan. We were getting ready to leave when they started testing the prop for takeoff.

Suddenly, Hogan said, "I don't want to fly on this plane."

I don't know if he heard something he didn't like or what, but Hulkster is one of the few guys who's logged more miles than I have, so I wasn't going to question him. Plus, hell, Hulk Hogan was Hulk Hogan; if he didn't want to fly on that plane, there wasn't anyone who was going to make him do it.

Hulkster asked to be taken back to the terminal at the little private airport we were flying out of, and Koko started following him off the plane. I said, "Koko! Sit back down! We still gotta make the show. Hulkster can do whatever he wants to do, but we need to get where we're supposed to be."

Koko brushed me off and said, "I'm gonna go see if Hulkster needs anything."

Me and JYD were sitting on the plane, like, "Jesus! Can you believe this?"

Finally, Koko came back onto the plane and said, "Vince told me to tell you guys to get on the plane and make the show."

Now, I was getting irritated. I said, "Koko, we never got off the plane!"

Koko might have been a little inebriated, but it was like he had no idea what was going on, and now he had ratted me and JYD out to the boss for something we didn't even do.

Koko and I argued back and forth throughout the flight. Koko especially was getting angrier and angrier, but he had me pretty pissed off by this point, too. We landed, and they had a big bus waiting to take us to the show. The three of us jumped on, with me and JYD sitting near the front and Koko picking a seat a few rows behind us. The whole bus ride, Koko kept arguing and yelling, telling me, "You don't mess with a street nigger! I don't care how big you are! I'll kick your ass!"

Finally, I said to myself, "Okay, I've had it with this."

I stood up and turned to face Koko. He stood up, too, and we met in the aisle about halfway between our seats. I gave him an open hand slap that knocked him down, and he wasn't rushing back to his feet. I chewed his ass out enough that it seemed like I was cutting a promo on him, and then I turned and went back to my seat.

Now, though, he was getting back up, and he was pissed.

"You bastard! You don't put your hands on me! I'm gonna get you!"

I could hear Koko moving as he started lurching toward me, one row of seats at a time. JYD glanced back and said to me, quietly, "Duggan, he's got a bottle."

Unfortunately for Koko, I had my 2x4 from the afternoon show down by my leg. Koko got about two rows behind me, and I jumped up and turned to face him again, this time towering over him (Koko stands about 5'7", and I am 6'3"). The bottle he had was about two inches long, one of those tiny liquor bottles you find in a hotel minibar! I just grabbed him and ran him into the side of the bus a few times, and then he settled down.

When we got to the arena, I was greeted by Arnie Skaaland, who was telling me something I heard more than once when we did the second half of a double-shot: "Duggan, hurry up—you're on!"

I had never changed out of my ring gear from the afternoon show, so I was able to drop off my bag and go straight to the ring for my match. After the match, I got to the back, and Arnie was waiting for me again. This time he was telling me that Vince McMahon was on the phone, and he wanted to talk to me.

I had only been back a few weeks, and I was convinced I was getting canned again.

I picked up the phone in the back, and Vince asked me what had happened with Koko.

"Vince," I said, "the guy backed me into a corner. I gotta stand up for myself. I can't let somebody talk to me that way."

"Well," Vince said, "I want you to give me your word that you will not fight Koko tonight. I want your word."

I said, "Yes, sir, Vince—I give you my word."

I went into the dressing room, where Harley Race and a few other guys were also sitting, and Koko came in a few minutes later. Koko walked up to me and said, "Duggan, this is not over. I'm gonna get you," and then he walked out.

A couple of minutes later, he came in again and repeated his threat, then left again. A couple of minutes after *that*, he came in a third time to tell me he was gonna get me.

Koko walked out for the third time, and Harley said, "If he comes in here again, I'll nail him. *I* didn't promise Vince anything."

Of course, Koko had some time to cool off, and nothing more came of it. Koko's a good guy, and he's someone I still consider a friend—this was just one of those things that can happen when you get a bunch of guys spending that much time together. It can really get to you, and before you know it, the guys are on each other's nerves. Looking back, the most surprising thing is that this kind of blowup didn't happen more often, with all the guys on the road for long stretches of time, away from home and family, along with the pressure of performing on such a big stage and the competition for the top spots.

I don't know if Koko knew how lucky he was that he didn't come back after that third threat, because Harley Race was one of the toughest guys ever in wrestling and a guy who learned how to bare-knuckle fight and began his wrestling career at age 14. You did not want to piss off Harley Race.

But it wasn't just me—Koko had a bit of a temper, and in 1991, he ended up losing his job with the WWF over a fight he had with a guy named Jim Troy. We were in Belgium as part of a WWF European tour, and a bunch of us were out at a nightclub that was connected to the hotel where we were staying. Even Andre the Giant came out, and Andre often kept to himself at that point in his life (he passed away in January of 1993 from health problems caused by the condition that also caused him to grow to such huge proportions). It was a huge party, with a lot of the wrestlers drinking and having a good time in the restaurant portion of the club, and even some of the WWF front office guys joining us.

One of those executives was Troy, a former pro hockey player who had gotten a job with the WWF because he was a friend of Vince's. He had kind of a chip on his shoulder when it came to dealing with the wrestlers. He had the attitude that he was a *real* tough guy, while we were all just fakers.

On this night, everybody drank quite a bit, but Troy got drunk as a skunk. I ended up saying good night to the boys and going back to my room early, because I was just exhausted.

Apparently, I left too early or just in time to avoid a catastrophe, depending on how you look at it. Koko and Troy got into a little pushing match in the restaurant. Koko went back to the hotel lobby and waited for Troy, and when Troy walked in, Koko just beat the hell of him, right there in the lobby. A bunch of guys separated them, but the hotel people were not happy about this, and they had words with a few of the WWF people who were there, including Shawn Michaels and Marty Jannetty, who were a tag team called The Rockers. The Rockers were already angry at the hotel people, because they were trying to call the States and couldn't get an outside line, and everyone else being drunk and obnoxious after a night of partying didn't help.

I got up the next morning and headed down in the elevator with Ray Traylor, also known as the Big Bossman, when *boom!* The elevator doors opened and six cops came on board.

Having no idea what had gone on after I left the party, I said, in a perfectly friendly voice, "Hey, how you guys doing?"

In response, I got nothing but silence and glares, as these cops locked eyes on me and Bossman. They did not look happy.

We got out of the elevator, and the lobby was packed with cops. And they were not putting up with any attitude, at all. They directed us all onto the bus and we rode off, with me still wondering what the hell was going on.

It must have been a pretty bad scene the night before, because as we found out the next time they were lining up a European tour, all WWF personnel had been banned from every hotel in Belgium.

The role of the 2x4 expanded after I came back to the WWF. Previously, I had a reputation for using a board if I needed one, but now I was bringing one out every night—it became a part of the Hacksaw package.

A lot of times when I got into the ring, I would use the board like those rifle-drill specialists in the military, tossing it up and catching it. And that's a lot harder than most people think. In 25 years of doing it, I've only missed it a couple of times, and never on TV. And that's more of a trick than it sounds like, because I'm close to blind without my glasses on, and here I am, throwing this long, heavy piece of wood up into the lights. The best part is, when I catch it, people pop! It's like for 25 years, they've consistently expected me to lose it in the lights or drop it.

One time at a house show, I was outside the ring and about to toss the board straight up. Sitting near me was Mike McGuirk, the WWF's first female ring announcer, who was a pretty lady. I tossed the board, turned to Mike, and said, "Nice shoes," and turned back to catch the board, but it hadn't gone as high as I thought, and...*boom!* It hit me right in the head and split me open. The crowd went nuts! I rolled back into the ring, and Jimmy Hart was yelling at my opponent Earthquake, "He's bleeding, baby! He's bleeding!"

After the match, I walked to the back, and the EMS people stationed backstage came running up to me, shouting, "What happened?"

Sigh.

"I hit myself in the head with a board."

I had to repeat myself, twice, because I was so embarrassed that I couldn't bring myself to say it without mumbling. Blackjack Lanza, one of the agents, came up to me and said, "Duggan, that was great! Can you do that tomorrow night?"

Most of the boards I used were brand-new lumber, boards that were in pretty good shape. But in Europe, everything is metric, and the dimensions on the boards were never quite right for my purposes. I know it sounds strange, but I guess every millimeter counts.

Debra's dad, Bill, made me a beautiful, green felt carrying case for my 2x4s. One time, we were flying into Italy, and the guy at customs pulled out my 2x4 case, I guess thinking it looked like a rifle case. He opened it and pulled out a 2x4, real slow, and he actually inspected the damn board! Honest—the guy was rapping his knuckles up and down the board, looking for a hollow spot so he could find what I was smuggling.

I'm standing there with all the other wrestlers, and the customs guy says, in his broken English, "What you do with wood?"

I said, "Well, I'm building a house over here, piece by piece."

I thought that was hilarious. Customs guy didn't.

He pointed at a chair against a wall and said, "Sit over there."

Two hours of waiting later, I'm calling out to the guy, "I'm sorry, I was just joking! I'm sorry!"

Finally, they let me go, and I walked out of the airport and onto the bus, which was packed with wrestlers who had been stuck there waiting for me for two hours.

As I got to my seat on the bus, I was serenaded by a dozen voices.

"Jesus, Duggan! Keep your mouth shut! Son of a bitch!"

But even though I had the 2x4 and other accessories, I never had much more of a gimmick than "Hacksaw," aside from the "king" thing, which was a temporary deal.

But I saw a lot of other guys who were given weird, new characters, and it was interesting to see how they responded. Perfect example—the difference between One Man Gang becoming Akeem and Terry Taylor becoming The Red Rooster.

Gang embraced Akeem, while Terry hated the Rooster. I know he tries to put a good spin on it when he talks about it now, but trust me, he hated the Rooster. Had Terry embraced the Rooster like Gang embraced Akeem, he could have gotten it over, as silly as it was.

Look, they were screwing with Terry when he got that gimmick. The British Bulldogs would screw with Terry constantly. We would be wrestling in Alaska, and they would take Terry's socks and dunk them in water, and then put them outside until they froze—which only took a few seconds.

One day, I was at the airport waiting for my flight, when here came Terry—with one pants leg cut off at the knee—just one!

Even though they were screwing with him by making him the Rooster, he could have made something out of it. He dyed a little strip of hair in the middle of his head red, and occasionally he'd do a little scratch and flap his arms. What he should have done was get a Mohawk and dye it bright red, strut around like a big rooster, and gone with it.

But if you ever see footage of Gang as Akeem, he was doing full-out dance moves on his way to the ring, looking all happy, with that goofy look on his face—they made him Akeem to screw with him, but he made the most of it.

CHAPTER 12

A RUMBLE AND A GIANT FEUD

IT WAS WILD THE WAY WRESTLING EVOLVED from a regional attraction to this big, national powerhouse. On Thanksgiving night in 1987, I was in the first match on the first Survivor Series pay-per-view, and it didn't really register with me at the time how the business was changing and going to this pay-per-view business model. All I knew was that it was an extra-good payday.

I never did think it would become the big worldwide thing that Vince has grown it into, with all these huge venues and shows. When I was in San Antonio, we would have looked at a crowd of 10,000 and thought, *Wow, this must be the biggest show ever!*

Now, the WWE guys see a crowd of 10,000 and say, "Where the hell is everybody?"

Meanwhile, that same Thanksgiving night, Crockett's NWA was running its first pay-per-view, but Vince aced him out of most of his pay-per-view clearances with the cable companies. Vince never mentioned the NWA, or anything they were doing, to the boys; we never really gave them any thought. They were doing their best, but Vince was just crushing them.

I never liked Crockett, because he had been rude to my dad. There was some function we went to, earlier in the 1980s, and I had my dad with me. I introduced my dad to Crockett, and he just brushed us off. I'm sure

Crockett doesn't even remember it, but to me, that was a big deal. He's lucky I didn't punch him in the nose. He might not have even realized what he had done, but it always stuck it my craw.

About two months after Survivor Series came the first Royal Rumble. Every Rumble since has been a pay-per-view, but that first show was a free special on the USA Network, airing January 24, 1988, which by complete coincidence, I'm sure, was the night of Crockett's second pay-per-view.

The Rumble was a 20-man battle royal, but with a guy coming in every two minutes, instead of everyone starting in the ring at once, as in a regular battle royal. The novelty of it reminded me of a match Watts had done in Mid-South—the blindfold battle royal. That one was a lot of fun, because we were wearing full hoods and could barely see. They drove people nuts, because the ending would be something like this: the last three guys would be me, Ricky Morton, and Hercules. The fans loved Ricky and me, but hated Hercules. So, as a babyface, I'd point toward Hercules, the heel, and the fans would cheer, so I'd walk toward him. But he'd start off in another direction, and we'd miss each other. We'd go back and forth until at some point, Ricky would walk in between us, and I'd grab Ricky and beat the hell out of him, while the fans were screaming at the tops of their lungs, "It's Ricky, Hacksaw! It's Ricky!"

And the Rumble was fun, too. The crowd really got into it, and the end came down to me and my old friend, One Man Gang. When I tossed him to win, the place really popped, which made me feel good to get such a warm reception in Canada (where the show was held), even though I was best known for being a 100-percent American patriot.

And just a few months after that, I was back on pay-per-view in the ring against my old pal, Ted DiBiase, as part of the first round of the WWF championship tournament at WrestleMania IV. Teddy ended up beating me in the first round, but the way it happened set up quite possibly the biggest feud of my career, no pun intended.

The finish came when Andre the Giant popped me while I was in the ropes, and Ted got the pin. "Macho Man" Randy Savage won the tournament that night, but I got a feud with Andre out of the deal, which worked out nicely.

The visual added to the feud, because when Andre hit me, he potatoed me and busted my lip. Hell, I didn't mind—it made for a memorable moment, plus it was Andre, so what the hell was I going to say, anyway?

Feuding with Andre transformed me from being a midcard guy into being a main event guy. Not long after the tournament, there was a deal on TV where Andre issued an open challenge to any other "giant." I ran out there with my 2x4 to confront him, even though the face-off was my chin butting against Andre's belly. The cameras caught my big line: "Hacksaw Duggan is not afraid of you!"

He went to swat me with his big paw, but somehow, his finger got caught in my lip and he almost pulled it right off. It worked out great, because the blood was just pouring out, much more than you could ever get with a blade. He was choking me down, and I was feeling around for the board until I found it. I reared back with it and whacked him. Andre went down like a giant redwood, and we went off the air with me standing over Andre, covered in blood, 2x4 in hand and giving a big "HO-OH!"

That segment alone elevated me, and I was off and running with Andre. I was really honored that Andre trusted me enough to do a bit with me where he would end up laid out like that—fans *never* saw Andre flat on his back. So it was a really big deal.

Behind the scenes, I got along with Andre. We played cards, and he liked Debra, too. And it was a big step up from the first time I'd worked with Andre, nearly a decade earlier. The Convict's matches against Andre in Hawaii (when he was on his way home from a tour of Japan) were short and consisted of me just getting crushed.

Andre also liked to play jokes on his opponent in the ring. Some were not pleasant. Once, I was wrestling him with Bobby Heenan at ringside. Andre knocked me down to the mat near a corner, and Heenan yelled, "Give him the mudslide, Andre!"

I was lying there on the mat, going, "Geez, I've been around a while now, and I have never heard of a mudslide. What the hell is this?"

Andre grabbed the ropes and flopped right down on me, butt first. I was like a great big suppository, because my head went right up between the cheeks of his ass. I was stuck in there, and all I could think was, *Mudslide...*

From then on, whenever I was selling on the mat with Andre and Heenan hollered, "Mudslide," I'd roll right out of the ring and work the crowd: "HO-OH! U-S-A!"

He had another spot he loved to do, where we'd be standing opposite each other and he'd say, "Duggan...step closer."

I'd think, *Oh god, here we go*, and take a few steps.

"Closer!"

Finally, he'd grab me by the hair and pull me in. Andre wore a singlet with one strap, and he'd pull down the strap and start choking me with it. One night, instead of going around my throat, it got caught in my mouth! So when he thought he was choking me, he was actually squeezing all his giant juice right into my mouth.

I swear, I never fought harder in my life than I fought to get out of that one. Andre just stood there, clamping down and chuckling: "Ho ho ho ho ho."

I finally broke away (more likely, he loosened his grip enough to let me go) and rolled to the edge of the ring apron, where I looked down and puked onto the floor. Unfortunately, puking from that height onto the floor meant a little splatter, so a few lucky ringsiders ended up with more than their money's worth that night.

Things were tough for Andre, though, because of his size. Pretty much anyone can disguise themselves if they want to be anonymous, but not Andre. And hygiene was difficult for him, because a standard shower stall was not going to accommodate him. There were times when Andre had, let's say, a distinctive aroma to him. You could be sitting in the locker room playing cards, and you'd know if Andre walked in even if your back was to the door.

But the feud got cut short by my own bad judgment. Andre and I were main-eventing the Meadowlands, and that day, Jake Roberts and I went to a gym in the area to work out. The gym had a basketball court, and Jake and I went to play a game, during which I ruptured my Achilles tendon.

It was the single most debilitating injury of my entire career. I had to call the office to tell them I was hurt, but I promised I would make the Meadowlands show. I got to the arena, but I could barely walk. Arnie Skaaland came to me and said, "Geez, I can see you're hurtin', but you gotta at least go out there."

Andre went out first, and as I walked to the ring, every few steps I'd stop to give a thumbs-up and a "HO-OH!" As I stepped through the ropes, Andre came over and kicked me in the leg, so that I would have a reason to sell the leg the rest of the match.

Jake actually inherited the Andre feud with me out of action. Makes you wonder...

No, Jake, if you're reading this, I'm just kidding! It was my fault, because I shouldn't have been out there playing basketball. What was I thinking?

A few months later, I got back into action, and in 1989, I had my next major program against Haku, my old friend from Hawaii. Now he was "King" Haku, having dethroned Harley Race for the sort-of championship. I beat him in April to become "King" Duggan, which really was where the Hacksaw character turned silly, although I had kind of been making that transition into a less intensely serious character since I started in the WWF.

It was easier being silly than going out there and chopping meat every night, that's for sure. I know that sometimes that character was over the top, but that character was working. Nobody ever gave me any creative input about which way to go with the character; it just kind of evolved that way. One of my most profitable times in the business was with my eyes crossed, my tongue sticking out, and my thumb up. It worked!

Early in my WWF tenure, I had worked a program with "King" Harley Race, and he was someone I greatly respected. I had never worked with him much before, but feuding with him taught me a lot. We became friends, and we're friends to this day. In the ring, he was the master—he knew a million little tricks to work the crowd and take the fans wherever he wanted to.

Harley and I also had the most damn fun of anyone at the first Slammy Awards, this WWF-themed award show Vince had come up with. I won the awards for "Best Hit" and "Best Vocal" for my "HO-OH!" They were nice trophies—although we had to give them back to the company after the show, so that they could use the same ones over and over.

When I got my Slammy for "Best Hit," Harley and Bobby Heenan were the presenters. Harley shoved me halfway off the stage, and we ended up in this huge fight. We fought through Trump Plaza, and they kept cutting back to us throughout the show. We'd actually taped all the backstage brawling the day before; it took all day, as we'd brawl in one place and then stop so they could pack up the cameras and get them to the next spot, and repeat. They even took Polaroids of us at various points, so we could make sure our clothes were torn in the same spots and the other details matched up. At one point, we were in a barnyard where they had chickens, a donkey, a camel, a pig, and some other animals. Harley actually picked up a chicken and started beating me with it. It turned out to be a big deal—he caught a lot of heat for killing that chicken.

We ended up in the banquet hall, where they had supposedly set up this big spread for everyone after the show. Vince had spent a ton of money on this prop door that was supposed to break when we brawled our way through it. Now, because of the expensive prop door and the fact that, unlike our all-over-the-place brawling, this part was happening as we filmed the night of the show, it was a one-take deal. Harley went to throw me through the door, but they hadn't secured it, so it just kind of popped open instead of shattering. Vince was *pissed*. He ripped that prop guy to pieces.

We finished up in the banquet hall, and I grabbed this giant tuna fish by the tail and whacked Harley with it. So, he got me with a chicken, and I got him with the chicken of the sea!

Harley and I did a lot of brawls after our matches that ended with me swiping his cape and crown, but he always got them back. However, after beating Haku, they became *my* cape and crown, although I admit I looked funny with that bucket-sized crown always falling over my eyes. Plus, I was always damn near tripping over my long, purple cape.

At one point, I was heading to ringside every night with the cape, the crown, the flag, the board, my tongue sticking out of the side of my mouth, the thumb turned up, the "HO-OH," and the crossed eyes. One night, Bobby Heenan was talking to Vince McMahon backstage as I was about to head to the ring. Heenan took a look at me and said, "Vince, he needs an eagle."

My kingship ended after about four months when Randy Savage defeated me to become the "Macho King." About a month later, in September of 1989, I got a call from the office, telling me I needed to turn in the cape and crown.

I said, "I turned them in already."

They said I didn't, but I knew I had, and we went round and round for a little while. I didn't really see what the big deal was, because they had given Savage a new cape and crown, but that didn't matter, because I clearly remembered turning them in.

A few years later, I was cleaning out my dad's attic, and I opened a trunk...and there were the cape and crown. I couldn't believe it. I really thought I had turned them in.

One of my big return matches with Haku was in Atlanta's Omni. He was already in the ring as I walked around with the cape and crown. I looked at him and pulled the cape up to my face, like Dracula, and for whatever reason, it struck him as funny. He just started cracking up, laughing. That got me laughing, and we were practically rolling on the mat. It was one of those deals where trying to stop laughing just makes you laugh harder. Soon, the people at ringside were laughing. It was just silly.

We got under control and did our match, and when I went to the back, Jay Strongbow was waiting.

He said, "Jesus! You wanna be a *little* serious in the ring?"

I said, "Serious? Let's see, I got the cape, the crown, the board, the flag, the thumb, the tongue, the crossed eyes...and I almost had an eagle!"

Strongbow just shook his head. My circle of friends and I got that reaction from him and the other agents a lot.

Sometime in 1990, I was in a battle royal with, among others, Curt "Mr. Perfect" Hennig, Big Bossman, and the Ultimate Warrior. Bossman was

133

legitimately a former prison guard and a big, mobile guy. Curt was one of the all-time greats in the ring and a great friend, but a notorious prankster. Warrior...well, he had a painted face and big, shiny muscles. To emphasize them, he wore armbands with fringe around his biceps.

Bossman and I got Warrior up against the ropes while Curt, selling on the apron, reached up and tied the fringe from one of Warrior's armbands to the top rope. Warrior didn't have a clue.

Bossman and I split, and Warrior started to come out from the corner but got jerked back to the rope that Curt had tied him to. I guess he thought he could use his mighty muscles to break free, but nylon is a lot more flexible than Warrior was strong. All he managed to do was tighten the armband to the point where it was cutting off the circulation in his arm.

I swear, you could have heard his scream from anywhere in the building. After a few seconds of Warrior squealing in pain, Strongbow came running down with a jackknife and sawed through the nylon to cut him loose. Curt, Bossman, and I all got a free trip to WWF headquarters in Stamford for a talking-to after that.

But even though no one particularly liked Warrior, Curt didn't mean any real harm—playing jokes on each other was just something we did to keep ourselves amused on what could be long, difficult tours. One of the favorite pranks was to put locks on someone's bags. We traveled a lot, and guys kept all their stuff in the bags they carried around, so you'd come back from working out or from your match and someone would have put 50 padlocks on your bag. But sometimes, guys used pranks, or "ribs," as we called them, to bully other wrestlers. The British Bulldogs were a good example of this. Remember the story about Terry Taylor and the frozen socks? Well, they never pulled any of their stunts on me or anyone who had a rep for being a tough guy. The Bulldogs picked their spots and their targets.

That's why I like guys like Brian Knobbs. He'll mess with the lowest guy on the totem pole, and then he'll wander over and mess with Hulk Hogan or Ric Flair, as well as everyone in between. He's an equal-opportunity offender.

The Bulldogs and Mr. Fuji (one of the heel managers) even screwed with one guy, an Australian named Peter Stilsbury who wrestled as Outback Jack, so badly that they drove him out of the WWF. Jack got there around the same time I did in 1987, but he was gone within weeks.

The poor guy ended up naked in a hotel lobby, and nobody knows for sure who Halcioned him into oblivion, but I know who had tormented him for weeks with some of the meanest ribs imaginable.

Some guys were even mean to other guys' "ring rats." And, you know, I hate using that term, because it has such a bad connotation, but the fact is there were girls for some guys in every town. And believe it or not, for a lot of these young ladies, it was not a sexual thing. I had a female fan in Boston who would pick me up at the airport. I could leave my bag in her car (which showed a lot of trust), and she would wash my gear and run me back to the airport when the show was over. It wasn't a sex thing (Debra even got to know her); she was a big fan and just a nice lady. But one night, the Bulldogs burned her dress with a cigarette at the bar. That was their style—pick on a woman, or even a male wrestler they saw as not as tough as them.

And a lot of the guys engaged in stupid stuff. We used to be able to get the best hotel rates at the Boston airport Hilton...until the night that some idiot took a dump in the elevator and thought it was real funny. Next thing you know, our rates were more than doubled, and because of that, we started staying at the Ramada. Not long after, a couple of guys got into a big fight at the Ramada, and now, to this day, the wrestlers have to stay at one of the hotels in Revere, Massachusetts, an hour away from the airport, because the hotels bumped up the rates on wrestlers.

CHAPTER 13

TITUSVILLE

WORKING FOR THE WORLD WRESTLING FEDERATION meant traveling all over the world, so they didn't care where you lived. I was still living in Pineville, Louisiana, which was near my old house in Ball. But my wife was from South Carolina and I was from New York, and since I wasn't working for Bill Watts anymore, there really wasn't any connection to Louisiana and no need to stay there.

This was in the days before guaranteed contracts; back then, if you worked, you got paid, and if you didn't, you didn't, so we all wanted to work as much as we possibly could. I know there were guys who did more consecutive days, but my longest stretch was 54 days without a day off. That was when I was working with Andre the Giant, and if Andre wanted to work, that meant a main event spot and main event money.

With all this travel, Debra and I sold our houses in Louisiana (our home and a rental property I owned), put all our other stuff in storage in Florida, and for a year, we both lived on the road together. If we were in the Southeast, we stayed with her folks. If we were in the Northeast, we stayed with my family. Out west, we'd just fly out and stay in hotels. Doing this let us bankroll some money, instead of having to make payments on a house we'd barely be in.

DEBRA SAYS:
Another benefit of us traveling together, at least for me, was that I didn't have to worry about him as much. Once, in October of 1987, when we weren't traveling together, he was heading

to Indianapolis for a show, and I saw a news story about a military jet crashing into the lobby of a Ramada Inn there. And it scared me to death, because I suddenly couldn't remember where he was, and the Ramada featured on the news was the one the wrestlers usually stayed at when they were in Indianapolis.

This was before cell phones, so I couldn't get in touch with him, and I wouldn't know anything until either he got in touch with me or someone else did.

Once we started traveling together, I got to see a lot of new places. I had never been anywhere outside of the Carolinas and our area of Mid-South.

If it was a road trip where we could do this, I'd pack a cooler with sandwiches and drinks, and we would picnic. Being in the car was easier, because we could basically live out of the car, whereas on the plane, you're stuck with whatever you can fit in your suitcase.

Finally, after about a year of saving, we decided to move to Florida. First, we looked at Tampa Bay, which was a hotbed for wrestlers. Hogan, Brutus Beefcake, Randy Savage, and other wrestlers who were friends of mine all lived there. I wanted to be close to my friends, but not so close that they'd be dropping by at 3:00 AM.

Debra, who was doing some house hunting, called me one day and said she had found the perfect place in Titusville, Florida.

I said, "Where? Did you say 'Titsville'?"

A few days later, I flew into Orlando and she picked me up. We had one of those big pimped-out Cadillacs, with the gold package and dark windows. We drove into the neighborhood in Titusville, a small community that was populated almost entirely by folks involved in the space program. There was an astronaut living right across the street.

When we reached the house, I got out of the car with the music still blaring. I had a tank top on, a ponytail, my pants tucked inside my boots, and I weighed about 310 pounds. Debra jumped out, a long-legged blonde in short-shorts and high heels.

We saw some folks out, and shouted, "Hi! We're your neighbors!"

The looks on their faces were like, "Get the kids in the house! *Hurry!*"

People were peeking out of their windows as Debra and I walked around the house. We sent that little neighborhood into a panic.

Things calmed down as we got to know the people a little bit. Some of them knew who I was, since I was on TV, and we made some friends. We still raised eyebrows from time to time, though.

One night, about two months after we moved in, Debra and I were out back, skinny-dipping in the screened-in pool that was part of our typical Florida home. After we swam for a while, Debra grabbed a flimsy little nightie, put it on, and said she was going to put out the trash. I said, "Sure, go ahead, honey."

She was walking the trash cans out when this pickup truck came charging down the street, knocked down my neighbor's trash cans, and kept coming. Debra ran back toward me (I was in the garage by then), and I said, "Let's get his license plate, that son of a gun!"

I jumped into my new Cadillac—the one I had bought with some of the royalties from my first action figure—fired up the car, still naked, and followed the truck. About two houses down, these idiots hit another trash can, but this one went underneath the truck, so they had to stop.

I pulled in behind them with my high beams on. I was scooched down in the seat, and Debra was in her nightie next to me, writing down the plate number. There were two guys in the cab of the truck, and one guy in the bed who started shouting, "Aw, these are two old bastards! What are they gonna do?"

He jumped out holding a length of pipe, and my first thought was, *My new car!*

I jumped out, screaming, and now this guy had 300 pounds of Hacksaw coming at him. He reached back with the pipe, but he hesitated before swinging, so I popped him. He went down, and my momentum caused me to fall over on top of him.

The other two guys in the truck looked at me in the mirror, and they were like, "Let's get the hell out of here!"

They took off in the truck, with the third guy running after them. I was standing with the high beams on me, screaming at them. Of course, all the neighbors were probably barricading themselves in their home, saying, "That wrestler finally snapped!"

Yes, our neighborhood had a very unique crime watch program—the naked Hacksaw!

I also enjoyed getting to know the local cops in Titusville. I had a friend who was a sheriff's deputy, and he'd let me ride along with him now and then. He'd always pick me up and then get on his radio and broadcast it—"Okay, fellas, I got the Hacksaw with me tonight!"

More than once, he'd arrest someone and stick them in the back of the car right next to me.

The guy would be screaming, "You sorry son of a bitch! I'm gonna..."

And then he'd look over at me.

"I'm gonna...Hacksaw Duggan? Hey, I'm a big fan, Hacksaw! Can you get me out of this?"

"Hey, kid," I'd say, "it don't work for me, it ain't gonna work for you!"

I even tried to branch out into business in Titusville. In 1995, I opened a gym, Hacksaw Duggan's Muscle & Fitness.

Catchy name, right?

For the TV commercial, Randy Savage and The Nasty Boys—Brian Knobbs and Jerry Sags—appeared with me, and when I had the grand opening, Hulk Hogan, who *never* took a day off, took a day off to come out and sign autographs, along with Brutus Beefcake, Knobbs and Sags, Savage, and myself. We had more than 1,000 people show up. And those guys, every single one of them, came down on their day off to do that for me, for free.

I could probably do a whole chapter filled with Brian Knobbs stories.

At one point in the late 1980s and early 1990s, it seemed like damn near everyone was on steroids (or "the gas," as it was known). I was 315 pounds, the heaviest I ever got, and I was benching around 500 pounds. A lot of guys were jacked up—I'm not saying I'm proud of it, but that's just the way things were.

One day in 1991, I was working out at Gold's Gym in Boston with a lot of the other boys, and we were all working out hard. Knobbs and Sags, at the time our tag-team champs, walked in wearing their duster jackets and their world championship belts. Those pudgy bastards were each working on a triple-dip ice-cream cone!

They came into the gym and announced, "Hey, screw you guys! We're the world champs!"

I was cracking up, but Hawk and Animal, the Road Warriors, were cussing them out. I guess I could see their point of view—the Warriors were huge power lifters, and here came two fat guys, making fun of them. But that was Knobbs and Sags. They were just goofing around.

They weren't the only ones. A lot of guys goofed around, because it was a way to pass the time with all the travel. After a 1989 show in Los Angeles, a bunch of WWF guys were catching a redeye flight to the next town. Everyone was in first class, and a lot of the guys had Halcion, which was very popular because it could put you to sleep in a flash, and when you woke up, there was no hangover. It was perfect for wrestlers who were always riding or flying and having to get used to different time zones—we suffered from permanent jet lag, and that alone will screw up anyone.

Anyway, it was about 1:30 in the morning, the plane was still boarding, and everyone on the plane was either half asleep or trying to zonk out. Next thing you knew, here came this big, banging ball of noise. It was Brian Knobbs, taking a minute to greet everyone on board in his own special way.

"Hey! Hey, how ya doin'? Hey, there!"

He messed with everybody—the crew, the passengers, the flight attendants. He sat down next to Curt Hennig, and they had this thing they used to do where they each took a bottle full of different kinds of pills, shook them up, and said, "Rainbow stew? Rainbow stew!"

Knobbs would grab a few of whatever pills came out, swallow a handful, and *wham!* He was out like a light.

As soon as he started snoring, everyone in first class had the same idea—*Let's get him!*

Everyone chipped in their blankets, so here was Knobbs, a very heavyset guy, buried under 20 or more blankets. Before long, he was sweating like a pig. Someone came up with some nail polish and painted Knobbs' nails a lovely shade of magenta, while someone else took a tube of lipstick, drew a big heart on his cheek, and wrote on his forehead. Someone else took a bunch of empty soda and beer cans and tied them to his shoes.

When we landed, a couple of us had to carry Knobbs off the plane; we couldn't just leave him there. Imagine the sight of two burly guys each hooking the arm of another big guy, dragging him through the Tampa airport, while the cans tied to his shoes clanked with every step, and people stopped to look at him and read the special message in lipstick on his forehead, which read, "I'm a dick."

We were taking Knobbs to Toni, his girlfriend (they later got married and are still together to this day). Toni was a really pretty lady, a very petite woman. But she was tough—she wasn't afraid of anything, and if she needed to, she would ball up her fists and could fight like a man. You did *not* want to mess with her.

We were still propping up Knobbsy, and she was waiting for us at the bottom of the escalator. She saw the heart on his cheek and must have thought it was something he did for her benefit, because she said, very sweetly, "Aw, Brian!"

Then we got closer, and the look on her face changed when she read his forehead.

Knobbs was awake but still out of it, and when she saw that and how messed up he was...*boom!* She nailed him! I was stuck in the middle of a pull-apart brawl (okay, a pretty one-sided brawl, but still).

We had three days off before the next shows, and when I saw Brian at the airport a couple of days later, he looked like he had been dragged behind a horse through a cactus patch. He had a thousand little cuts all over him. I asked him what happened.

He said, "Toni was so mad that when we got home, she took a picture off the wall and smashed me right over my head."

Another time, when we were all in WCW together in the mid-1990s, the two of them were traveling together in their car, with Brian driving and Toni next to him in the passenger's seat. (I wasn't the only guy who took my special lady out on the road with me, but I don't think anyone did it for as long as I did, except maybe Randy Savage with Elizabeth, and that was a different deal.)

Knobbs was one of those guys who loved cars and always had a nice one. They pulled into a gas station, and he opened his door and got out. But he had pulled too far ahead of the gas pump. Before you knew it, they were fighting.

"Toni, back the car up!"

"*You* back the car up!"

"Dammit, Toni, back the car up!"

This went on for a while. Finally, Toni leaned over from the passenger seat, put it in reverse, and gave it a little gas. She only did it for a second before braking, but her foot slipped off the brake and hit the gas again accidentally.

The open door clipped Knobbs and actually hit an artery under his arm. They had to airlift him out of there, because he needed urgent care. He was fine, but it was a scary moment, and it just shows Brian Knobbs lives a life that's crazier than any movie. Seriously, have you ever heard of anything like that happening to someone?

Actual movie people even got the Knobbs experience, more than once. There are a lot of celebrities who are wrestling fans, always have been. Brian came to me one night after we'd done a show in Los Angeles and asked if I wanted to go with him to this Hollywood cigar bar that Hulk Hogan had shown him. Knobbs had gotten chummy with the owner.

Now, we're talking spring of 1991, and the top people in Hollywood came to this place—Arnold Schwarzenegger, Sylvester Stallone, and Bruce Willis, among others. Knobbs and I jumped into our rental car and headed over there.

I can't imagine what people thought, smoking cigars in this fancy Hollywood club, and here came two huge, crazy-looking wrestlers. The owner, Knobbs' pal, came up and greeted us, and Knobbs had him take some pictures with the WWF tag-team belts, which he'd brought with him.

It was a hell of a night—big stars all around us, and we were making the most of the free food and booze.

Knobbs looked around the club and said, "Hey! There's that guy from *Robocop*! I gotta go talk to him!"

He got up and walked over to where actor Peter Weller was, and I could hear him halfway across the room: "Hey! Guy from *Robocop*! How you doin'?"

About two minutes later, Knobbs came back to our table, sat down, and said, "You know, that guy's really an asshole."

Nearly two hours later, we were still in there when another movie star walked in.

Knobbs' eyes got big, and he said, "Hey, that's Alec Baldwin! I gotta go talk to him!"

I was like, "Knobbs, Jesus, leave the guy alone!"

But Knobbs went over, and I sat there for five minutes, expecting the worst. But then I heard Knobbs again, this time hollering at me: "Hey, Duggan! Come on over!"

As I always say, you either love Knobbs or you hate him. And believe it or not, Alec Baldwin *loved* him. We ended up sitting there talking with Alec Baldwin for most of the night, and he was a great guy.

Knobbs was also tight with Dennis Rodman, the Hall of Fame basketball player who ended up doing some stuff for WCW. Like I said, Knobbsy got on a lot of people's nerves, but a lot of other people just loved the guy.

Even though the WWF didn't project a kayfabe/"protect the business" mentality, we still ran into people who wanted to test out a wrestler way too often.

After one show, I was pulling into a parking lot when I saw Marty Jannetty getting the crap knocked out of him by a group of guys. I parked and started to get out when I heard someone shout, "Get the gun! Get the gun!"

I went back to the car and reached under the driver's seat, yelling, "That's fine! I'm gonna get *my* gun!"

Of course, all I had under that seat was a wrapper from McDonald's, but my bluff worked. Those guys all got into their car and drove off.

Debra and I finally got married in April of 1989, right after WrestleMania V. All the wrestlers got two weeks off after WrestleMania, and we decided to use that time to have our wedding.

Back in January of 1998, Debra and I were on our property in Louisiana, out by a pond that was at the edge of our land, where we lived in a brick house, the one we had bought from Bill Dundee when he had been Bill Watts' booker back in 1984. When he moved out in 1985 to go back to his old stomping grounds in Memphis, we bought his house and had been there until our move to Titusville.

It was a pretty day, and I couldn't imagine a better opportunity to take Debra's hand and ask her to marry me as we stood underneath one of the big, old trees that stood around our pond. One minute, we were just walking and talking, and the next, I had fished a diamond ring out of the pocket of this long winter coat I'd been wearing. She said yes!

And, you know, I still have that coat.

DEBRA SAYS:
After getting engaged, we had to decide if we wanted to get married in three months or wait a year until after Wrestlemania. We decided to wait so we would have time to plan the wedding we really wanted.

That year was the second in a row where WrestleMania was at the Trump Casino in Atlantic City, and we made our plans to take off straight from Atlantic City.

>When he asked, I didn't have to think about it, I just bounced
>up and said, "Yes! Yes!"

The only person who knew ahead of time that I was going to propose was the Junkyard Dog. He had turned me onto his jeweler in Baton Rouge, and that was where I had the engagement ring made.

The wedding turned out really well. Jake Roberts was a groomsman, and so was Ricky Ferrara, the cranky little referee from Mid-South who had been so supportive of me over the years. But when it came time to decide on a best man, there was really only one choice, and I was so proud to have my pop standing up there with me.

DEBRA SAYS:

>We ended up getting married in a church that's just a few
>miles from where we're living now in South Carolina. We had
>the reception at a Holiday Inn, where we reserved 26 rooms,
>plus another 10 rooms at a neighboring hotel. The out-of-
>town guests added up quickly, because aside from the few
>wrestling people who were there, only my family was from
>around the area. Jim's side was all coming down from New
>York, except for a few relatives who had settled in other parts
>of the country.

Several wrestling people came, but for the ones who couldn't, especially the WWF people, I understood—this couple of weeks was the only time off we had all year. Still, it was good to see some familiar faces. Even though one of my most vicious feuds was with the One Man Gang, away from the wrestling ring, George Gray was one of the nicest guys in the business, and someone I've been proud to call a friend for years.

I was also glad to see Magnum T.A., who had left Mid-South in late 1984 and headed to Crockett Promotions on Superstation WTBS. By 1986, Crockett was just about the closest thing Vince McMahon had to competition for a national wrestling audience, and Magnum was one of

Crockett's most popular stars. Magnum had it all—he had the look, the work ethic, the talent, and the interviews.

However, in late 1986, Magnum lost control of his car on a wet road and ended his wrestling career when the car wrapped around a telephone pole. His biggest sin was that he liked to drive fast, but hell, we all did. But Terry Allen was a real-life tough guy, and he defied every doctor's expectations, first by surviving the crash, and then by learning to walk again. He was never able to wrestle again, but he's had some success in the business world, and I have all the respect in the world for Terry Allen.

In addition to Jake Roberts being part of the wedding party, his dad, "Grizzly" Smith, was also there. Griz had been a wrestler in the 1960s and 1970s, but I got to know him when he worked backstage for Bill Watts in Mid-South. He was another person who'd been incredibly supportive of me. Grizzly, Ricky, and Gang all came to South Carolina, all the way from Louisiana, to be with us.

There was one other wrestling-connected person there, although she was not in the business at the time. When I got back to the WWE in 2005, ring announcer Lillian Garcia came up to me one night and said, "You know, I sang at your wedding reception."

I thought she was kidding, but she told me the name of the band and the hotel where we had the reception. Turns out that before she became a singing ring announcer, she and her band played local events in the Carolinas, including weddings.

DEBRA SAYS:
The next morning, we headed to Hawaii for our two-week honeymoon. We went back to Hawaii for a week for our first anniversary. Then we flew to Los Angeles, where Jim filmed an episode of the TV show *Harry and the Hendersons.*

Debra actually met me in Hawaii for that trip. I was coming back from Japan, where WWF had done a tour, and she flew out from our home in Florida. It wasn't the most romantic anniversary, because I spent most of my days tanning, training, or learning my lines, all for the show. But I felt good, because after all that studying, I had my lines down.

The first day we went in for the TV shoot, one of the guys from the show came in and said, "Script change!"

I couldn't believe it—I'd been studying for days to get these lines right, and everything was changed. And if I have a major weak point, it's doing stuff verbatim. It's kind of like today's WWE wrestlers. Who are the good promo guys? Who the hell knows? None of them speak from the heart—those kids are out there worrying about repeating their scripted dialogue verbatim, and none of their own mannerisms, their idiosyncrasies, the things that show their own personalities—none of that shows through.

I don't know if I'd have made it in wrestling if I'd had to do that. I couldn't really be "Hacksaw" if I was constantly worried about what I was saying. I was able to just let it roll, and that always worked pretty well for me.

But my *Harry and the Hendersons* experience gave me a lot of respect for actors. They bust their asses to memorize their stuff and then deliver it exactly right, with the exact right feeling behind the words. It's a lot harder than it looks.

CHAPTER 14

THE END OF THE ROAD

THE DOMESTIC TRAVEL WITH THE WWF WAS INSANE, but a few years into my stay there we started making regular tours of Japan and Europe. In 1990, we did some shows in Japan, and one night, I was in downtown Tokyo with referee Mike Chioda. We were pretty drunk when we walked into a McDonald's, and the place was jam-packed. We had just gotten our food and stepped outside when a group of Japanese guys just slammed right into me.

The lead guy made me spill my soda, so I was not happy. I grabbed my French fries and hit the guy with them. What I thought a regular order of fries would accomplish, I have no idea, but the guy got mad and started coming at me in some kind of kung fu stance. Of course, he was not a big guy—if I'd had a *large* order of fries, I probably could have held him off.

The guy hit me and knocked my glasses off, so I reared back and really unloaded on him. The guy couldn't have been more than 100 pounds, so he went completely up, over, and back. But as soon as I hit him, it was like the radar went off for every Japanese person within a quarter mile, and I was swarmed.

Of course, I was 20 years younger and drunk as a skunk, so I was ready to take them all on. Chioda, who had found a cab, was pulling on me and pleading, "Come on, Jim, get in the cab! Get in the cab!" (That was the way we had to get a cab over there: we'd have to send one guy out, because cabs wouldn't stop for groups of wrestlers.)

Another time, we were in England, and one night we ended up at Stringfellows, a really popular London club that had to be like what Studio 54 in New York had been in its heyday. One of the other guys there was Hercules, and he was making out with this tall person who, to me, was clearly not a lady, even though this individual was in a pretty dress and makeup.

The bouncer came over to the table where a bunch of us wrestlers were sitting, and he said, "Hey, um, you know your friend over there is making out with a guy."

I just looked over and said, "I don't think he cares."

In August of 1992, we headed back overseas for one of the biggest shows of my career. We went to Wembley Stadium in England for SummerSlam and performed in front of more than 80,000 fans—one of the biggest crowds I'd seen since WrestleMania III.

Debra and my dad went to England with me. A day after the show, we got to Heathrow Airport, and right before passengers were divided between trips to the U.S. and trips to Europe, I said, "Pop, big surprise! We're not going home—we're going to Ireland!"

He was excited, but he still had his sense of humor. As we went through security, he started saying, "They're kidnapping me!"

Unlike my dad, the security people had *no* sense of humor about that. Even in those pre-9/11 days, they took that stuff pretty seriously. They pulled us aside, but we assured him my dad was just kidding around.

Debra had tracked down the Duggan family history to a town called Fermoy in County Cork, Ireland. We flew into Dublin and drove into Fermoy, making a weeklong trip out of it. More than once, I guess I forgot where I was and started driving on the wrong (or right, depending on how you look at it) side of the road.

And more than once, I heard screams of, "Go to the left!"

In Fermoy, we found Duggan's Grocery Store, so we had to stop. Pop was dressed in shamrocks, Debra was all in green, and I was taking pictures in the grocery store. The clerk came up to us and said, "Hmm, you must be Americans!"

How could he tell?

I did my second Royal Rumble match in 1991 (I was on the 1989 and 1990 shows, but in separate matches on the undercards), which was also the first Rumble for a talented kid who I knew would go far—although I didn't know how far.

Mark Calaway had been in wrestling for a couple of years before he came to the WWF as The Undertaker in 1990.

I still remember wrestling a short series of matches against him not long after he started. He was wound as tightly as he could be. I guess it was nerves or wanting to make a good impression with this great gimmick he had, but he was so tense that when he started choking me, he *really* started choking me. I wanted to snap him out of it, so I grabbed two handfuls of his stringy hair, pulled them straight up, and yelled at him, "You got devil hair! Devil hair!"

He damn near laughed out loud, but he kept his composure. Still, he understood what I was trying to do, and we worked fine the rest of the match.

Like I said, I knew he was going to be a big star. But no one could have predicted that would be the start of a 20-year (and counting) run; seriously, it might just be the greatest run of any wrestler, ever. No one will ever touch Undertaker's mark again.

That's partly because the days of the 30-year guys, like Terry Funk and Ric Flair (and myself), are over. The guys in it today won't stay with it that long; with the stuff some of them do, it's not physically possible to do it for 30 years.

By 1993, I could tell that my WWF days were winding down. They were featuring me less and less, and I was being booked in lower spots on the card. I understood the need to freshen things up with different talent, but I still had to make a living.

One of the last major things I did there was an angle with this 500-plus-pound kid named Rodney Anoia, who wrestled as Yokozuna. He had beaten Hogan for the WWF title at the King of the Ring pay-per-view in June of 1993, and he was doing a heavily Japanese, anti-American gimmick, so a match against me was a natural.

He pinned me with his finishing move, the banzai drop, where he would flatten opponents with his huge butt, right on their chests after bouncing off the second rope. To cap off our first match, he did the move several times for effect. It made for a pretty powerful visual after the match, when Yokozuna's manager, Mr. Fuji, draped an American flag over me as I lay in the ring. Unfortunately, because Fuji had laid the flag over me and Yoko couldn't tell exactly where I was underneath it, he couldn't tell where he was dropping and legitimately left me with some cracked ribs.

This led to a TV segment a few weeks later, where Vince had a camera crew at my house, interviewing Debra and me, with Debra trying to talk me out of a rematch with Yokozuna. Of course, as a proud American babyface, I was determined to fight again.

I thought we had a couple of decent rematches, but I could see the writing on the wall, especially when Lex Luger started doing the heavily patriotic gimmick. Apparently, the WWF saw it, too, because they let me go not long after the Yokozuna matches.

I would have liked to work more with Yoko, and not just because he was champ; it would have meant working for main event money. I also liked him, just as I'd made friends of Haku and pretty much all the Samoans and other guys from the islands. They were tough as nails, but you could not find a more gracious group of people...at least, until you messed with them. I never could understand it, because the guy was just deadly, but Haku was a moron-magnet—he seemed to attract the most foolish people. For whatever reason, these idiots were constantly trying to mess with him and challenge him. He would let it slide, at first, because he really was a good-hearted guy, but some people just couldn't take a hint. Once, I saw him try to wave off a guy who kept challenging him and insulting him. Haku even told the guy he didn't want any trouble, because we were all out just trying to have a good time, but the guy kept hassling him.

Finally, Haku grabbed the guy and told him, "First, I kill you; then..."

Haku's eyes got real big.

"...*I eat you!*"

I'd try to warn people away from him. I'd tell folks who hassled Haku, "You know, brother, about three generations back, your liver would be on a stick right now, so you might want to knock that shit off."

Haku never went out looking for trouble, but he knew what we all knew—you couldn't back down in our business.

. Ultimately, Luger was not a success, with his "Lex Express" bus tour, his fancy gear, and his All-American gimmick, because as I said before, it wasn't from the heart, and people can sense when that's the case. You might think I'm full of myself, but I honestly think I'd have done better feuding with Yokozuna in that situation, because even in 1993, my gimmick was still working.

A lot of people have tried to make heat between Lex and me over the situation, but there was never any heat between us, personally. I knew it wasn't his call.

So I wasn't exactly thrilled about being let go, but I never had hard feelings over it, because I understood it was just business, and I have a lot of respect for Vince McMahon. I think back to that night at the Slammys, when Harley and I brawled all over the place. You might remember Vince getting onstage at one point and doing this song-and-dance number with the showgirls, but that was the least of it, for him. He knew every word that everyone was supposed to speak. He knew where they needed to be, when they needed to be there, and what they needed to do. He was like the director, producer, and one of the stars, all at once.

And that's what has made him a success—he's an unbelievably hands-on guy, and no one works harder than he does. And Vince even sent us a gift when our daughter Celia was born in 1993, even though he surely knew by then that he wouldn't be keeping me much longer. He sent a silver teething ring with the old "WWF" logo on it.

Celia's birth was a huge moment in my life. I never thought I'd be married, and I sure never thought I'd be ready for children, because it's a real sacrifice. You have to put yourself second, third, or fourth. Debra and I always talked about having kids and figured we eventually would, but I kept putting it off. I figured we had time, since Debra is nine years younger than me, but she started telling me we needed to go ahead and have kids.

"Don't worry," I'd say. "It'll be like ordering a pizza. When the time's right, bing-bang-boom, we'll have a kid."

But she persisted, and finally, I agreed. One month...nothing. Two months...nothing. Three months...nothing.

I started thinking, *Uh-oh, maybe we did wait too long.*

I went to the doctor to get tested, and I was okay. The problem was I was on the road all the time, working. So Debra was at home, always taking her temperature, and one day she called me from our home in Florida and said, "Jim, I just took my temperature, and everything's right! It's perfect, right now!"

"That's great, honey," I said. "I'm in Indianapolis."

But Debra stayed positive; she even picked out an outfit that she told me she would wear when she became pregnant, a yellow dress with some blue highlights—a hot outfit, since she said it would probably be the last time she'd get to wear it.

Then came one of the most unbelievable days of my life. I had to appear for FBI questioning in New York City as part of a federal steroids case against Vince McMahon. I was sitting there with my expensive lawyer, in this big meeting room, when two FBI agents walked in. One of them—I'm not making this up—was named Inspector Flagg.

Flagg threw a thick folder down onto the conference table. I said, "Wow, that's a pretty good-sized folder on the WWF."

One of them opened it up, and my picture was on top. It wasn't their WWF folder; it was their *Jim Duggan* folder.

They asked me all about the WWF and steroids, because their theory was that Vince was encouraging guys to get on the gas and then getting them access to it. But I'll tell you what I told them—in six years in the

WWF, Vince McMahon never once told me to use steroids. I did them, but it was because I knew a lot of the top guys were on them, and if I wanted to compete and be stronger, I needed to use them. But nobody told me to, and Vince absolutely *never* gave me access to them or even discussed them with me. Never.

They asked me about Randy Savage, and about all this weight he had recently lost.

I said, "Well, I know he's going through a divorce. But I don't know anything about his personal habits."

By this point in late 1992, the feds had already convicted Dr. George Zahorian, a Pennsylvania doctor, for distributing steroids to WWF wrestlers. I remember seeing Zahorian at shows as far back as 1980, when I was first there as "Big" Jim Duggan. He was supposedly the commission doctor, but he had suitcases with him filled with Valium, uppers, downers—whatever you wanted.

That evolved into steroids; before that, there were probably only a few guys juicing (not to name names, but if you remember some of the physiques back then, you're probably looking at the obvious suspects).

Nothing ever happened with me; I never ran too much with Hogan or McMahon, the original targets of the investigation. For what it's worth, when it went to trial in 1994, Hulkster ended up testifying reluctantly for the government, and Vince was exonerated by the time it was all over. I was signing with WCW by then, so it's not like I was privy to what was going on behind the scenes in the WWF, but, well, Vince is a master. He showed up to court every day in a neck brace, because he'd had this neck surgery he had needed for a while. He played for sympathy well.

But the bottom line is I never once saw Vince encourage anyone to take steroids. And I think the right thing happened when he was found not guilty.

But that day in 1992, I left the FBI building, drove to the airport, and flew home. This was back when they had those phones on the backs of the airplane seats, and I had a million questions about how the legal process worked on something like this, so I called my sister, Angel, the prosecutor, and we ended up talking the whole flight. What I didn't realize until I got my credit card bill was that the phone rates were so high, that call cost me more than the lawyer in New York had.

When I landed at the airport, Debra was waiting, which was kind of weird; she usually would just wait outside the baggage claim area. She was wearing a yellow dress with blue highlights. I was so drained after a day of lawyers and questioning that it didn't even register with me right away.

I gave her a hug and a kiss. She said, "Well, how do I look?"

I stepped back, and it clicked.

"You're pregnant?"

She was.

DEBRA SAYS:

It was kind of funny. Mike Rotunda (who wrestled as I.R.S.) and his wife, The Undertaker and his wife, and Jim and I were all expecting children at the same time.

I had a due date in the first week of August, which was about the same time that the other two women were due. Undertaker's son ended up being born a few weeks early, and our daughter Celia was born two weeks early. Rotunda's son was born a month late, but for a while, it looked like we'd all be having our kids at around the same time.

Debra ended up being the best mother for my kids that I could have asked for. I changed a few diapers, and the one time I watched Celia, I dozed off, and the poor thing rolled off the ottoman like a little Tootsie Roll. Fortunately, Debra has great maternal instincts and was very hands-on.

My old joke about it was that I got bumped from No. 1 to No. 2, and then down to No. 3 when Rebecca was born in 1995. These days, I think I'm sixth, with the dogs coming in third through fifth. But I wouldn't have it any other way.

CHAPTER 15

WCW

AFTER I LEFT THE WWF, I spent the next few months working sporadically on the independent circuit.

I had fun on the indies, and especially at first, I did well, because I was just coming off years of TV exposure. Even though guys tend to overvalue themselves on the indie circuit, a wrestler's highest value is when he comes right off TV.

If you've never been to an indie show, most of the time there is one "name" guy in the main event, and the rest of the card is filled with local kids. Once in a while, they'd have two or three guys with TV names, and on rare occasion, someone would try to do a big show with lots of names, like those shows Insane Clown Posse does each year with 50 old-timers.

But I had fun working the indies—they have smaller crowds, which took some getting used to, but that just gave me a chance for more interaction with the fans, and I really enjoyed that.

I probably would have been happy doing it for more than a few months, but in the spring of 1994, I got a call from Jimmy Hart, whom I'd been friendly with in the WWF. Jimmy said that Hulk Hogan wanted to talk to me. This was before the days of cell phones, so Hulk wanted to make sure I'd be home.

Hulkster talked about starting up in World Championship Wrestling and said, "Hey, we're gonna be in Orlando. You wanna come on over?"

You bet I did!

I actually stood next to Hulk while he was making his announcement about coming into WCW, and while I was in town for that event, I had

157

my first meeting with Eric Bischoff, which went great, and I started in WCW.

WCW was owned by Turner Broadcasting System, which got into the wrestling business when Jimmy Crockett's NWA went under in late 1988. TBS didn't want to lose one of its best-rated shows, the Saturday night wrestling program, so the company bought what was left of the promotion from Crockett. In the following five years, they hadn't managed to compete against Vince McMahon much more successfully than Crockett had, but when Eric Bischoff took over in 1993, he made it his mission to take on the WWF. That meant getting some big-name talent, and there was no bigger name than the Hulkster.

That period was a busy one, not only because of my impending WCW debut, but because we were adding a new member to the family. I was home from working an independent show in April of 1994, laying in bed with little Celia, when Debra came in and told me, "You are going to be a daddy again!" I was so surprised! After the hard time we had getting pregnant with Celia, I thought it was going to take a while for us to have another child—but not this time. Rebecca was born January 12, 1995, two days before my birthday—best birthday present ever! Even though I know taking care of the girls was a lot of work for her, Debra did great with them and never complained to me about my being on the road so much. Debra always embraced the business and knew that all the travel and time away from home was to make a living for our family.

I started out on a modest nightly deal, $1,500 per show, but soon after I started, WCW's schedule really picked up and we were working almost every night. Guys on contract were griping, but I was as happy as I could be.

I was also making friends. Although we had known each other back in our WWF days, WCW was where I got to be really good friends with Jerry Sags and, particularly, Brian Knobbs. When I first met them, I had heard stories from a few guys about how obnoxious they were, and I hate to admit it now, but I'd pretty well decided I wasn't going to like them before I even met them. At first, we never socialized or even talked. Eventually, I think we got each other's humor, but the friendship didn't really take off until we were in WCW and ended up traveling a lot together.

As for the WCW travel itself, it was easy, especially compared to Mid-South or the WWF. I got to know Atlanta real well, especially "The Dungeon," the nickname for the Ramada Inn by the Atlanta airport, where all the guys would stay. They really took care of us, letting us check in early and stay late when travel circumstances messed with our schedules. It's kind of funny that Atlanta, of all cities, has played such a huge part in my life. From the Atlanta Falcons, to Georgia Championship Wrestling, to WCW, to the WWE Hall of Fame—it all happened in Atlanta.

Knobbs and Sags had come into WCW in late 1993, but it was almost like they were the advance wave for the Hulk Hogan group, which came in during 1994, and that was the group I was part of. There was actually a lot of tension in WCW, where it was like two factions opposing each other, even though we were all supposed to be on the same side. There was Hogan's group, which consisted of us newcomers with plenty of prior exposure with the WWF, and there was Ric Flair's group.

I have nothing but respect for Ric Flair as a performer, but the fact is those guys were doing their TV tapings at Centre Stage, a TV studio that was part of the TBS facilities. The place held something like 300 people, tops. And there were plenty of WCW shows where they had to block out 200 of those seats.

In a way, it just goes to show what a mastermind Vince McMahon is. At the time we got there, WCW had Jean-Paul Levesque and Steve Austin, and they were solid workers, but not really box-office draws. But when they got to Vince McMahon, within the next couple of years they were Triple H and "Stone Cold," two of the hottest stars in the business.

But in 1994, Steve Austin wasn't the hottest star; hell, he wasn't even "Stone Cold" yet. He was "Stunning" Steve Austin, holder of WCW's secondary singles belt, the United States championship; he was also my opponent for my debut, at October 1994's Fall Brawl pay-per-view.

We were supposed to go about 10 minutes but we ended up only going 35 seconds. I gave Austin a backdrop and we just went right to the finish.

The truth is he just didn't want to do the job and pass the belt to me. He was pissed off because he was part of the Flair group and I was part of the Hogan group.

Referee Nick Patrick helped Austin back to the dressing room. I followed them, but they didn't know I was right behind them. When they got back there, Patrick said to Austin, "You should get an Academy Award for that."

I said, "What the hell?"

Now they knew I was there.

I ended up just trying to make a joke out of that entire debacle. I just said, "That's right—I beat 'Stunning' Steve so bad that he had to shave his head and change his name! I oughta be getting a kickback—he'd still be 'Stunning,' not 'Stone Cold,' if I hadn't beaten his ass!"

But as Austin himself now likes to say, the "bottom line" is, I'm sorry if you don't like the way you're being booked, but I didn't book the damn thing, so don't take it out on me, and don't punish the fans by cheating them out of a match they paid to see just because you're not happy.

All these years later, while I think he could have handled it better, I don't have any hard feelings toward him. It was just the nature of the business at that time. Back in the regional days, you'd pass the torch; if a guy does you the favor, you do the favor for the next guy. But when it was as business-oriented as WCW was getting in the 1990s, everyone was nervous about protecting themselves, because there was a lot of mistrust, especially between the different groups.

I think there was some resentment because a bunch of us came in around the same time, and there was a perception that we were "WWF" guys. Plus, the fact that business picked up almost as soon as Hogan got there, and then kept getting stronger and stronger, probably created even more tension. The whole thing was dumb, because in theory, we were all looking for WCW to succeed, but those of us in the "Hogan group" got to a point where we didn't care about the other camp getting pissed off. Our attitude was that it was all about the business and business was going up, so anyone who didn't like it needed to put the business ahead of his own hurt feelings.

One day, Knobbs and I got onto the elevator at CNN on our way to the TV tapings. CNN talk show host Larry King got on with us.

Knobbs turned to King and said, "Hey, Larry! How're your ratings?"

Our ratings were blowing away his ratings.

Not only was I working with a lot of familiar faces, but I also got to meet some quality guys who would go on to be big names.

By 1994, I wasn't nearly the wild child I had been in the 1980s, but I still liked to go out and have a good time. One night, I was in one of the hotter nightclubs in Atlanta when I got spotted by the club's manager, a guy I'd recently had words with at a different bar. It was just an argument, nothing major, and I didn't know he ran the place I was in now.

I was drinking when I started looking around and noticed a guy standing to my left, one standing behind me, and another standing to my right. Another one stepped in front of me, and now they were starting to circle and close in.

I was ready to go at them if I needed to, but I knew I might be in a real bad situation. Just then, I spotted Harlem Heat—two enormous guys who were really powerful and great athletes, two brothers from Houston named Booker T and Stevie Ray.

I called out, "Hey, Heat!"

I didn't know them that well, but I damn sure knew them well enough to say, "Hey, Heat, come on over, and let me buy you a couple of drinks! C'mon!"

They stayed long enough for me to talk to the manager and get things smoothed over, and nothing happened. The next day, Booker and Stevie came up to me and said, "Gee, Hacksaw, you were awfully nice to us last night. Just wanted to say, we really appreciated it. Thanks a lot!"

I smiled and told them, "What you guys don't realize is that I was in a pretty big jam until you showed up. You were like the cavalry, man!"

I ended up working with them a lot, and I really thought a lot of both those guys—just really good people. And they were a great team, a good blend of Stevie Ray's power and Booker T's quickness.

My partner in a lot of those matches was a good kid who, unfortunately, became one of those guys who kind of lost his own identity to his wrestling character. Marcus Bagwell was a good-hearted guy, just a nice guy with a big heart. I always got along with him, but a couple of years later, he became a villain as part of the New World Order faction that rode roughshod over the WCW. And while Marcus was a good dude, his NWO alter ego, Buff Bagwell, was an incredible pain in the ass.

Looking back, I don't really blame Marcus, and I don't have any hard feelings. When you work very hard to become successful, and then all of a sudden you're on TV, you're making money, everybody knows you, life is good. It's only human nature to get a big head for a little while. But you've gotta come back down to reality at some point.

I'm no different. I had a big head back in my Mid-South days. We were doing Superdome shows, the people in the area loved me, and it probably did puff up my ego more than it maybe should have.

But there was no ego-puffing that could match the feeling I had when Debra gave birth in 1995 to Rebecca, our second daughter. Although I wasn't as home as much as I'd have liked for Celia's infant days, with the lighter WCW schedule, I was able to be very active with my three ladies, and that's always something I've treasured. Even when touring and working has made our time scarce, all of us, as a family, have really worked to make every second count.

I was also lucky to have Debra, who was no less the fantastic mother to Rebecca that she'd been and still is to Celia. That's probably a big part of why I never had to spend a lot of time dealing with discipline—having that structure at home really helped keep the girls on the right paths in life, and they've never been troublemakers. I've been very lucky with my three ladies, including Debra, of course.

Celia and Rebecca have both grown up to be wonderful young ladies, in my unbiased opinion. Of course, I haven't grown up much at all, and I'm occasionally prone to terrorizing their houseguests—but it's always in good fun.

Once, when Rebecca was in high school, she was in her room with a couple of boys from her class, and I came in the house, voice booming, "Rebecca! Do you have boys in your room?"

I think one of them was about to cry.

A few years earlier, I was doing some work out in my yard, as Celia was in the house with a young man. I was shirtless, with an axe, gloves, shorts, and boots on. I went to the house, kicked open the door, and howled.

The boy took a bump out of his chair!

Another time, I was loading up my car when I saw Celia and her date coming down our driveway (this is rural South Carolina, so we're talking about a looooooong driveway). I ducked down, because I wanted to see if they were gonna play kissy-face, because if they were, ol' Hacksaw was coming out, and he was gonna be pissed.

But they just sat in the parked car and talk...and talked...and talked. I was bent over so long I was getting a backache when they finally got out. As he was walking her up to the house, I came charging at them, growling like a madman. Celia knew it was me, but the boy didn't...and he split! He ran off!

I was like, "You'd leave my daughter to some psycho? Throw yourself in front of her, or something."

Chivalry, my ass!

Parent-teacher nights were always interesting, too. I always got one of two reactions. Either I was treated like a celebrity, because they knew me from TV, or it was some poor, horrified teacher watching this big guy with the long hair and beard walk in. One look at the teacher's eyes said it all, and often, that was, "Who the hell is this guy coming into my classroom?"

But in 1994, parent-teacher nights were still ahead of me, as was Starrcade, WCW's December pay-per-view and traditionally its biggest show of the year. I was in one of the semifinal matches with a guy I enjoyed working with, Leon White. Leon, a massive man and a great athlete, wrestled as Vader.

I thought we had a pretty good match. Terry Taylor always used to tell me that if I had someone who would challenge me physically, I would always knock off the goofy stuff and put on a physical match. And Vader fit the bill—if you didn't fight him back, he would eat you up. Plus, he was massively strong; I used to do pretty well at arm-wrestling, but he put me down in about one-tenth of a second.

I was also there for one of Vader's more infamous moments, his 1995 backstage fight with Paul Orndorff. Paul was another wrestler who was a tough guy and a hell of an athlete, and he was someone you did not want to mess with. I was talking with Vader when Orndorff walked up to us and told Vader, "They need you for interviews. Get down there now."

For some reason, Vader didn't want to go; I don't know if it was a personality clash, some problem with the company, or what, but Vader ended up going anyway. I saw Orndorff later, walking along a backstage corridor with a cup of coffee in his hand. Vader walked up to him and shoved him, causing Orndorff to spill his coffee on the floor. They had a little punch-up, until Vader stepped into the puddle of coffee and slipped onto the floor. Orndorff put the boots to him for a few seconds before it was broken up. I saw Vader later that night, and he was more embarrassed than hurt.

Vader was gone by the end of 1995, but in his place stood an even bigger monster—7'0" Paul Wight, the man that WCW called The Giant. I actually wrestled him in several of his very first matches for WCW (which were the first matches of his career). One night, a few months into his WCW tenure, we were working in Little Rock, Arkansas, and there was a spot in the match where I could almost see on his face that the light had come on, just as it had for me in San Antonio back in 1982.

When he started, Paul was always solid in the execution of his moves, but everything he did was very mechanical. I remembered a spot I'd done with Andre, and decided to try it with The Giant. It was a spot where my opponent would toss me into the corner and then hold onto the ropes while bumping his butt against me, like he was crushing me.

The way Andre and I had done the spot, after the first two bumps I'd roll out of the ring, causing him to miss the third one. Paul Wight and I did that spot, and when I rolled out and he landed into an empty corner, I knew right away he had figured things out.

I knew because he sold the ass bump into the corner like it really hurt, instead of just turning away and going on to the next thing. I knew he had taken that step of understanding the performance end, and selling an idea to the audience.

But what impresses me still about Paul (who works today as WWE's The Big Show) is that he could have gotten by on his size and never bothered to learn a thing. But he cared about what he was doing, and he worked his ass off to get better. And he has—he turned out to be a hell of a worker.

And what a great athlete! He's not as imposing as Andre the Giant was, but he's a much better athlete. If there's any knock on Paul, it's that he worked too hard—he didn't capitalize enough on his size, and busted his ass to do moves that smaller guys did. He didn't need to do that stuff, but he was and is such a great athlete that he's always pushed himself.

We also made a lot of trips to Europe, just like I'd done in my WWF days. Once, I believe in 1999, we flew to London. When we landed, I went right to the hotel, went to bed, and slept all day. That night, I was good to go for our show, but Curt Hennig and The Nasty Boys had gone out for sushi and apparently never made it to bed.

After the show, we went to Stringfellows, the same London club where Hercules had his transvestite encounter. About 3:00 AM, Knobbs had finally gotten on my nerves. Because he's always talking, always playing a prank, people always had different time limits with Knobbs—some people could only take an hour. The Big Bossman had about a two-minute limit. Hulk Hogan has a month-and-a-half limit.

But at that point in the morning, Knobbs had reached my limit, and after one smartass remark too many, I said, "Enough, Knobbs! I'm outta here!"

I went back to the hotel, then got on the bus the next morning to move onto the next show in the next town. Steve Borden, better known as Sting, was sitting in the second row, with an open seat in front of him. Ring announcer Michael Buffer was across from Sting, and I was sitting behind Sting, talking.

I looked out the window, and here came Knobbs, half staggering and half rolling down a hill toward the bus. He hadn't been asleep in two days, he had a beer in his hand, and he was screaming, "Hey, you guys—wait for me!"

Knobbs staggered through the aisle on the bus and found an empty seat a few rows behind me.

At the time, WCW had the Harris Brothers working for them. Now, these were two gigantic biker-looking guys, twin brothers with shaved heads and sleeves of tattoos. And they were just about as scary as they looked, which goes to show—the best gimmicks are the ones closest to the heart.

The Harris boys got on the bus, got to where Knobbs was sitting, and...

Boom! Boom! Boom! Boom!

They each landed three or four punches on Knobbs in the blink of an eye. They had already pummeled him pretty good in the couple of seconds it took me to hear what was happening, turn around, and say, "Hey, come on! That's enough!"

The Harris Brothers stopped and walked together to the back of the bus, where they grabbed a seat together. Knobbs turned around, big goose egg growing out of the top of his head, blood streaming out of his nose, and beer still in his hand (I don't think he spilled a drop). He looked at Sting and said, "So, how'd I do?"

I hollered back, "You got your ass kicked, Knobbsy!"

They could have cut his legs off and he wouldn't have known it.

Meanwhile, Michael Buffer was scared half to death. This was a guy who was used to fancy sports shows, like those glitzy boxing championship fights on pay-per-view.

Another time, we were flying over to Europe, and Ric Flair got on the plane and announced to everyone on board: "I got a big day tomorrow. It's very important for me, and it's very important for my company. I don't want anyone messing around on the plane, okay? Now, I gotta get some sleep!"

You could hear about 30 guys muttering some variation of, "Oh, screw you, Ric, get your goddamned sleep."

Ric went to sleep, and pretty much all the other wrestlers on board did, too. I remember waking up after feeling something on my face. I felt my face and went, "What the hell? Half my eyebrow's gone!"

A few minutes later, Flair woke up, screaming about the same thing—someone had shaved off his left eyebrow.

"Knobbs, you son of a bitch!"

But *both* of Knobbs' eyebrows were gone!

He pointed at his missing brows and told Ric, "It's not me! Look! They even got me!"

I looked at Knobbs later and was just amazed at how thorough that shave job had been. Seriously, only Knobbs would shave off his own eyebrows just to throw Ric off his trail.

WCW was doing strong business already, but when they started the New World Order feud, things got even bigger.

A lot of fans really viewed it as the World Wrestling Federation invading WCW, and it all grew out of WCW signing two guys who had recently been part of Vince's main event roster: Scott Hall and Kevin Nash.

Scott Hall had wrestled all over the country since debuting in 1984, and as a tall, well-built guy with athletic ability, he seemed to have all the tools needed to be a star. But he'd never really hit it big until he got to the WWF in 1992, after Vince McMahon turned him into Razor Ramon.

Hall ended up being a sad story, though. He really was one of the most talented guys in the business, with a great look, and he could cut a great interview. But he was also one of the most detrimental guys a company could have. He had a lot of substance-abuse problems, and they made him impossible to deal with.

And I don't just mean with people in wrestling, either. In 1998, WCW booked a tour and had chartered a plane to get us to the tour cities. When we boarded the plane to return home at the end of the tour, we found the same flight crew that we'd had on the flight out. Scott had been such an asshole on the way out that they refused to let him onto the plane, and they called a whole team of security to make sure he didn't cause a scene.

A lot of the rest of the guys started cheering when Hall got kicked off the plane. You could hear, "Yeah, get him off the damn plane!"

But Scott Hall, Kevin Nash, and Hulk Hogan (following a shocking heel turn in the summer of 1996) formed the New World Order, an anti-WCW group. The gimmick was a huge hit at first, although WCW ruined it by diluting their main event heel group with guys like Scott Norton and Virgil—nothing against those guys, but they weren't exactly main event caliber wrestlers.

In a way, I guess it was kind of an insult that WCW never even approached me about joining the NWO, especially considering that I'd match up my own credentials against at least half the guys they had in there, but the truth is, I was pretty happy with my own corner of the WCW universe.

CHAPTER 16

MR. SATURDAY NIGHT

ONE THING THAT I WAS ALWAYS PROUD OF was my time on *WCW Saturday Night*. Even though *WCW Monday Nitro* was a big success, both that show and *WCW Thunder* (which debuted in 1998 on Thursday nights) had big budgets out the ass. Meanwhile, in a way, I had come back to one of my earliest wrestling homes—the original Saturday evening slot on WTBS, or just TBS as it became known. The show originally called *Georgia Championship Wrestling* was now *WCW Saturday Night*, and WCW pretty much gave it to Jimmy Hart and me to do whatever we could with it, scraping together the WCW guys who were not being featured on the "main" shows.

WCW Saturday Night did great in the ratings, with practically none of what Eric Bischoff thought of as "main event talent," and on a shoestring budget. In 1998, our little weekend show was getting better ratings than WCW's new, heavily pushed *Thunder* show and often rivaled *Nitro* ratings, with an eighth of the budget that those productions had. I even went out on one of those shows and proclaimed that Saturday night was *my* night! I turned it into a positive, and we made it into a wrestling show that actually had *wrestling* on it.

We were able to pull that off, in part, because Bischoff and the other top management put all their focus onto *Nitro* and *Thunder*, and they didn't really care what we did on Saturdays—Bischoff even told us as much. Jimmy and I had kind of become castoffs, but we were under contract, so they had to put us somewhere, and they had those two hours of programming to put on, so they turned us loose on it.

I give Jimmy Hart a lot of the credit for that show's success, because he put a lot of energy into making that show good. If I was starting a business right now, I would want Jimmy Hart working for me, because the guy never stops. Jimmy is not happy unless his cell phone is ringing while his pager is going off, and he's going 100 mph, at all times.

One of the feuds that kept drawing those ratings was me against Dave Sierra, who wrestled as The Cuban Assassin. He was a lot of fun, and that feud worked for the same reason that it would work today: American fans want to cheer for America. They want a chance to chant, "U-S-A! U-S-A!"

I even used to be able to get that chant going when we wrestled on those international tours in Italy, Germany, and Spain. These days, with all the turmoil in the world, I've found that I can get that crowd support more from a show of solidarity. I'll usually come to the ring with my American flag, accept my lukewarm reception, then spot a kid in the front row with his country's flag and do a deal where I motion to the kid's flag and mine before offering to swap in a grand gesture. Yeah, I know, it's a cheap pop to then run around the ring with that country's flag, but I figure we're all on this Earth together, and if you're at a wrestling show, you're there to have fun.

Actually, the hardest place to be a proud American was in Quebec, Canada—they *hated* my ass! Of course, they hated the other Canadians, too, so I didn't feel too bad about it.

While I made a home for myself on the Saturday show, Bischoff also put me on the big shows, but before the tape began rolling.

"Hacksaw," he'd say, "you do a good job of getting the crowd fired up, so we'll send you out there before the shows officially start to get the people rocking, and to help build up the atmosphere for the broadcast."

I couldn't understand why they wouldn't put the guy who got the fans fired up on the actual shows, but what do I know? They even gave me a WCW flag to bring to the ring, purple and gold, instead of the old Stars and Stripes. I even had to wear purple trunks and gold boots to match it. Their idea was that since I was so good at getting "U-S-A!" chants going, I could start up a "W-C-W!" chant. That didn't work out so well.

The NWO success carried WCW through the summer of 1996, and Bischoff was trying some new things, although not all of them were necessarily strictly done from a business perspective. Bischoff, a motorcycle guy, decided to hold a WCW pay-per-view during the annual Sturgis, South Dakota, motorcycle rally, the biggest event of its kind in the United States.

This surprises a lot of people, I guess because of my appearance, but I am not a biker, so I was not as excited about this as a lot of the wrestlers who were big Harley guys (Davidson, not Race—I'm still a big Harley Race guy, to this day).

Management told all the wrestlers, "If you have a motorcycle, bring it to Atlanta. We'll load it up on an 18-wheeler, and we'll take all the motorcycles in the truck. When we're about 100 miles out, we'll pull the truck over, get on our bikes, and ride into Sturgis as the WCW crew."

I traveled to the show with Bill DeMott, who also lived in Titusville. As we got close to the rally, we pulled by all the biker wrestlers and waved from the air-conditioned comfort of our rented Lincoln.

Of course, all those guys were macho to the core, so not one of them used a windscreen. I remember going by, reclining with the passenger's seat as far back as it would go, watching all these tough guys get bugs in their teeth and thinking, *Looking good, fellas!*

Bill and I got to be friends when he moved to Titusville in the mid-1990s; he's got two girls who are the same age as my daughters, and our wives got to be best friends, too.

Bill went on to train a lot of guys, and a lot of those students really learned to hate him. If you've ever watched him on that *Tough Enough* show where he trains wrestlers, that's pretty much him. He's extremely tough on the guys, and he was always intense. Like I said before, I'm not a big fan of forcing kids to do thousands of situps, because that's not professional wrestling, but he has produced a lot of guys who have gone on to become stars.

WCW's top homegrown star—and aside from Diamond Dallas Page and Bill Goldberg, pretty much its only homegrown star—was Sting, a guy I had first seen as a rookie when he and his muscle-bound partner formed a tag team known as The Blade Runners. It was 1986, we were in Mid-South, and they were not good. Watts decided early on he didn't like those guys, but I guess Sting grew on him, because when the other Blade Runner (Rock, later more famous as the Ultimate Warrior in the WWF) left, Sting stayed around.

I respected Sting for his loyalty; he was the one guy who remained with WCW, from 1987 (when Crockett owned it) until 2001, when WCW finally went under. Even Ric Flair, who symbolized WCW to a lot of fans, left in 1991 and stayed in the WWF for about 18 months. In return, WCW always took good care of Sting, but that's as it should be. He became an icon in our business, but I don't think he reached the level that he could have in WWE. On the other hand, he's probably financially better off than 99 percent of the WWE guys, because he was smart and saved his money.

Even as the Flair and Hogan camps learned to coexist in WCW, there was another clique coming up—Eddie Guerrero, Perry Saturn, Dean Malenko, Chris Benoit, and Shane Douglas (who came over from ECW in 1999). I'd met Eddie in passing in the mid-1980s when his brothers, Hector and Chavo, worked in Mid-South and for Paul Boesch in Houston. I didn't know the others real well, even though we all worked for WCW for years; they kind of kept to themselves.

There was also a sense that the younger guys, like those five, resented the older guys. To be fair, those guys were really good in terms of the mechanics and the psychology of what they did in the ring. But one thing I thought they didn't grasp—and a couple of them would never grasp it—was that the in-ring moves only make up a small portion of what it means to be a pro wrestler. You've got to be able to interact with the people in the audience, to draw some emotion out of them. I'm not saying everyone should go out there, make a goofy face, and yell, "HO-OH!" but every wrestler should find his or her own way to relate to the fans.

That attitude reminded me of Buff Bagwell. In 1998, Buff and I were on the Bruise Cruise; WCW put together cruise-ship packages where fans could hang out with the wrestlers, and we were on board. We were doing a Q&A session, and Buff got on the mic and said, "Well, it's time for these older guys to move on and make room for the younger guys."

I waited until he finished and then said, "Well, us 'older guys' ain't goin' anywhere. If you 'young guys' think you can carry the ball, then carry the ball. We ain't gonna just give it up to you."

Aside from having to listen to Buff, that Bruise Cruise was a great experience, and I did it two years in a row. WCW let me bring Debra and the kids, so we turned it into a working family vacation. I'd spend my days in the kiddie pool, and people would say, "Aww, look at Hacksaw, playing with the kids in the pool—isn't that sweet?"

Meanwhile, the truth was I was in shallow water because I couldn't (and still can't) swim worth a damn. And even there, those kids were damn near drowning me. I wasn't "playing with the kids"—I was fighting for my life!

I think the cruises were so fun because they were the perfect format for me—I got to interact with people. I wrestled a little, did a lot of interviews, and played it up for the folks who'd paid good money to meet some of the wrestlers. I think they had a lot of fun with it.

Meanwhile, Perry Saturn was another one of the WCW "stars" on that first cruise, and he was miserable the whole time. He came up to me on the second day and said. "I'm going crazy. These people are all over me."

I said, "Well, hell, Perry—that's why you're here! Hey, watch this."

I turned around, and there was this little boy waiting to talk to us. I said, in my best Hacksaw voice, "C'mere, kid!" and grabbed him and put him in a headlock. The kid's dad must have shot half a roll of film with the kid in the headlock, then the kid choking me, all kinds of stuff, all playful, and it was obvious the kid was having a great time goofing around with one of the wrestlers he saw on TV.

I'd walk into the dining room and demand everybody give me a big thumbs up and join me in a mighty "HO-OH!" And people got with it! They had a blast, and I guarantee you that I made a few new Hacksaw fans every time I did something goofy like that, because people got to see my personality, and they could see I was having fun with it, too.

And that's what I was trying to tell Saturn—you can do 375 different variations of flying Japanese armdrags, picture-perfect every single time, but if you don't give the fans a chance to care about who you are, they're going to sit on their hands while you perform your technically beautiful moves.

If you remember, Eddie Guerrero really got over in WWE only after he found a personality that he had fun playing. Once he started that "Latino Heat" persona and made people care about who he was, he quickly became a huge star until his sad passing in 2005.

One of the young guys in WCW who understood the business completely was Chris Jericho. I watched him early on and even looked out for him a little bit in the early days of his WCW career. I could tell right away that he knew he had to find a way to click with the audience. He really cared about being good and about reaching the fans, whether as a fan favorite or as the most hated villain he could be, and that commitment is what made him a huge star in WWE after he made the move from WCW in 1999.

But Jericho never changed from that good-hearted kid I first met in WCW, no matter how big a star he became. Years later, at the end of 2008, Jericho and I were supposed to do a bit for WWE's *Raw* program, where I was supposed to wrestle him. I would be in my gear and I'd hit the ring when my music played. He'd come out in street clothes and say how he wasn't going to waste his time with me, calling me "old," "dried up," and whatever other insults they had laid out for him, which all would lead to a physical altercation.

When we got our scripts from the show writers, Jericho came to me and said, "Hey, Hacksaw, I can't say this to you, man."

I said, "Chris, it's okay. Say what they've got for you. It's an honor for me to be in the ring with you. Let's go ahead and do it like they have it."

And we did, and it went over well. But to me, that shows what a class act Chris Jericho is.

WCW had another up-and-coming talent who I thought had a world of potential, a German kid named Alex Wright. Alex was really polished inside the ring, but he didn't seem comfortable in terms of creating a character for himself. However, before long he had developed a great gimmick: he would come to the ring doing this German techno-music dance, with his bright-orange trunks, leather jacket, and blond hair slicked into a pompadour like something out of *American Graffiti*. It was so goofy, but everyone in the crowd was doing the dance when he came to the ring.

WCW's brilliant idea was to remove all the goofiness from his persona and make him into the deadly serious Berlyn, with his head shaved into a black Mohawk. He'd gone from someone the fans had fun with to being someone that nobody cared about. It was like he was the symbol of WCW's creative stupidity.

The Berlyn gimmick came with a sidekick, a massive partner called The Wall. Get it? Berlyn/Wall? The Wall was Jerry Tuite, another young guy who I thought had the potential to go far in the business, although he unfortunately had his demons.

Jerry had a bit of a stutter—not a major speech impediment, just a little stutter. But as minor as it was, it really embarrassed him.

I told him, "You should embrace that, buddy."

Heck, I used my crossed eyes to make a definite visual impression on fans. And yeah, at first I did have a problem with people calling me "Cock-eyed Dugan," but I finally figured, "Well, okay, you guys paid to come in, so..."

You gotta take what you've got and make it work for you. Jerry was a big, impressive guy, and he would have been memorable had he gone out there for a promo and said, "I'm gonna k-k-k-k-k-k-k-kick your a-a-a-a-ss!"

I'm tellin' you, he would have had fans going, "K-k-k-k-k-k..." every time he went to the ring! But he was so self-conscious about it that he couldn't bring himself to play it up.

I worked a match with Jerry in Europe, and we were talking about it beforehand. Now, this alone tells you how far the business had come—back in the 1980s, you'd never catch wrestlers mapping out their matches before they went out there, but this was a different era. And nowadays, it's evolved to the point that matches (at least, TV matches) are totally scripted.

So, Jerry and I talked over our spots, but early in the match, I saw something in his eyes that concerned me—the guy had gone completely blank. Trust me, I had been there myself many times, and I could tell, he was *lost*. He charged and just crushed me. He had me in a clench and said, "What do I do?"

I said, "Don't move. Just keep the hold for a second—I'm thinkin'!"

We were able to get back into the flow, and he was able to pick up enough that we finished the match without a major hitch.

It goes without saying that being able to improvise is a skill every wrestler needs to have. For example, I used to carry a deck of cards in my kneepads, because being a wrestler means doing a lot of waiting in the dressing room. We played a lot of Crazy Eights and gin. One night, I was wrestling a guy and went for the Old Glory kneedrop. When it hit, my whole deck of cards went flying out of my kneepad.

People were floored; it was like I had just pulled off some major illusion! I didn't sell it—I just got the pin and got out of there.

Of course, it could have been worse. I remember a six-man match involving The Freebirds against me, Ted DiBiase, and Steve "Dr. Death" Williams. It was a street fight, so guys could use weapons and wear street clothes, and when Michael Hayes pulled off his boot to hit Teddy, a bag of weed flew up in the air! It landed in the middle of the ring, and it was damn near a six-man knockout as everyone dove for it to keep Michael from getting busted.

Then again, as part of their gimmick (and in real life), The Freebirds were wild partiers, so maybe it wouldn't have hurt!

A lot of people lose money playing cards; I (and most wrestlers) lose track of time. At one WWF show, I was the first one up after intermission, but I got so engrossed in a locker-room card game with Brian Adams, who wrestled as Crush, that I completely zoned out on hearing the first intermission announcement. The guy running the arena sound system decided to fill the intermission time by playing the wrestlers' themes over the loudspeakers.

Guess whose music played first?

Adams looked up from his cards and said, "Duggan! Your music!"

I went, "Oh, shit!"

I jumped up, grabbed my flag and 2x4, and hurried through the curtain, yelling, "HO-OH!"

I took about five steps before I started wondering why half the seats were empty. One of the agents had followed me out and caught up with me. He got in my ear and said, "It's not your match!"

CHAPTER 17

FIGHTING FOR MY LIFE

ONE MORNING IN 1998, I WOKE UP, went into the bathroom, and pissed blood. I decided a trip to the doctor's office might be a good idea.

They did some tests on me, and my prognosis came back quickly, although it was not good. I had kidney cancer, and the doctor told me I would have to undergo surgery to remove the afflicted kidney. The procedure was quick, and was scheduled for 15 days after my diagnosis.

I heard from a lot of people when I was diagnosed with cancer. It was really something to realize the impact I'd had on people's lives, because we got tons of calls and letters (sent to WCW) with well-wishes from fans, even though I hadn't been featured on a pay-per-view in quite a while.

I give Terry Taylor credit for the TV announcement, which ended up being a powerful moment for me. I wasn't about to go on TV and talk about this, but Terry said, "These people, these fans of yours have known you all these years. You should share this with them. They'd want to know."

I had just gone into a cocoon. I didn't want to talk to anyone, I didn't want to see anyone, and I sure didn't want to broadcast my health problem. Plus, I was focused on getting better and spending time with the three people most important to me—I sure wasn't giving a damn about wrestling at that point.

But Terry convinced me. He said, "You really should come on TV and do it. If you do, I think in the long run, you'll be glad you did it."

And he was right—looking back, I am glad I did that. But giving the spiel on *Nitro*, all I could think of was Gary Cooper from *The Pride of the Yankees*, the 1942 movie about baseball legend Lou Gehrig, who had to go before his fans and announce that he was leaving the sport because of a terminal illness.

As I talked to the fans, thanking them for their support over the years and telling them I was getting treatment, all I could hear in the back of my mind was Cooper saying, "Today, I consider myself the luckiest man..."

I thought about the real Lou Gehrig, and how his making that announcement must have been a horrible, difficult thing to do. And now, here I was, a wrestler standing in the middle of the ring and telling these people that I might be dying. It was hard. When I finished, I went backstage, and as soon as I got past the curtain, I almost collapsed. I was really distraught.

But it turned out to be a great deal, because the fan support was amazing. This was before email really took off, so I still have boxes and boxes of cards and letters from people. To this day, it's something that really makes me appreciate the power of wrestling. More than once, when I've done appearances or worked an independent show, I've had tough-looking grown men come up and shake my hand and tell me, "Hacksaw Duggan, let me tell you..." And he'll share with me something from his own life, a loved one who fought cancer, the whole ordeal, and it's those moments that make me realize how much what we do affects people.

DEBRA SAYS:
I got flooded with calls. They aired that segment on TV the day of his surgery. The hospital pulled his name from their public records and wouldn't tell anyone he was there, at our request. We wanted Jim to have some privacy while he was in the hospital. Not that we didn't all appreciate the good thoughts from people, because we truly did.

The whole thing went quickly, just like the doctor said. But that doesn't mean it was easy. I was scared to death the whole time—not just of the cancer itself, but also of having to go through chemo and radiation. Thankfully, since the cancer was encapsulated in the kidney and hadn't spread, I was spared from having to endure either. I remembered my dad fighting stomach cancer and beating it, but it really wore him out.

As terrifying an ordeal as the whole thing was, I thank God that Debra and I didn't have to worry about what to tell the kids. They were only five and three at the time, and we decided not to tell them anything, because they were just too little to understand. In fact, we'd decided not to tell my sisters or my dad until just before I went on TV to make the announcement. We didn't want to have people worrying for all that time.

Debra's support meant everything to me. I spent all those years cutting promos where I called other people "tough guy," but she turned out to be as tough as anyone I've ever known. Debra was there with me every step of the way, even while she ran our household and took care of the kids.

But during my surgery, Debra was terrified, although she didn't let on until much later. The doctors had told me that it would be a short surgery, "unless something goes wrong."

Of course, when you combine the time you spend in pre-op, the procedure, and the time you spend in recovery, it adds up to several hours. Debra was expecting some news within the estimated time of the procedure itself, and as the hours ticked by, she started getting very scared.

But Debra was a real trouper and showed me nothing but love, support, and strength. And my sister Sheila came down shortly after the procedure to help take care of me in the hospital, which freed Debra to stay at home with the girls. Having an actual nurse like Sheila looking after me personally was a real godsend.

It was about five months before I felt well enough to come back to work. Returning to wrestling was never in question—I still had to make a living. Debra understood, but my sisters and my dad were terrified about what could happen if I were injured, having just one kidney. My doctor told me I should never wrestle again.

I won't lie; ever since I came back, I have taken it easier on myself physically than ever before. If you buy a ticket to see me today, you're not going to see the hard-brawling Hacksaw of 1985. Hell, you won't even see me take a hard charge into the turnbuckles. But I've always tried to do things to keep the crowd entertained, no matter what my physical limitations are.

Of course, this was WCW, so they found a way to screw up what had been a very powerful moment for me and piss me off in the process. Just a couple of months after I made my announcement, they did an angle where Ric Flair supposedly had some kind of fake heart attack and collapsed in the ring, and it was treated like it was a shoot, a real deal.

I really thought that cheapened my whole situation, because mine had been genuine. At first, when we saw it on TV, Debra thought he'd actually had a heart attack, because of how they played it. I just thought they took advantage of my life to get sympathy for someone else in a worked situation.

And when I came back to WCW months later in 1999, that was when I really started having problems with Eric Bischoff, and then with Vince Russo, and then with both of them. Russo had been a *WWF Magazine* writer who got added to the creative team that presided over Vince McMahon's most successful run ever.

Russo quit the WWF in September of 1999 and came to WCW, presumably to sprinkle some of that same genius on our company and to break it out of the rut it had gone into. My first impression of Russo, right off the bat, was that he was full of himself. I realize that having an ego is kind of a requirement for a successful booker; you've got to have incredible confidence in your own ideas to be able to do that job effectively. But Russo took credit for other people's success, and pretty soon, I knew that bringing him in had been a mistake.

Shortly after he took over, Russo flew me out to Atlanta to discuss things WCW wanted to do with me. What they were actually trying to do was push me out of my contract. Just a year after some of its biggest successes, WCW was getting its ass kicked by the WWF and looked like it was going to go under. It was actually a year earlier, while WCW was still riding high, that I started getting the feeling that its days were numbered.

There was just so much political bullshit going on, with guys like Scott Hall and Kevin Nash pulling power plays, and everyone was protecting himself and his pals at the expense of the company.

I want to say that while he definitely did some things I thought were self-serving and probably hurt WCW, I never saw Kevin Nash as being as bad as Scott Hall. Nash was a big, tough guy whom I respected as an athlete, and he had some creativity. I know those two get lumped together all the time, but it's really not fair to Nash, if you want to know the truth.

In the summer of 2000, I got to play victim to Russo's latest brainstorm—he was going to turn Bill Goldberg heel. Goldberg was like me, a college and pro football player with a competitive athlete's mind-set.

I got along with Bill, and he was a great athlete. I didn't think at first he'd be the superstar he'd turn out to be, but even though he might be considered a flash in the pan because of how brief his career was, his short run was amazing.

I think Goldberg was kind of like Ultimate Warrior in that he had no real love for wrestling; he just saw it as a stepping-stone to other things. I don't mean that as a knock, because I like Bill; it's just the way he felt about it. With me, even though I wasn't a fan growing up, I came to love the business and the whole act of performing. I loved being able to get people that excited.

From 1997 to 2000, Goldberg shot up quickly to become WCW's biggest star, and then Russo decided to "shock" everyone by turning him heel. To emphasize the point, Goldberg won our match, and then punched me in the kidney a few times while the announcers reminded viewers of my recent health problems. I didn't mind doing it, because I liked working with Bill, plus it was a good payday.

I got to do the internal bleeding bit again, although this time there was no condom filled with my own blood. WCW actually used blood capsules. Times change.

I know WCW's ratings and pay-per-view numbers plummeted in 2000, but I still think the salaries they were paying guys were just insane. Tank Abbott, an Ultimate Fighting Championship (UWF) guy who'd had moderate success, and even Ernest "The Cat" Miller got big money! These guys never sold a ticket—they can't even get booked on indie shows these days.

They had all these young guys that they were spending a fortune on, and they wanted to get rid of me to clear up the money they'd save on my contract. But if they fired me, they'd have been in breach, and they would have had to pay me anyway.

However, if they could get me to quit, then I'd be the one in breach, and they wouldn't have to pay me. So, to get me to quit, they came up with one attempted humiliation after another.

Their first idea was to make me the janitor of WCW, which was a dumb idea, if you think about it. I mean, janitors usually work in the same buildings. How many traveling janitors do you know? They told me I'd have to wear a janitor's outfit on TV each week, and I just said, "That's fine."

"So, Jim, we're going to have you clean Vince Russo's toilet...with a toothbrush."

"Okay, that's cool. You guys are supplying the toothbrush, right?"

They couldn't believe it—they just looked at me like, "What the hell is up with this guy?"

When the time came to clean the toilet with the toothbrush, I took a can of Diet Coke and poured it into the bowl. They were expecting me to be suffering through the indignity of cleaning this toilet. Instead, I had my whole head in there, thrashing around and splashing that nasty-looking brown water everywhere. Finally, I looked up with a big, goofy look and yelled, "I'm cleanin' the toilet! I'm cleanin' the toilet!"

And damned if it didn't get over. I still hear from people who loved that goofy stuff. I was wearing one of those big, brown, padded janitor outfits—they even had to custom-order me one, because the double-extra large was too small for me.

A few weeks later, I was playing the happy janitor when I found the WCW TV title in a trash can. I took the belt, proclaimed myself champion, and actually defended the title until the company finally did go under in 2001. (That's right, folks—by trying to embarrass me into quitting, Vince

Russo created a situation where I ended up in the history books as the last-ever WCW World Television Champion.)

I had a lot of fun with that, too. I wore the belt upside-down and backward, did my Hacksaw thing, and defended it mainly on the *Saturday Night* show until that show ended in 2000. When McMahon bought out the last of WCW in 2001, Vince's people asked for the belts back...except for the TV title. No one ever asked me for the belt back, and it ended up in my coat closet. Every time Debra's nephew, Nathan, came to visit, he'd get it out and play with it. He'd challenge me to matches, and we'd roll around on the floor. He even got a couple of pins on me. (Did I maybe let him win? Uh...I don't recall.) So maybe *he* was the last WCW TV champion.

Exiling me to Saturday nights had turned into something I really enjoyed, and the janitor thing had failed to make me quit, so they came up with their next genius idea: "Hacksaw, we're gonna turn you heel!"

I was determined not to let on that they had found something that bugged me, but inside, I was thinking, *Aw, man—where's this going? Am I supposed to come out in favor of Iraq? Iran?*

Russo said, "We're gonna put you with Team Canada."

Team Canada was the team of Lance Storm and Mike Awesome, and the two of them were pro-Canada and anti-America—you know, because of the years of conflict and tension between Canada and the United States. And before you ask, yes, I'm aware that I had been a proud American patriot in matches against Canadian athletes like the Rougeau Brothers and Dino Bravo in the WWF, but the country vs. country heat in those situations wasn't really strong, and we all knew it—we were just having fun with it. But WCW was trying to present Team Canada as this serious threat to the American way, which was just stupid.

Next, they wanted me to cut my hair, shave my beard, and wear a suit. I'd had long hair my whole adult life, and my beard also had been part of me for 30 years (minus the couple of months in 1984 it took to grow back after Nikolai Volkoff and Krusher Darsow/Khrushchev shaved it as part of an angle on Mid-South TV).

I actually went to a barber who recognized me and asked for the shave and haircut, and he looked at me in silence for a few seconds.

Then, he shook his head a little and said, "Really?"

DEBRA SAYS:
He called me and said, "They want me to cut my hair," but he didn't say anything about the beard. I didn't get to see his new look until he came home a couple of days later.

I did it all—I even bought a new suit, since part of this angle would be Team Canada trying to make me more "presentable." Then, I took my well-dressed, short-haired, clean-shaven self to where we were doing that week's TV tapings. I saw guys I had known for 10 years or more, and they had no idea who I was! A couple of guys thought I was one of the state athletic commissioners.

When I got home, Debra didn't know what to think, plus Celia and Rebecca were still little kids. I walked into the house and introduced myself to the girls as Mr. Neal, an old friend of their dad's, from Glens Falls. Even *they* had no idea who I was! For the longest time, there was a picture of Debra and me from that time on the refrigerator, and our own daughters had no idea who was in that picture with their mom.

Lance Storm was a good wrestler in the ring, but as a personality, he unfortunately was about as bland as unsalted crackers. He'd be standing in the middle of the ring for our Team Canada promos, and in a voice like Robocop, he'd say, "May I please have everyone's attention..."

Meanwhile, I was behind him, being "Hacksaw," bobbing back and forth, pointing at fans with my face all twisted and screaming, "Shut your mouths! Aarrrggghhh!"

A week or two of that got me another trip up to the office in Atlanta.

"Uh, Jim, we're trying to feature the kid. You want to try dialing your stuff down a little bit?"

I couldn't believe what I was hearing.

"Dial my stuff *down?* Tell the kid to dial his stuff *up!*"

Jimmy Hart and I used to describe that period in WCW as being like going down on the *Titanic*. We knew the ship was sinking, but we wanted to stay on board as long as possible.

But when WCW hired Vince Russo, it was like the company was driving the nails into its own coffin. When he came aboard in the fall of 1999, he was taking the credit for being Vince McMahon's chief writer and idea man in the WWF. Russo tried to pretend that he was the genius who created The Rock and "Stone Cold" Steve Austin, but come on. The idea guy in the WWF was named Vince, no doubt, but his last name was McMahon, not Russo. McMahon's creative mind-set is a lot like Bill Watts'. Bill had success in Mid-South with different bookers (Ernie Ladd, Buck Robley, Bill Dundee), because Bill Watts had the last say and made the final decisions on any ideas or angles that his bookers came up with. But Watts was smart enough to know that if someone else had a good idea, he should run with it.

McMahon is like that—he could have 20 guys feeding him ideas, but they all get filtered through his mind, and he makes the final calls and puts his own touches on them, and that's why McMahon has been so successful—it damn sure wasn't because of Vince Russo.

I always tried to stay positive and professional, but I admit that last year of WCW was one of the worst times of my professional life. I reached a point where I would get to the arena and check in, and then go out and sit in my car until it was close to showtime.

And it wasn't just me—as Russo came up with one dumb idea (like world champion David Arquette) after another (like world champion Vince Russo), the gossip backstage was that McMahon had sent Russo over to tank WCW! I'm sure that's not true, but Russo could not have done a better job of screwing it up.

Even Arquette, a Hollywood actor who was also a wrestling fan and a really nice guy, thought it was a bad idea to put the title on him. It's pretty sad when folks outside the business understand it better than a promotion's "creative force."

WCW lost tons of talent from 1999 to 2001, and among those who stayed, the sense that the young guys resented the old guys was stronger than ever. I understand a guy wanting to prove himself in the eyes of those who came before, but that's not what this was. This was guys like Dallas Page, Buff Bagwell, and Ernest Miller walking around all puffed up like they were superstars while the ratings were going down the crapper.

WCW was falling apart, and the top concern for a lot of these guys was that they wanted their own private dressing rooms. A few guys had done that for years, like Bret Hart (and I liked Bret) when he got to WCW at the end of 1997. I couldn't understand it. To me, that seemed like a penalty; everyone else is playing cards and laughing, and you're sitting in your private little room with your bottle of water? Yeah, *that* sounds like fun.

Still, I'd be lying if I said the last days of WCW didn't have any bright spots. One was a tour of Australia we did in October of 2000, and what made it a bright spot was that I was able to bring Debra with me.

She and I had a good time—Brisbane has a beautiful marina, there was a lot of great stuff to see, and just having Debra with me made it a great trip. One morning, a few days into the tour, we were having breakfast in the restaurant at the fancy-dan hotel where WCW had booked us. I told her, "You know, these guys are doing pretty good. Usually, at least one guy goes crazy on these long trips. Sooner or later, somebody pops."

Not five minutes later, the elevator went *ping*, the doors opened, and Debra and I watched as Juventud Guerrera came running out, completely naked, screaming, "I'm God! I'm God!"

He ran around the lobby, with Terry Taylor (now working behind the scenes for WCW) and WCW head of security Doug Dillinger chasing him; Dillinger was carrying a sheet, I guess to cover him up with. They didn't catch him, and within seconds, a nude Juventud Guerrera was running through the streets of Brisbane, Australia.

By now, Debra and I'd completely forgotten about finishing breakfast, because we had to see how this turned out. As Naked Juvi ran, cops were running toward him from every conceivable direction—it seemed like they called in patrol guys from all over the city. The first cop to catch up to Juvi got popped in the face for his trouble; I mean, Juvi just *dropped* him. For the dozen or so cops who saw this as they were closing in on

Guerrera, it must have been piñata time, because they all got out their nightsticks and beat him like a drum. They not only beat the hell out of him, they maced him and tossed him into their paddy wagon. If you've never seen one of their paddy wagons, they're not like our American ones. The Brisbane version was a pickup truck with a cage over the top of the truck bed, the type of vehicle we use for captured animals here in the U.S.A.

They tossed Juvi in the back of the truck, inside the little cage, and he was howling like a wolf. He wouldn't stop, and one of the cops got a hose from the hotel and sprayed Juvi with it.

By now, I was standing outside watching, and while I understood that Juvi needed to be brought under control, the hose was too much.

I said, "Come on, Officer. He's had enough. That's wrong."

The cop looked at me like I was an idiot and said, "We're trying to wash the mace off of him."

I just kind of muttered, "Oh. Um...sorry."

Debra and I had plans for the day, so we didn't stick around to see if there would be any further drama at the hotel. She had gotten behind-the-scenes passes to the zoo, and when we got to the kangaroo pen, we found they had the fence set up so that you could pet the kangaroos. Debra was petting one of them, and then I did, too, saying, "Nice kangaroo...nice kangaroo."

I looked down and saw the size of the kangaroo's tail—it was bigger around than a can of tennis balls and nearly three feet long. I was fascinated by it, so I gently grabbed the tail—I mean, I wasn't looking to abuse any animals—and that kangaroo straightened up and gave a *very* angry hiss. It kept straightening up like something out of a cartoon, getting taller and taller, until finally it was at eye-level with me. And I didn't need a kangaroo whisperer to tell me this thing was pissed off.

I was trying to back out of this situation without having the kangaroo kick the crap out of me with those powerful legs. I had my fingers against its chest as I was trying to keep my legs away from it, so he didn't kick my legs out from under me.

I managed to back away safely, but I learned something very valuable that day. Kids, take it from me, Hacksaw Jim Duggan—don't ever grab a kangaroo's tail, tough guy!

I got to do some other interesting things around that time, like a series of *Family Feud* game shows in 2000. We were almost late to the tapings. Jimmy Hart had drilled into my head that I had to be on time for the show, so the morning of the flight, I was set. I usually get dressed like a fireman, anyway—when the alarm goes off, my stuff's packed, and I just have to get dressed and go. The whole process takes 30 seconds, tops.

Within a couple of minutes I was knocking on Knobbs' hotel room door, since we were to leave together. Knobbs opened up...and he was half-asleep with his stuff thrown everywhere. Maybe I should have made him get a cab instead of waiting on him, but I was always told never to leave a brother behind, so I waited for him to get his stuff together and we got to the airport. There, I had to drop him off and return the rental car, so he actually made it to the gate before me.

But we made it to the studio in L.A., where we taped five shows against *Playboy* playmates; it was billed as "Beauties vs. Beasts." All the winnings went to charity. The playmates won two, and we won the other two, so it came down to the last show as a tie-breaker, which we won. That got us to the bonus round, called "Fast Money." Host Louie Anderson asked one of us five quick questions, with points based on how many people surveyed gave the same answer. A "family" got two cracks at the questions, and if their totals were 200 points or more, they won the big jackpot.

We had some real geniuses. When Bill DeMott was asked to name a state whose name was two words, he said, "New Orleans." I'm not knocking Bill—that game's a lot harder to play for real than it is when you're coming up with answers at home. Trust me, the pressure will make you say some goofy things, especially since you only have a couple of seconds to come up with an answer. Even though people bust Bill's chops to this day about that, especially since he was from *New Jersey*, the truth is, that pressure makes it tough.

If you've never been to a *Family Feud* taping, they tape five shows in a row, so it's a little bit of a grind. By the end, we found ways to amuse ourselves, as we always did. At the end of the last show, Knobbs made a big presentation to Louie Anderson, giving him one of their Nasty Boy trench coats. He told Louie that he was making him an honorary Nasty Boy. Louie actually looked really excited as they went off the air. Of course, as soon as they stopped rolling, Knobbs told Louie, "Okay, c'mon—I need the jacket back."

Louie was like, "What?"

"Yeah, that was just for TV," Knobbs said, putting his coat back on.

CHAPTER 18

A LONG VACATION

WHEN WCW FINALLY DID FOLD IN MARCH OF 2001, I sat home for six or seven months, collecting my checks, because I was still under contract. WCW might have been gone, but Turner Broadcasting had been its parent company, and when AOL/Time Warner took over TBS, it inherited all those wrestling contracts, including mine. As it turned out, I made the most money of my career in 2001, per wrestling match.

I actually talked to the WWF about coming back right after the buyout, or at least I tried to. Jim Ross, who used to sleep on my couch back in the 1980s when he was Bill Watts' announcer and office guy, was now director of talent relations for the WWF. I called Jim's office, but his secretary told me he wasn't in, so I left my name and number.

A week later, I'd heard nothing, so I called back and said, "Jim Duggan for Jim Ross."

The lady said, "Mr. Ross is aware of your call and will get back to you when he has the opportunity."

I never heard back from him, but I don't blame him for that, because that's part of his job description. You have to be the asshole, the axe man, the person who has to be kind of a dick, and some guys excel at it.

A few weeks later, I was doing an independent show in Canada with Roddy Piper when I got a call at the building. It was John Laurinaitis, who had wrestled as Johnny Ace and now works as one of the WWF executives who had come over from WCW when Vince bought out the company.

John said working indie shows violated my contract. I said, "John, I'm sorry—I swear, I didn't realize that."

He said it would be okay to quietly work this one show but not to accept any more bookings. So I stayed home for the rest of the year. Once the contract expired, I went back on the indie circuit. Once again, the indies were where the true wrestling fans were. They were incredibly loyal.

My old friend Jimmy Hart also contacted me near the end of 2001, shortly after my WCW contract expired, with an opportunity to join Hulk Hogan and some familiar faces in a new venture—the XWF. The "X" was supposed to represent what was missing in wrestling ("X-citement"), with only one other company/vision remaining, but what it was really missing was a long-term business plan that would allow it to remain afloat.

Curt Hennig, The Nasty Boys (Knobbs and Sags), and Greg Valentine were also going to be involved, and the basic idea was to do frequent pay-per-views that were cheaper than what the WWF was offering. It was actually the same plan that ended up being used by Total Nonstop Action. They were going to do tapings at Universal Studios in Florida, the same place WCW had done a lot of its syndicated tapings in the 1990s. Even though they looked to have signed every major piece of talent not under contract with Vince, I don't think Vince was very concerned about this upstart group.

Before they even had put on a single show, the company bought these extravagant offices in Tampa Bay, with a receptionist who had worked for WCW, and a huge refrigerator that was always stocked with beer. They even hired Doug Dillinger, WCW's head of security.

Knobbs and I went to Dallas to meet with the owner, and while we were there, we ended up meeting Willie Nelson, who was already good friends with Knobbs, on his tour bus. Willie was really cool, and we ended up talking with him for a couple of hours. Knobbs then asked if Willie would cut an interview with me, and Willie said, "Sure."

Willie was sitting there while I was pounding on the table, going into full Hacksaw mode, and when I watched it later, I could see Willie's expression, like, "What the hell planet did this guy come from?"

A Long Vacation

As part of the promotion for the XWF events, we were going to do Farm Aid, the annual farmer's benefit concert put on by Willie Nelson, John Mellencamp, and some others. Knobbs asked me if Debra and I wanted to go with him, Sags, and their wives. Did I? You bet, tough guy!

Knobbs had gotten VIP parking for a bus directly from Willie himself, but we couldn't find a good rental until Debra found us this old Winnebago. So there we were, pulling up to this big event like the Clampetts going to some fancy-dan Hollywood shindig.

They waved us in, and we were in between Hootie and the Blowfish and all these other superstars, with their million-dollar buses, and ours was backfiring to where it sounded like shots were being fired.

These big-name artists looked at us like we had walked out of the swamps of the movie *Deliverance*, but man, were the roadies excited to see us.

"Wow! The wrestlers are here!"

We partied pretty good with Willie, but by the end of the concert, Sags' feet were hurting because of the new cowboy boots he had been wearing all day. He went back to the Winnebago, leaving me, Knobbs, and our wives on the wings of the stage. Willie's concert was about over when he motioned for us to join him onstage. We walked out there as Willie and the band were performing "May the Circle Be Unbroken."

They had microphones for us, but I'm pretty sure they cut mine off, because I was so ripped that I wasn't going to be anywhere near in tune. Still, I was belting out those words as loudly as I could.

The XWF never really got going, and I'm not entirely sure why. Maybe the investors got antsy, and like I said, there didn't seem to be a firm, long-term plan. We did three shows that seemed to draw okay. We even went to Las Vegas for the NATPE convention, where TV programmers from around the country see the various offerings for syndication and decide which programs to buy for their stations. The XWF had an extravagant booth with several of the wrestlers, including myself, and they even brought in Sable (who had been the WWF's most popular female performer in 1998 and 1999). Meanwhile, the World Wrestling Federation had a tiny display, just a small booth with some packets of information for the TV people, but Linda McMahon definitely noticed the XWF spread. The second day of the convention, it was like magic, because now, the World Wrestling Federation's footprint was much bigger. They had a ring set up, a sound system, and everything else.

A few months later, Curt "Mr. Perfect" Hennig made a surprise appearance at WWE's Royal Rumble pay-per-view in January of 2002. His return got a huge reaction, but this time, his WWE stint was brief, and he was soon gone.

Just a little more than a year after his Rumble appearance, Curt was dead of a heart attack caused by cocaine use, but the medical examiner also said other drugs contributed to his death. I hate to say this, but there are several guys who, if I got a call to tell me they had died young, I wouldn't be all that surprised, but Curt dying at age 44 really did surprise me.

Others were not as surprising. Ray Traylor was a good guy, but he wasn't what you'd call a health nut, and when he died at 41, just about a year and a half after Curt, I wasn't really shocked.

Even "Macho Man" Randy Savage's passing of a heart attack at age 60 in 2011 didn't catch me by surprise. In real life, Randy was wound just about as tightly as the "Macho Man" character you saw on TV.

But by the same token, a lot of guys have done all right for themselves. George Gray, the One Man Gang, works as a prison guard, and he's spent some time working on death row, which has got to be one of the most grueling jobs you could have. I wrestled Gang in 2010 at an independent show in New Orleans, and I'm proud to say that he's every bit the gentleman he always was. I always liked Gang, even if he did put a dent in my head. We did the show for a guy named Marty Graw, which is a great name for a wrestler, especially in New Orleans.

Back in 2002, life on the indie circuit meant I had a lot of time to be at home with my family, something I really enjoyed. A couple of times, stuff at home was as wild as anything I'd encountered on the road. Maybe the wildest of all was the guest swimmer I found in my pool in the summer of 2002.

Debra and I were at home, watching TV. Outside, we had a swimming pool enclosed by a screen partition that went all the way around, mainly to keep the kids and our pets safe from falling in when we weren't around.

Our TV program was interrupted by a hissing sound. We turned and saw one of our cats near the back door, hissing, with its fur standing on end like it was on red alert. I figured the cat had spotted a raccoon or something. I mean, we were in a Florida suburb, not deep in the wild. How bad could it have been?

When our show ended, I walked out back to the pool. I turned the lights on and saw a big shape in the pool. Acorn, my golden retriever, loved fetching the Frisbee, and I often tossed it into the pool so the dog could enjoy making a water rescue.

I remember thinking, *Dammit, I told the girls to pick up their floats when they get out of the pool.*

And then the big shape moved—it was an alligator, about five feet long. Good thing I didn't throw the Frisbee in there! The alligator was just swimming in the pool, back and forth, happy as a lark. We woke the girls up to come see this thing (from a safe distance, of course).

The alligator had pushed its way through the screen to get into the pool. What drew him there, I couldn't tell you, but we watched him for a few minutes, then gathered up the kids and pets, made sure all the pet doors were secured, and went to bed. Debra and I figured it would enjoy its swim and then wander off—in the morning, it would surely be gone.

I got up the next morning, and there he was, still swimming back and forth in the pool. We ended up calling the news and the county's animal control people to get the alligator out safely. Remember, this was Titusville, where we were surrounded by all these space-program people, and I could just hear some of them: "Oh, it's that crazy wrestler again! What now?"

I thought it might be a neat little item for local news, but the press ended up being huge. Out of my entire career, the alligator in the pool ended up being the only time I ever made it into *Sports Illustrated* magazine.

The next day, after animal control had removed the alligator and relocated it, I got a call from Brian Knobbs: "Hey, Duggan, how long it take you to lure that alligator into your pool?"

But in 2002, my family also suffered a major blow when my dad passed away. His health had been declining for a while, but it was still devastating to lose the guy who had been my hero, my friend, and my biggest supporter. He was as tough in his last days as he ever had been; my dad never lost his sense of humor. One night, toward the end, I had him with me for a match in Glens Falls. I was standing at the top of the ramp, getting ready to come to the ring, with him next to me in his wheelchair. My music started playing, and I had the 2x4 in my hand. I looked down at him and gave out a big "HO-OH!"

My dad cowered, like he was terrified of me. Now he had everyone thinking I beat my poor dad. I just looked at him and went, "Pop! Jesus, you're killing me, here!"

Later, we had a big laugh about it. He always said he was proud of me, no matter what, but I couldn't have been prouder than to have a dad who worked as hard as he did for his family and his community. His values— charity, love for family, and patriotism, among them—are things I've tried to impart to my own kids.

CHAPTER 19

COMING BACK TO THE WW...E

WITH THE DEMISE OF THE XWF, I needed to look around and see what was next. In 2003, I worked a couple of shows for Total Nonstop Action, a group that started out in 2002 as an attempt to compete with Vince McMahon on the national stage. They hadn't (and still haven't) been very successful.

TNA boss Jeff Jarrett and I weren't exactly buddies, but we were always congenial to each other when we were in the WWF and, later, WCW together. So, when someone from the TNA office called about having me come in for a show, I was willing to listen.

At the time, Mike Sanders and Disco Inferno (two lesser WCW guys) were doing a gimmick where they would handcuff their beaten opponents. TNA wanted to have them do this to me and my partner for that match, Larry "Moondog Spot" Latham. I said, "Gee, that's a little strong for one payday." So they agreed to pay me double.

They also said not to worry, because they were planning to make an angle of it and bring me back for some revenge down the line, so I agreed. Well, they did the whole thing, putting me out of the building, and I have to say, everyone in TNA treated me fine the whole time I was there.

That was eight years ago as I write this, and I'm still waiting for TNA to call and let me know when my revenge will be. Actually, Jimmy Hart called me about a year later to tell me TNA wanted to do something with me.

"Jimmy," I said, "not a chance in hell."

But I thought about it and realized I owed Jimmy Hart more than one favor, so I told him, "Well, Jimmy, for you, I'll come up and do the deal."

This time, I was supposed to get the big *El Kabong!* from Jeff Jarrett with the guitar. Jarrett had used a guitar as a gimmick in the WWF, WCW, and now TNA. This time, I knew I was in for a onetime deal, so I just did the spot, and that was that. I saw Vince Russo backstage, because he was now writing for TNA, but he wouldn't even make eye-contact, much less say hello.

The thing about TNA was, they shot their TV show at Universal Studios in Florida, and their TV production is kind of an all-day affair. Well, I figured, my hotel room was only a quick hop down the interstate from the arena, and there were hours to kill...

Before you knew it, I was back at the hotel, catching a nap. I made sure to set the alarm to give me plenty of time to get back. Everything was ahead of schedule...until I stepped outside and saw that traffic on the freeway, heading to the amusement park, was standing completely still, a traffic jam that went all the way from Universal to the hotel.

I remember looking at that paralyzed line of cars and thinking, *I am so screwed. Sorry, Jimmy...*

I got into my car and slogged through the traffic to the show. I got there, but I was really late, and when I got out of my car, Jimmy Hart was in the parking lot, looking frantic.

He cried out, "Hacksaw! Oh, baby, I am so glad to see you, baby, I thought you'd walked out!"

So I got the big *El Kabong*, and Jarrett nailed me on the forehead instead of the top of the head, where it should have been. I didn't take it personally—at 5'10", Jarrett's arms probably couldn't reach all the way up there.

Afterward, I cut an interview where I threw a chair, which bounced up and hit a fluorescent light tube in the ceiling. The tube shattered and little sparks showered down on me as I finished my interview. I thought it was great TV; Jarrett said, "Eh, I don't like it." They actually made me cut another interview, which was okay, but not nearly as good as the first one.

Actually, you want to know the truth about my promos? Here's my secret—every promo I cut is spontaneous. I don't plan a thing. I just let it roll, brother, and once it starts rollin', sometimes I can't turn it off!

I think that spontaneity has helped me in wrestling, although it's not something that works for me in restaurants.

In 2005, I got my second crack at working for Vince McMahon, whose company was now called World Wrestling Entertainment. It all started with this pay-per-view called Cyber Sunday, where the show's gimmick was that fans got to pick who would be partners and what the match stipulations would be. One of the choices would be who would team up with Eugene against Tyson Tomko and Rob Conway. The options were Kamala, Jimmy Snuka, and myself. Snuka won, but I was a close second, and both Kamala and I got involved at the finish of the match. We all had to be there, because it was legit—no one knew who was going to win the vote until the show was under way.

Even though I wasn't the fans' choice, Vince McMahon was impressed enough with the response I got that he brought me back a week or so later, for a bit with Edge. Edge was one of WWE's top villains, and his "girlfriend" Lita got some great heat from the crowd. I did a deal where I got on the mic and said Lita was a "HO-OH!"

Finally, they put me in a match with Edge, and I was wondering beforehand how it would go, because I knew it was an important match for me, and I didn't really know this young guy I'd be wrestling. What I knew was that a lot of young guys had the attitude of, "Eh, I'm in with this old guy; I'll give him my 'C' effort."

Well, Edge gave me his "A" effort. He was at the top of his game, and he even let me shine in a situation where he could have easily made me look bad. After the match, I thanked him for giving me the chance, because he made it a good match, and that launched me into some other things for WWE, including working with Umaga and Randy Orton, the company's other top heels. It became a good gig; I would come in to WWE for short stretches and then be phased back out, like an inactive reservist who gets called up to active duty from time to time.

During the Edge feud, we even did a bit where he attacked me offstage, and I remember thinking how different things were from the old days. In Mid-South, it all would have been off camera, but WWE's production crew had me covered in (fake) blood and made a whole visual out of it.

That wasn't the only difference. For my 2005 run in WWE, I had to get used to having scripts tell me what to say, instead of coming up with it on the fly like I'd done in the 1980s.

I was backstage for the first night of my return to *Raw*, WWE's flagship show, when this young fellow (who I later learned was part of the writing staff) handed me some papers and said, "Uh, Hacksaw? Hi, this is your verbiage for tonight."

I went into "Hacksaw" mode, right then and there!

"How's some punk kid gonna tell Hacksaw Jim Duggan how to cut his interview?"

"Well," he said, "this is what we want you to say."

I read it over and thought, *Well, what the hell—I'll read this, you guys send me my check, and we'll be good.*

I wasn't crazy about it, but wrestling's always evolving, and you have to be able to roll with the times. Even if you don't like something, you can't fight city hall.

In April of 2008, I was participating in the World Sailfish Championship tournament, and just before the tournament, WWE called to tell me they needed me to head to London, to work a *Raw* taping.

"But I have this charity event—I can't just miss it," I said. "I asked for this weekend a couple of months ago."

But the agent I was talking to said they really needed me, so they made arrangements to get me to England for the show.

At the time, there was this big marathon going on in London, so I had a shuttle take me as close to the arena as we could get, and I walked from there. It was one of the most unique experiences of my life, as I walked for blocks through a completely deserted downtown London. There were no shops open, no cars, and no other people on the streets. It was eerie.

Finally, I walked up to a cop, who first wanted to know how I had gotten through their security perimeter. I explained I was lost and American (actually, he figured out that last part before I explained it). He told me how to get to the arena.

When I got there, I was eager to find out what I'd be doing, because I figured that if they were bringing me this far and even having me cancel an event to do it, it must be something significant. I waited in the catering area, while Vince and his creative and TV people had their production meeting. After it was over, Barry Windham (a former wrestler who was now a WWE agent) came over to me and said, "Jim, we're going to have you working with Paul Burchill tonight, and he's going to beat you in about 45 seconds."

I sat there, stunned, and then I said, "You know what, Barry? I'm not gonna do it. I come all the way over here, and I don't mind being used to build up these other guys, but this just isn't right, to pull me out of an event on a weekend I lined up months ago, for *this*? Send my old ass home—I don't care."

Barry nodded and said, "Well, you gotta tell Vince."

I said I would, and I went to Vince's makeshift office. I was waiting outside, and I was pacing back and forth. Finally, a guy came out of Vince's office, and he could tell I was pissed.

A lot of Vince's personal security team was made up of ex-cops, and I've always gotten along with cops, so I was friendly with a bunch of them. One of the main security guys, Jim, came up to me, and he could tell I was steaming. We talked, and I was cordial, but I was still pretty ticked off.

After a few more minutes, one of the production guys came out and said Vince would be with me when he had a minute, and I said, very deliberately, "I ain't going anywhere. I'll...be...right...here."

My temper was snowballing, and Jerry Brisco walked over to try to smooth things over, but I wasn't about to be smoothed over. I was getting madder and madder.

When I finally got in to see Vince, I walked into the office with Barry, and Vince was texting someone. Barry said, "Hey, Vince, you want me to stay with you?"

Vince looked surprised and said, "No! I've known Jim for nearly 30 years! No problem! Come on in, Jim! Sit down—take a load off! I just have to finish texting this."

He focused on his texting for a few seconds, and then asked if I knew how to spell a couple of words. I won't say what they were, because I don't want to be disclosing anything he might have been corresponding to someone else, but I didn't know how to spell them, anyway, so I said, still in kind of a huff, "No."

"This thing drives me crazy! Do you text much, Jim?"

"Um...no."

We had another few minutes of small talk, and I just couldn't bring myself to stay mad at Vince. I was calming down a minute at a time. Finally, I realized I wasn't even angry anymore, and then he said, "Okay, so what's the matter, Jim?"

"You know," I said, "I just didn't think it was right..."

I laid out my case, but very calmly.

He listened intently, nodded, and said, "Well, I'll tell you what. I'm starting this legends program, and we're going to make you one of the legends, and we'll have you do a lot of P.R. for us as part of that. I certainly don't want you to think I don't appreciate what you've done."

We chatted a few more minutes, and then I excused myself so I could get ready for my 45-second match with Paul Burchill, which by now I was happy to do.

I got to thinking about all the times I'd seen guys go into Vince's office over the years, furious, only to come out calm and confused. I came out of there feeling like that stormtrooper from *Star Wars* who got Jedi mind-tricked by Obi-Wan Kenobi.

Seriously, when I walked out of that office, I might as well have been muttering, "No, these are not the droids I was looking for."

And I also understood that one of my main purposes there was to work with the younger guys and maybe teach them a little. I tried to teach them to relax in the ring and try to enjoy what they were doing. Andre the Giant had been the one to teach it to me.

"Slo-o-o-o-w down," he'd say. "The people come to see us. Let them enjoy."

Like a lot of wrestlers, my natural tendency was to go fast. But you weren't going to go fast with Andre. You were going to go at the speed he wanted to go, and that speed usually was *slow*.

The young wrestlers I worked with and tried to teach a little included Ted DiBiase Jr. (it's funny how things come around, huh?) and Super Crazy.

I had fun with Ted; once, I had him in a headlock, and I leaned into him and said, "Give this to your old man."

He said, "What?"

"I said, give this to your old man!"

"What?"

While still applying the headlock with my left arm, I reared my right fist back.

"I said, give this..."

Pop!

"...to your old man!"

"Ow! Jesus, Duggan!"

But that shot was delivered with love.

Super Crazy was a high-flying Mexican wrestler, and we actually got to be buddies, even though he spoke very little English and I spoke even less Spanish. We tagged up for a while and traveled together, but I dealt with people at the hotels and car-rental companies, because Crazy couldn't communicate with them...or so I thought.

After about a month of us working together, we were on a flight and the stewardess was passing out sandwiches. She passed our row when Crazy turned to her and said, "Hey, lady, I didn't get my sandwich."

My jaw dropped. I stared at him for a second and then went, "Crazy! This whole time, you been working me?"

He gave me this really confused look and said, "*Qué?*"

Something I noticed during this stretch, which I would notice again every time WWE brought me in for a few shows, was the sheer scope of what Vince had put together. When I had been there full time, I'd never really stopped to appreciate how massive the operation was becoming, but now, I did take a second to look at everything, and I was just amazed. My industry had gone from two cameras and a ring to satellite linkups, digital recording equipment, stage lighting technicians, catering, trucks of equipment, and so on. It was really cool to be part of such a huge production.

Sometimes, on the road, I'd even stop to take in a sight, like if we were traveling past a canyon or mountains. I'd usually notice guys whizzing by me in their cars, just as fast as we used to go, although now, everyone had their own car, instead of six guys piled into a sedan the way we used to be. I like a lot of the young guys, but I really think they're missing something by not traveling together.

I even had a lot of fun working with the Spirit Squad kids. These guys were doing a gimmick of being a team of male cheerleaders, which a lot of people thought was dumb, but those kids busted their asses. I don't know what happened there, because they were pushing Kenny Dykstra pretty hard, but as of 2011, the one getting the big push out of that group is the one who now wrestles as Dolph Ziggler. Every now and then, I do interviews to plug local shows I'm doing, and the interviewer asks me for a prediction; one I have given out more than once is that Ziggler is going to be a big star. He's got great presence, he works hard, and he's a great natural athlete. In a way, he almost reminds me of a young Shawn Michaels...in the ring, that is. He's not the pain in the ass that Shawn was as a young man.

CHAPTER 20

A DARK DAY

I WAS BOOKED ON *RAW* ON JUNE 18, 2007, which was the night they blew up Vince's limo in one hell of a production. It was going to be this big angle about someone trying to take out McMahon, and it would turn into a whodunit. They had an effects crew rig the car and they were ready to do the stunt, so they warned all the talent to stay away from a certain set of doors. We could use pretty much any exit but that one.

So, of course, I went out that certain set of doors, trying to get out of there and beat the crowd (yeah, I was leaving a little early; give me a break, I'm an old-timer). I went around the back toward where I'd parked. I saw a security guard and stopped to chat with him for a minute, when all of a sudden, *boom!*

I was about to jump out of my skin. "What the hell was that?"

"Oh, didn't you know? They're blowing up Vince's car," the guard said.

Had I not stopped to talk to that guy, I could have ended up in the background of that shot...which probably would have led to another explosion, when Vince blew up at me. Good thing I'm a friendly guy!

The next week at TV, actor Bruce Campbell was scheduled to be the guest host of *Raw*. Both the wrestling show and Campbell's spy show, *Burn Notice*, aired on the USA Network, so USA was planning on doing a little cross-promotion. I taped a segment with him that afternoon, where he and I were huddled over a casket, talking about Vince "dying" in last week's limo explosion.

At one point, when talking about my memories of the WWE's head honcho, I mistakenly referred to him as "Vince," which caused an immediate cut and retake. Behind the scenes, Vince likes to be called Vince, but his TV character was this ruthless hardass who, among other things, demanded to be called only "Mr. McMahon."

Anyway, we got through it, and Bruce Campbell did great—he was very funny and a really good guy, very easy to work with. Campbell was a real class act.

Unfortunately, the segment never aired, because just a few minutes after we finished taping one of the bits, one of the TV production guys came into where we were shooting, grabbed Vince, and the two of them walked off—briskly.

About a half hour later, Vince came back and announced he was shutting down the shoot and that there would be a meeting in the (still-empty) arena. Everybody knew something bad had happened; only something major would cause Vince to shut down a shoot like that.

All of us—wrestlers, TV crew, agents, everyone—were sitting in one section of the arena. Eventually, Vince walked up to us, visibly shaken, his eyes red and watery.

He took a breath and said, "Ladies and gentlemen, Chris Benoit and his whole family have just been found dead."

Everyone was still and silent for a second, just stunned. Then, I could hear a couple of quiet sobs.

For the rest of the day, a lot of the people were walking around in a daze, while more and more folks backstage were starting to speculate on what might have happened. Was it some crazed fan? A gas leak?

I was one of the people stunned by the news, but I was from a different generation, and even though we both worked for WCW at the same time during the mid- to late 1990s, Chris and I didn't work together and certainly didn't socialize. However, the guys who were closer to Chris really took it hard. The whole company took it hard.

Vince made the call to do a memorial show, as he'd done on a couple of occasions when guys had passed away. I know a lot of people have since criticized his decision, but I was there, and he had only a few minutes to decide what to do. At that point, *no one* thought it was possible that Chris Benoit had killed his own family, which included his seven-year-old son, Daniel. Chris loved that little boy; he used to bring him to shows, and I can remember him coming up to me in his little suit and tie and saying, "Hello, Mr. Duggan."

He was such a polite young man, and his father adored him; no one saw it coming. As more information started coming out, people were getting uneasy, but no one knew for sure until well after the show went off the air that night that Benoit had apparently snapped and killed both his wife and son over the weekend.

It's hard to process something like that, but sadly, it's one of those things in life that happens. You see it on the news—police officers go nuts, postal workers become suddenly violent, students riot—and whether his actions were influenced by repeated concussions, as several doctors who examined Benoit speculated, it was an awful tragedy.

Vince ended up making another call, and this one was kind of a no-brainer at that point. He squashed the whole angle of the Mr. McMahon character getting "killed" in a limo explosion, because with a real tragedy going on, it would have been totally inappropriate. Even though Vince had invested a lot of money in making that explosion work as a Hollywood-type stunt, he did not delay at all in dropping the angle.

I think Vince McMahon gets a bad rap sometimes, wrongfully blamed for things caused by the wrestlers' own bad habits. Somas are a good example. Somas are a muscle relaxer, a drug that can have therapeutic uses but is also easy to abuse. I never took somas, never even understood the appeal (maybe because I never took them), but I used to see guys get the "soma shakes."

In WCW, there was a kid who wrestled as Louie Spicolli, a nice kid, but he took so many of those that he would forget how many he took. He would start shaking while he ate dinner, and the next thing you knew, food was flying all over the place. I would offer advice if asked, but no one wants to be preached to, and that's the kind of thing you've got to want to fix yourself. I remember looking at him and thinking, *Geez, this guy's killing himself right before our eyes.*

And in 1997, he finished the job, dying a drug-related death.

Another really talented wrestler was Lance Cade, a Shawn Michaels trainee with a ton of potential. What started his slide toward getting released by WWE was a plane ride, where he got the soma shakes so bad that he started convulsing. They got medics to take him off the plane when we landed, because they thought he was having a seizure. When the company found out it was drug-related, they let him go, which started the downward spiral that led to his death.

A lot of guys had problems, but they would have had problems no matter what they did, because of their tempers, personalities, or whatever was in their heads. In the mid-2000s, I was working an indie show in Texas with Brian Knobbs, among others, when Knobbs came into the dressing room and said, "Hey, the dude that killed Chris Adams is here."

I had known Chris from the regional days, and to be honest, I wasn't a big fan of his. But I had thought he was an okay guy, and everyone in the locker room was kind of pissed off that this guy would show his face at our show.

This very unassuming guy came in, not what I was expecting at all. And then, he started to tell the story of what had happened the night Chris Adams died.

I knew "Gentleman" Chris Adams as a British wrestler who earned some popularity in the 1980s, working in Fritz Von Erich's territory. But what this guy was describing sounded like a different person completely, and what he showed us was even worse. The guy took off his shirt, and there was a big hunk of meat gone from his chest where Adams had bitten him. He said Adams was beating him so bad that he was killing him, so he grabbed the gun and hit Chris with it. That didn't faze him, and Chris kept coming at him, so he fired once, hitting Chris in the middle of the chest and killing him instantly.

The guy never went to jail, because it was self-defense, justifiable homicide, and I hate to speak ill of the dead, but I believe it was because Chris was out of control on drugs.

A lot of tragic stories are centered around guys I loved. Some of my closest friends in the business died too young, because of their own choices. I think back to the WWF days of the early 1990s, and I remember Rick Rude, Big Bossman, Curt Hennig, and Kerry Von Erich. The four of them got tight, and they all partied together. And none of them lived to see 50.

Kerry, in particular, broke my heart, because his death was such a waste. He killed himself in 1993, and he was only 33 at the time. He was looking at a few months in jail for a probation violation, but he'd have been out before he knew it.

On the other hand, there were guys like Steve Williams, a guy I loved like a brother, who overcame a lot of obstacles, only to die young from cancer that would have gotten him even if he'd never touched anything harder than an aspirin.

A lot of bad news stories that get blamed on wrestling have nothing to do with wrestling, because a lot of guys who are called "wrestlers" really shouldn't be. If you don't make your living in wrestling, then you shouldn't be identified as a professional wrestler. If some semipro football player gets in trouble or has some tragic accident, he doesn't get identified primarily as a football player. But take a guy who works as a welder all week and then wrestles on maybe two independent shows a month—if that guy attacks someone and goes to jail, you better believe the headline is going to start with, "Pro wrestler..."

And a lot of that is that many people just don't like wrestling, or to put it better, they have no understanding of it, and no respect for what it takes to be involved in the business.

Look, I'm not a fan of ballet, but I appreciate how hard those dancers work, the amount of time they put in, and the talent that's required to do it well, and I don't walk around looking for excuses to knock ballet.

So if someone doesn't like my business, that's fine—heck, my own sister doesn't like it and never has. But don't be critical when you have no idea what it takes to make it. So many guys with great athletic ability can't make it in wrestling, because they could never cut an effective promo.

Think about what passes for a good interview for an NFL player: "I had a good game, and he had a good game, and I hope I have a good game next week."

If I cut a promo like that, I'd have been out of the business! As a wrestler, you've got to say what you're gonna do, who you're gonna do it to, in what arena, and at what time, tough guy! You gotta sell tickets, and a lot of guys had the physical ability but couldn't talk on camera, and that's a huge part of our business.

Some guys have the physical ability and can talk on camera, but they can't handle the road life. All that travel can be very hard. Almost all my family videos have a shot of the family sitting down for Christmas or Thanksgiving dinner, with me in the background, carrying a suitcase out of the house and telling everyone good-bye and that I'll see them in a couple of weeks. I missed my daughter Celia's 18th birthday, and I'm just lucky that she understands the business and knows that when I'm gone, it's because I'm providing for our family.

I would never want my girls to go into the business, and fortunately, they've never shown much interest in doing so. My youngest, Rebecca, accompanied me to the ring a few times in my WCW days, as a little kid carrying the flag for me, and she had fun doing that. The girls do always have fun whenever I work a show close to home and am able to bring them backstage with me. That's one reason I was so thankful to have a chance for a second run with WWE in 2005, because during my first run, I was traveling too much to slow down and enjoy it, and the girls weren't even born yet.

Twenty years ago, I was flying down the road to make the next town. This last time, I'd be pulling over at rest stops, taking pictures with my cell phone to send to the family.

On one of those trips during that time, I was driving from Reno, Nevada, to Sacramento, California. The morning I left Reno, a snowstorm had shut down Donner Pass—which you pretty much have to go through to get to northern California—to all vehicles without snow chains on their tires. Unfortunately, I didn't know how to put chains on.

I bought some chains and got to a truck stop, and offered a trucker $100 to put the chains on. He put the chains on, and I headed for the pass. It was really something—I could actually see the storm heading my way, and then it hit while I was on Donner Pass. I was calling everyone: "Hey, you gotta see this. I got pictures on my phone...good thing I'm by myself. If I get trapped in a snowstorm, I might end up having to take a bite out of somebody to get through it!"

But the joking stopped right around the time all the traffic stopped. I was stuck in a line of traffic, all these cars, completely stopped, and the snow kept coming...and coming...and coming...

I had to keep getting out to wipe the snow off the top of the car, and it was getting pretty scary, because we were going maybe a mile an hour, and the snow kept piling up. Meanwhile, my gas tank was going empty, quickly—I could literally see the fuel gauge moving steadily toward the big "E" at the bottom.

It went from being a funny situation to one of the most terrifying moments I've ever experienced on the road. I kept picturing the car running out of gas, and me standing outside my car asking other drivers, "Hey, could you let me in?"

And I could only imagine their reactions to hearing that from some long-haired wild man the size of Sasquatch.

It took all night just to get over the highway pass, which was only a couple of miles long. I had to stop at the very first gas station I saw, and I called Debra at home to let her know I had made it through. I also said, "Honey, if you had ever worried about me in my career, last night was the night. That was a tight one!"

Some even blame Vince for their own failure to plan. I was doing an interview in 2008 or 2009 with some guy who had recently been released from WWE, and this guy said, "That Vince McMahon, he treats us like pieces of meat."

I said, "Well, kid, who the hell do you think you are? If you want a friend, go buy a puppy." What nearly everyone in WWE needs to realize is that Vince is your boss, and when the time's right, he'll flush you down the toilet—welcome to the real world.

Of course, there are a lot of guys on the scene who seem to live in their own fantasy worlds.

In the mid-2000s, I went up to Halifax, Nova Scotia, to work an independent show, and there was a guy there who was a complete asshole, telling me (and everyone else within earshot) how much better his stuff was than anything on TV, and how he would never degrade himself by working for Vince McMahon.

"Never!" he said. "I would never go to work for that damned WWE!"

Well, I thought, *you're right about that*—there was no way WWE would even have given this guy a second look. And he was getting on my nerves from the time I first walked into the parking lot. At first, I didn't even realize he was one of the boys—I was talking to some folks, and he kept chiming in with "I don't care who you are!"

I finally turned around to him and said, "Well, that's fine, because I don't care who *you* are, buddy!"

I went up to one of the bouncers working security (here's a tip for traveling wrestlers: always get to know the bouncers as soon as you get to a venue) to ask what the deal was, since none of the security guys were quieting this idiot.

Come to find out, the loudmouth was some local big-shot for the company up in the Maritimes. Anyway, I said, "Okay, I'm out of here—I don't need trouble from some idiot who thinks he's a star."

I walked out, and he followed me into the parking lot, jawing the whole way.

"Look," I said, "I'm trying to be decent here. I'm walking away from you, because we don't need to have a problem, but enough is enough!"

There were a few people watching us argue in the parking lot, and before I knew it, we had 20 people recording our entire dispute on their cell phones. Nothing happened, and it was a good thing—both for the sake of that guy's teeth, and my not needing the legal bills from a lawsuit.

Even when I talk to my NFL buddies, a lot of them don't get it. I'll hear stuff like, "You mean 32 years in that business, and you guys don't get a pension?"

And, you know, maybe the wrestlers should. In a perfect world, they would be taken care of. But the reality is, they're not, and that shouldn't be a surprise to anyone. I knew that before I started, and I tried to save a little, knowing I was going to be responsible for my own retirement. It may not be a perfect system, but as Bobby Heenan used to say, "It's more money than you'll make moving refrigerators at Sears."

The one season I was with the Atlanta Falcons, I made the league minimum, $23,000, and I was living like a big dog. When I got cut, I was in debt up to my ass. It took me a long time to get out, and I thought, *Well, I don't think I'll do that again.*

And ever since, I always managed to put away a little money, here and there, and now, as I close in on my late fifties, my retirement is pretty well set. Of course, if you'd like to help, please feel free to buy extra copies of this book for all your friends!

I was never one of those guys who wore a lot of fancy jewelry or Rolex watches, and aside from my Trans Am back in the early 1980s, I never got into buying fancy cars. There's an old adage that I'd advise young wrestlers to keep in mind: "It's not what you make; it's what you save."

I'm not saying that I was the most frugal guy in the world. Actually, that honor probably went to Randy Savage, although Nikolai Volkoff was another guy who was extremely thrifty; he was always very careful about how he spent his money.

A lot of guys saved money by splitting hotel rooms, but that was always the one luxury I did allow myself: I always wanted to get a hotel room by myself. I was (and still am) always happy to ride with a carload of guys, but when we get there, I just need a little quiet time to myself.

So, all you young WWE superstars, take some of that money and set it aside. Savage, Volkoff, and I were not the only ones who managed to do that. Tito Santana, a good man who might never have been a marquee name but was still a solid star in the business, saved his money, made some smart choices, and he's doing well for himself. When he left wrestling, he went into teaching and coaching, and his kids are lucky to learn from someone who has as much character and work ethic as he has.

Granted, there might be more sad stories than Tito Santana success stories, but if guys fail to plan for life after wrestling, that's not the business' fault, and it's not Vince McMahon's fault.

CHAPTER 21

FAMILY, FILM STARS, AND COMMUNITY

WE NAMED OUR FIRST DAUGHTER, CELIA JOYCE, after my mom—who had been such a great influence on my life—and my mother-in-law, Brenda Joyce. We named our youngest daughter Rebecca Sue because Debra always loved the name Rebecca and Debra's middle name is Sue.

Celia and Rebecca are both very good athletes. They both turned out to be such great kids that I really feel like I got lucky, because I was gone so much. I tried to be the best dad I could be, every minute that I could be with them, but I know Debra worked like crazy while I was out on the road, and I know that our kids are great kids because of all the time she put in with them. I can't even put into words how proud I am of those three special ladies.

Having a dad who's a wrestler is tough on a kid. Birthdays, holidays, whatever it was—we celebrated them when we could celebrate them. In a weird way, though, I think that while my lifestyle as a wrestler made that difficult, it also helped my girls separate the superficial from what was important. The day we celebrated a birthday or holiday might not have been on the actual date, but the day we *could* all be together was what we all knew was important—being together, as a family.

DEBRA SAYS:

And I really think that the reason our family is still together, while a lot of other families in the wrestling business have split up, is that we did remember what was important. Family was what mattered, not a number on a calendar.

Sometimes, the kids even got a little extra because of how hectic things were and how hard it could be to get everyone together. It would be nothing for the girls to get three or four birthday parties or Christmas mornings per year, because we might have one at home, then one with Jim's family in New York, then with my family in South Carolina, then with their friends, if the friends couldn't make it to one of the other ones.

In 2004, Debra and I were on the board of directors for the Children's Home Society, which has become the largest child-welfare agency in the state of Florida. Someone suggested that we do a golf fund-raiser, and the Hacksaw Duggan Celebrity Invitational Golf Tournament was born.

I called up Mike McBath from the Orlando chapter of the Retired NFL Players Association, as well as some of my buddies from wrestling (Knobbs, Sags, and Brian Adams, among them). It ended up being a pretty successful fund-raiser. There was a casino night before the day of the golf tournament.

Of course, having wrestlers around meant there was never a dull moment. Once, I was with some of the folks from the society when from across the fairway, Knobbs mooned the entire crowd as his wife, Toni, drove him across the course in a golf cart.

I just shook my head at the thought of all those poor people confronted with Knobbs' big, white, pimply ass, and thought, *Oh my God, this is not the right place, Brian.*

A year later, I had a much more significant mishap at a charity event. I also have been very involved in benefits for the law enforcement community, largely because of my dad. In 2005, I got a call from Ben Johnson, the Volusia County, Florida, sheriff, asking if I'd participate in a charity school-bus race.

216

He explained how it worked, and I thought the idea was a little wacky, but it was for a good cause (the Florida Sheriffs' Youth Ranches, which work with troubled kids), so I said, "Sure, I'll be glad to do it."

It was a huge event; about a quarter of all the sheriffs in the state of Florida were participating. They asked if I would do the media day prior to the main race, so I drove up to New Smyrna Beach, just outside of Orlando. I couldn't believe how much media there was for this thing, but I wanted to help put on a good show, so I cut a promo in full "Hacksaw" mode: "Lemme tell ya somethin', Ben Johnson! You been winnin' this race, but Hacksaw Duggan is comin' up here, and I'm takin' over!"

Everyone got a laugh out of it, but then Sheriff Johnson said, "So, how about we take a couple of laps, Hacksaw?"

I pulled him aside and said, "You know, Ben, I've never actually driven a bus before. That interview was just for the media."

He said, "Don't worry—you'll be okay. It's easier than you think."

I reluctantly got into my school bus, and they had me strap into a seatbelt. Good thing, too. A young lady, a reporter for the *Orlando Sentinel*, asked if she could ride with me, so she piled onto the bus, and off we went. A third bus with a TV crew was following Johnson and me.

I actually got ahead of Johnson, but pretty soon I felt a bump.

Ben Johnson was bumping me from behind! I steered away to get him off of my tail, and we did get clear, so at that point, I thought we were okay. But then we hit the first turn, and I didn't bank enough to the right (which I should have, because the pavement went at a slight incline as you made the curve), and we went up and over onto our side.

I was holding onto the steering wheel as the bus rolled over, and I didn't lose my grip, but I did tear my rotator cuff from holding on so tightly. As the bus slid on its left side, that poor reporter and I were getting pelted with asphalt, and she was getting bounced around the inside of the bus. I was sure we were going to hit the retaining wall. But instead of hitting the wall, we rolled into the infield.

I'm pretty sure I was in shock. They asked if I was okay, and I distantly remember saying, "Yeah, sure, I'm okay."

I even managed to cut another promo for TV and went home. As I was heading home, I called Debra and told her what had happened.

Of course, as you've probably figured out by now, I tend to joke around a lot, so she said, "Yeah, right."

"No," I said, "I really wrecked the bus."

"Oh, come on, Jim!"

But when I got home, she took me to the hospital, where they put my shoulder in a sling for the torn rotator cuff. Two days later, I showed up for the event, but told them I didn't know if I could do the actual race. One of the organizers looked at me and said, "Yeah, that shoulder looks pretty bad. Hey, I know—why don't you skip the race and just do the demolition derby instead?"

"Look at me," I said. "I can't be doing *anything!*"

Demolition derby!

Sadly, in 2006, the very next year, Lake County Sheriff Chris Daniels was killed in the race on his 47th birthday. He got bumped and fell out of his bus, because he wasn't wearing a seatbelt. They stopped doing the races for a couple of years before bringing back the event with some new safety requirements.

I've always been happy to use my fame as a way to help out, but sometimes, fame makes you a target. Around 2006, someone showed up on my website and contacted me, saying, "Hacksaw Duggan, I'm your son. I don't want nothin' from you. My mother is so-and-so, and I'm living in Las Vegas. All I want is recognition. I want to be a wrestler."

Not long after, I went to the Cauliflower Alley banquet (an annual event where a lot of wrestlers, families, and some fans get together) in Vegas, and this woman came up to me and asked if I wanted to meet my son.

"Lady," I said, "I don't have a son."

This kid came up and hugged me, saying, "Aw, Hacksaw...Dad!"

I knew something wasn't right—I looked at this scrawny kid and thought my middle-school-age daughter Rebecca could have kicked his ass!

I had known this kid's mother. She was a stripper when I was in Mid-South back in the mid-1980s. A lot of wrestlers knew strippers—they were often wrestling fans, they often had the best drugs, and a lot of them were bisexual, which were three things young wrestlers were looking for in a party back then.

By the time I got home, I was kind of worried, and I talked to Debra about it.

"I really don't think this is my kid," I said. "There's no resemblance, at all."

Also, I figured if I really was the kid's father, the mother would have hit me up in the late 1980s, when I was in the WWF making the big bucks, not 20 years later.

But Debra said I needed to get tested, just to be sure.

I ended up spending $700 on some damn blood test, which proved I was not his father, and even after that, he kept wrestling around Las Vegas, using the "Duggan" name. And that pisses me off, because it makes me look like a heel (a real one, not just a wrestling bad guy)! If he had turned out to be my son, I would have embraced him. He'd be at my house, and he'd be a Duggan. But the way this guy carries on, people hear him and go, "Ah, that Hacksaw Duggan, he doesn't even take care of his own kid."

On Twitter and Facebook, there are apparently hundreds of people claiming to be Hacksaw Duggan, and people follow these guys! It never ceases to amaze me how blurry the line between wrestling and reality can get sometimes.

For example, when the movie *The Wrestler* was released in 2008, Mickey Rourke, who plays the film's washed-up title character, started hanging out with a few of the wrestlers, and I had a bit of a run-in with him.

That spring, I'd decided to do WWE's Fan Axxess event, held every year right before WrestleMania. Fans show up to attend Q&A sessions, to buy merchandise, or, in some cases, just to meet their favorite performers.

After a full day of festivities, Debra and I went to the hotel's bar to have a drink and unwind. I finally decided to head upstairs to check on the girls, who had also joined us for this trip. I got off the elevator at my floor and made it to the room. My daughters were asleep.

I shut the door and turned back toward the elevator. Now, in all fairness, I was a little inebriated and I didn't have my glasses on, so I couldn't see too well.

As I headed back down the hall, I saw three big guys coming my way. I moved over to the right, trying to be polite, and one of them changed positions so that he was still coming right at me.

When we passed and accidentally brushed shoulders, I turned and said, "So, you got enough room there, buddy?"

The guy in the middle spun around and said, "What did you say to me?"

"I just mean you seem to have plenty of room, asshole."

"Yeah? Well, you don't talk to me that way!"

At that point, I was thinking, *Who the hell is this guy?*

Then it hit me—I was being screamed at by Mickey Rourke.

Still, movie star or not, he *was* talking a little trash, and since he was a short guy, I used one of my old standby lines: "Hey, buddy, you stand up when you're talking to me!"

He started calling me a son of a bitch, and we were starting to get into a square-off in the hotel. As it turned out, the two guys with Rourke that night were two UFC fighters, and those guys were really cool. They knew me right off and kept saying they just wanted to get Rourke out of there, peaceably.

Within hours of word of our "altercation" getting out, I had more than 80,000 hits on my blog.

That made me realize that what I should have done was punch Mickey Rourke's lights out, because even if those two had ripped my arms off, just think of the amount of press I would've gotten for that!

Rourke was there because he was going to do a bit with Chris Jericho at WrestleMania, WWE's flagship pay-per-view. Earlier in the day, Jericho was going over spots, and Rourke said, "Just so you know, I got my boys here, in case things don't go right."

Jericho said, "Hey, I'm playing a part, just like you, you ass!"

But their bit went off without a hitch, and we all went to the post-WrestleMania party. One of the WWE's office guys came over to me and said, "Hey, Hacksaw, if you get a chance, go on over and talk to Mickey, just smooth things over."

I said, "Well, okay, it's a big party. If I see him, I'll say something to him."

About half an hour later, that same WWE office person came over to me and said, "You're right, Hacksaw; that Mickey Rourke *is* an asshole!"

As for the movie *The Wrestler*, I watched part of it, but after my run-in with Rourke, I never had any desire to see the rest of it. If you haven't seen it, it's about a (fictional) wrestler who was a big name in the 1980s, but who's down and out in the present day, and the basic message of the film is that wrestling destroyed the guy.

But what I saw of the movie, I didn't like, and based on what I've heard about it from other people, I wouldn't have liked the rest of it, even if the lead part hadn't been played by a guy I thought was a jerk. I thought it gave wrestling a bad image, which the business doesn't deserve. Sure, there are a lot of train wrecks in our business, but that is not the whole story. There are guys who live normal, productive lives with their families, but I know that the ones who are down on their luck are the ones that people like to hear about, which I guess can be chalked up to morbid curiosity.

One of the ways I've managed to save money is that I never got divorced. A lot of wrestlers' marriages don't survive, and boy, talk about a way to slash your nest egg right in half!

I've always been proud of the fact that Debra and I have managed to stay together and in love for nearly 30 years now, in a business that eats up a lot of relationships. Not a lot of my friends have managed to pull that off. Ted DiBiase hung onto his wife, Roddy Piper and his wife have stayed together, and even Jerry Sags and his wife, Lara, have stayed together for all those years, and I think that's a pretty special thing.

A lot of times, problems arise because a guy will have a one-night stand in a strange city somewhere, with a woman he'll never see again. All those admiring female fans can be a temptation. I know it seems like kind of a double-standard, but the affairs that usually end the marriages are the ones carried on by the wives. A lot of men and women look at relationships differently. Some guys can have one-night stands, but a woman will often really start to care about the guy who's always around while her husband's on the road. And, of course, the opportunistic guy is there telling the wife, "Hey, your husband's out there banging away, but I love you, and I'm the one right here with you."

I've seen a lot of relationships come and go, and I've watched a lot of friends try to deal with broken hearts, and one thing's for sure—a jealous relationship will never work. You've got to have trust, or you're doomed.

A girl I lived with before Debra was paranoid. We lived near Alexandria, about two hours from New Orleans. I'd make it in an hour and 45 minutes, and she'd be screaming that I must have been out, screwing around. I knew that wasn't gonna work out.

And a lot of guys just ask for trouble. They get married three or four times. They get married too young, or too quick.

One thing I love about my life now is that I can pick my shots, instead of always being on the road, and I love being home for Debra and the girls. I still do my share of air travel, but in my life as a wrestler, I've managed to rack up more than 2 million miles on Delta Airlines alone. Thanks to the airlines' frequent-flier programs, I've been able to keep track of my miles in the air, and if you add up all my totals from the different airlines, it's more than 6 million lifetime miles—and this is from a guy who had never flown before his college recruitment trips.

I'm a lot luckier than a lot of guys in wrestling, because I was eligible for membership in the NFL's retired players' association, which gives me (among other things) health coverage, which most wrestlers don't have. It started for me in the early 2000s when I was doing some appearances for the Orlando Predators, an indoor football team. The team's co-owner was Mike McBath, a man who has had a big effect on my life and who played with the Buffalo Bills from 1968 to 1972.

Mike and I ended up having dinner a few times, and we hit it off pretty well. After we'd known each other for a little while, he said, "Well, you had something to do with the NFL, didn't you?"

I told him I had played a season with the Falcons but had spent most of that time on injured reserve. He said I should join the players' association; but I said I couldn't because membership required a person play for four years.

"No, no, no," he said. "You have to play for four years to be eligible to receive a pension. But if you got paid for one year by an NFL team, you can join the union."

Turns out, there are a lot of guys in my situation, who only played a year or two, and didn't think they were eligible to join. It was a blessing, because as a wrestler, I'd had problems getting health insurance, but I was able to get it through the retired players' union.

I go to the association's annual meeting each year, and 2011 was the first year in which current players (including big-name guys like Drew Brees and the Manning brothers) were at the convention. At one point, they were discussing the lockout that was then under way, and one of the association people on the mic said, "But before we discuss this further, we want to take a second and recognize one of our members, Hacksaw Jim Duggan, who was recently inducted into the World Wrestling Entertainment Hall of Fame."

I got a standing ovation from these guys, players past and present that I admire and respect, and it really moved me. It was so ironic; as a kid, I'd always admired football players and wanted to be one. Now, at this point in my life, I was honored just to be among these guys. It's not as bad as it used to be, but a lot of people in mainstream athletics have been critical of pro wrestlers and wrestling, looking at us like we were phony athletes. But these guys really appreciated me, and it meant a lot to me.

And being in the players' union means that when I have to get my right knee replaced (which is inevitable, I think), the NFL will take care of it.

It'll never happen, but an association is one thing I think would be good for wrestling, or at least for the wrestlers. It wouldn't hurt Vince McMahon; all he'd have to do is set a little aside, to match retirement fund contributions, just something to help the guys out a little bit. It's a publicly traded company, so it's not like it's coming out of his own pocket. But like with everything else, what the WWE does is up to Vince, and guys know when they sign up what they're getting into.

In the summer of 2011, I attended a meeting of the players' association, and I had people asking me, "You *still* wrestle?"

I do still enjoy appearing on the independent circuit, even if I can't do everything I used to do. Other guys will come up and ask me, "So, Hacksaw, how's the ring?"

I just shrug and say, "Well, my feet don't hurt."

These days, that's the only part of my body that's touching the ring!

Like I said before, a lot of the young guys working independents are green, but hell, I used to be green. Every now and then, one of them will ask me something like, "Mr. Duggan, sir, are we on TV tonight?"

"Geez, kid," I say, "I hope not. Just try to relax out there, son."

"But it's a really big crowd! There's gotta be like 200 to 300 people out there!"

I'm thinking, *God help me. Where's my 2x4 when I need it?*

Given my physical limitations, both from 32 years of physical abuse in the ring and from the loss of a kidney, I tell the kids I work with that they should think of our matches like an episode of *Dancing with the Stars*. You're gonna have to dance around me, but if you do and you listen to me, we can put on a hell of a show. We'll have the place rockin'.

And I do still love being in the ring. I love performing. The people at these little indie shows seem to have fun, and I'd like to think part of that is because they can see I'm legitimately having a good time myself.

In 2011, I worked on one of the wildest independent shows I've ever seen. This two-man rap outfit called Insane Clown Posse, who did some stuff with both the WWF and WCW in the late 1990s, puts on an annual outdoor event for their fans, with concerts, food, drinks, and wrestling matches. In a word, this was, well, insane.

They had my old friend and Georgia booker Buck Robley booking their show, and Buck called to see if I'd be interested in working the show. I said I was, and he asked me if I'd be interested in a match against Matt Borne.

Borne trying to kick my head off in White Plains a year earlier was still a sore spot for me, but I said, "Buck—I'm 57 years old, I got two kids, and these days, I get hurt getting off the couch. And it's a no-win situation; if I win, I beat up Matt Borne—big deal. If *he* wins, he beat up Hacksaw Jim Duggan, and it's the biggest thing that's ever happened to him. If you guys want me to wrestle him in a shoot, I'll do it, but we're gonna have to negotiate another price. If you want a shoot match, you're gonna have to train me for a shoot match and pay me a shoot fee!"

Buck kind of grunted softly and said, "Aw, never mind."

Instead, I was one of 10 guys in a battle royal, where the idea was to put guys from different eras into a "battle of the generations."

When I first arrived, I thought I was going to be in a fight before I even reached the building. I was walking from my car, when I saw this stocky, bearded guy with longish hair. He yelled, "Hey, Hacksaw!"

I thought, *Oh, man, it's Borne—we're about to go, right now!*

I dropped my bags and got my hands up, when I heard him yell, "Whoa, Hacksaw, what's going on?"

It was Nick Dinsmore, who'd been my tag partner in WWE in 2005, when he was "Eugene." He was just walking up to say hi, being friendly, and here I was, ready to clean the poor guy's clock!

I actually got to see a lot of familiar faces at that show, like Tito Santana, whom I'd first met in Southwest Wrestling nearly 30 years before. Tito had always been a true gentleman, and I think that reflects in his family, which has been very stable. His sons didn't go into wrestling, but they found their own way and have both been very successful, and I think that's a testament to the quality of their dad's character.

Most indie shows are a lot smaller than those Insane Clown Posse events. It's funny to see things come full circle, because I started off working in high school gyms and National Guard armories, and now, my bread and butter is in high school gyms and National Guard armories. And it's a different feeling than WWE. WWE is a spectacle; it's like Barnum & Bailey. It doesn't matter who's on the card—WWE is coming to town, and it's a show you have to see, because it's a package of entertainment. A lot of times, WWE announces a show without even announcing one wrestler who's going to be there, and it succeeds anyway.

But on independent shows, one name can make a difference. And I enjoy it because, first, I truly enjoy interacting with the fans. I get a chance to thank them for being a part of my life for 32 years. And second, the people going to independent wrestling shows are often the most loyal fans of all. These people really love the guys, and they'll come out to see us, because a lot of them grew up with us.

I do admit that one thing I see more and more is starting to bug me. I'm starting to get old guys coming up to me at shows and saying, "Hacksaw! I been watching you since I was a kid!"

Sometimes as I look at them, I want to say, "Been a rough few years, huh, buddy?"

But seriously, I enjoy the fan interaction, and I enjoy working with the next generation of wrestlers. As much as I complain about some of them in the ring, you want to talk about people who truly love wrestling? These are your guys.

When I go to these shows, I get questions from a lot of the young guys, and I try to pass on what I can, just as guys like Bruiser Brody and Gino Hernandez tried to pass on some knowledge to me when I was starting out. These are people who either have 9-to-5 jobs or are trying to find jobs, but they still go out and wrestle at night and on weekends, because most of them will never have the opportunity to go any farther than the indie circuit. If you're reading this and want to be a wrestler, I'll tell you what I tell the young indie guys when they ask my advice: Chase your dreams, but realize it's a numbers game, and right now, there ain't a whole lot of guys making a living in this business. This year, there are 1,500 NFL football players. There are 500 NBA basketball players. In WWE, there are only 120 wrestlers under contract. It's a television show, and it's more competitive for each spot than any sport. It would be like trying to get on *CSI* or *Law & Order: SVU*. It's an extremely competitive business.

And people lose sight of that, because all they see is that it's a work, or fixed, or whatever term you want to use. It's still an incredibly competitive business, and if you want one of those 120 spots, you gotta take my job, or another guy's job, to get it. And I'm not going to just roll over and give up my job that easy, and none of the guys on *Raw* or *SmackDown* is going to give them up, either.

Once, a guy brought his young son to my table at an indie show for an autograph. He told me his son wanted to grow up to become a wrestler and asked me what I thought.

"Well," I said, "get him some golf clubs. That's where the real money's at. And it's a lot easier on the body!"

I stay involved in the community, too. In Lugoff, South Carolina, where Debra and I live now, I talk to kids in schools and do charity appearances. It's just something I think is important to do.

I went to my daughters' high school, Lugoff Elgin High School, the day of the big game with their rival school, Camden High, in 2011. That day, the kids got two speakers: Jim and Hacksaw.

First, Jim stood up and told the kids, "I still remember my high school football days, and you guys will always remember this time in your lives. Play hard, play well!"

I sat down, but then Hacksaw shot right back up and said, "Now just wait a minute, Coach! I gotta tell these boys what it's really all about!"

I tore off my shirt and got louder and louder, more pumped up as I went: "Camden is coming into your house! To kick your ass! What are you gonna do?"

The coach was standing there wondering what kind of madman he'd gotten involved with, but the kids were picking up my energy, and they were all on their feet, chest-bumping and getting worked up.

I kept going on: "Are you gonna beat 'em?!"

"Yes! *Yes!*"

"I can't hear you! Are you going to beat 'em?!"

Every kid in the room, at the top of his lungs, answered back, "Yes!"

Of course, whether I'm Jim or Hacksaw, to my daughters, I'm just Dad, so when Celia and Rebecca heard about it, they gave me an embarrassed "Aw, geez, Dad," like any teenager would.

But hey—it worked. They beat Camden 21–7.

CHAPTER 22

HALL(S) OF FAME

IT TRULY MEANS A LOT TO ME that enough people remember Hacksaw Jim Duggan that they've released five different action figures of me over the past 20-plus years. And, yeah, I do sometimes still have to tell the nice folks, "They're not dolls—they're action figures." But even I have a hard time getting that out, because I flash back to when the first ones came out. I'd be in my daughters' rooms, and there would be a miniature little tea party set up, with four Barbies and a Hacksaw.

In 2009, I even got to relive one of my professional highlights, if only for a few minutes, when WWE invited me to be one of the mystery entrants in the Royal Rumble. This time, I was the 29th wrestler to enter the ring, and even though I was already excited just to be back on the show, the loud pop I got from the crowd really amped up my excitement. Looking back, I'm even prouder of the respect the guys in the ring showed me—I couldn't have asked for more of a class act.

I know it sounds corny, but hearing that crowd cheer and chant for me is my lifeblood. And the 2009 Rumble crowd was really going strong. I used to jump in the ring, but these days, I roll in, so I rolled in and got to my feet to find myself face to face with The Undertaker. *Boom!* I hit him. *Boom!* I hit him. *Boom!* I hit him.

Undertaker said, "Give me the big one, Hack!"

I wound up and hit him, and he went down like he'd been shot! Everyone else in the match looked my way...and then Kane came over.

Boom! He went down. HHH came over.

Boom! He went down.

Every single one of those guys fed me, and it really meant a lot to me that these big stars would give an old-timer like me a chance to shine.

Finally, here came my old friend Paul Wight—WCW's The Giant, now wrestling as The Big Show. By now, I was sucking wind from all the brawling in the ring. I landed some hits on him, and he did the Kamala-patented weeble-wobble. Finally, he casually tossed me over the ropes as he yelled, "Get the hell outta here!"

I headed down the aisle, and as soon as I got through the curtain to the backstage area, I saw Vince McMahon looking at me. He was sitting at his table where he produced the show while wearing headphones to communicate with the announcers. He said, "Jim, come here."

I walked over to him.

"That was a hell of a sign of respect those guys showed you tonight," he said.

"Yes, sir, I realize that," I said.

Later that night, I came across Undertaker and said, "Hey, man, I just wanted to say thanks for taking that bump for me. You set off a chain reaction with all those guys."

He said, "Hey—nothing's too good for 'Devil Hair'!"

I kept making occasional appearances for WWE, and then I got a call in 2010 from John Laurinaitis, who had replaced Jim Ross a few years earlier as WWE's talent-relations guy. He said, "Jim, I don't want to take up too much of your time, but I just wanted to let you know we're going to induct you into our Hall of Fame this year, if you'd be interested."

Every year for nearly a decade, WWE had done a Hall of Fame induction during WrestleMania weekend. I know some people have some issues with who's in and who's not, and I know a lot of people in wrestling are jaded about everything in the business. Still, I don't care what anyone says, it's a very big deal, and I think anyone who's been a part of it will say so, if they're being honest. Guys who say it doesn't matter are either lying to you or they're lying to themselves.

I can tell you, it meant a lot to me. The way I see it, wrestling history is not as well kept as history in other sports, and WWE at least makes an effort to recognize people who have devoted years to the business and have made a real contribution to its success.

At indie shows and public appearances for the past couple of years, I'd had fans coming up to me and asking, "When are they gonna put you in the Hall of Fame?"

That tells me that it means something to a lot of fans, too. It also tells you something that the induction ceremony has attracted live crowds of 10,000-plus the last few years. In the past, they used to do it at much smaller banquet halls, like the one Harley and I had brawled through during the 1987 Slammys.

WWE asked me to send some memorabilia for their display; a lot of times at the pay-per-views, they'll set up big Hall of Fame exhibits that fans can visit. And the company told me they were discussing creating a permanent display, possibly at the corporate headquarters in Connecticut. The other idea was to add a trailer to the traveling caravan of rings and TV equipment, and make the Hall of Fame a permanently traveling attraction that would accompany every TV taping. Either way, I'm all for letting the fans see some of the amazing stuff they've accumulated.

The company asked me for robes, but I never used any, aside from my brief stint as king (and that king's cape is long gone). Boots? I only had one pair, and I was still using them.

"I do have some old kneepads I can send!"

Debra ended up sending them some old 2x4s and a couple of the flags I'd carried to the ring on one occasion or another. The UPS guy was like, "What the hell? Is this *lumber*?"

Believe it or not, that's not the only hall of fame I'm in. I'm also in the Glens Falls High School Hall of Fame, thanks to my high school football career. WWE even sent me up there for that event, which I thought was really nice of them, because the company doesn't get a lot of publicity out of doing that kind of thing.

The Glens Falls folks gave me a red jacket with the "Indians" logo on it, which could be a historical artifact, because sports teams with names like "Indians" are becoming rarer and rarer. It's a shame, I think, because even though I understand where they're coming from, the folks who are against the name seem to miss the point that the schools are *honoring* their namesakes. You don't name your team after something you want to insult; you ever hear of a school calling its own team "The Fightin' Morons?"

I even got recognized in New York's Division II Hall of Fame for high school players; I wasn't able to attend that one event, but it's still nice to be appreciated.

Like my 2009 Royal Rumble appearance, the WWE Hall of Fame was almost like "Hacksaw Duggan, This Is Your Life," as I saw dozens of guys that weekend whom I'd known professionally over my 30-plus year career, including some I hadn't seen in years. Some others were guys I'd seen mature in the business over time, like Shawn Michaels. I first met him in 1984, when I was on top in Mid-South and he was just breaking in, having been trained by Mexican star Jose "Supersock" Lothario. I got to see him as half of a Rock & Roll Express–influenced tag team, The Rockers, in the WWF of the late 1980s and early 1990s. And when I was winding down my first WWF stint in 1993, he was on his way up as a heel.

While I always had a lot of respect for his ability in the ring, Shawn was not exactly one of my favorite people, for several years. The last few times I've worked with WWE, from 2005 on, I've noticed he's grown up a lot, and I think he'd be the first to admit he wasn't always the easiest guy to get along with in the 1980s and especially the 1990s.

In Shawn's defense, he has often attracted heat through no real fault of his own, unless you want to blame him for being a good-looking guy. Whenever Shawn walked into a bar, he was a chick magnet—nearly every woman in the place would go over to him, and every guy in the bar would be pissed off at him. Shawn has had his share of sucker punches landed on him, and he's been attacked more than once by jealous idiots who nailed him from behind. That's definitely not fair to Shawn; if you and your lady are at a bar, and she starts chatting up some other guy, don't blame that other guy—that's the girl's fault.

I was never like that. If I was out somewhere with Debra and some guy tried hitting on her, I was never worried, because I have always been able to trust her, and I also know she's a big girl who can take care of herself. Now, if somebody is coming on too strong and crossing the line (like putting their hands on her), that's a different story. If she gives me the sign, I'll get involved, but that's out of me wanting to protect her, not jealousy because she's talking to a handsome guy.

And one more thing about Shawn Michaels—I respect the way he was able to keep himself relevant. I always used to joke with my good friends Ricky Morton and Robert Gibson, "I actually kind of feel sorry for you guys. You may be the pretty boys now, but in 20 years, that's gonna be a tough sell. In 20 years, I'm still gonna be the same big, hairy guy that people love now!"

But even though he started out in one of those pretty-boy tag teams, Shawn kept himself going through the strength of his work, and he emphasized the pretty boy stuff less and less over time. Today, he's not remembered as a pretty boy; he's remembered as a guy who went out there and busted his ass to put on a hell of a match. And even though we were never buddies, I was proud to be part of the same WWE Hall of Fame class as Shawn.

I was even prouder of the reception I got from the crowd in Atlanta the night before WrestleMania XXVII. I was a little nervous beforehand; even though I was used to speaking in public, speaking from the heart about what this business has meant to me, not just to Hacksaw, but to Jim Duggan, was not something I got to do very often.

Apparently, though, my speech went over pretty well. One of the TV people there from one of the networks came up to me after it was over and told me, "Wow, Hacksaw, that was great! I didn't know you had that in you!"

WWE suggested that Ted DiBiase, my good friend and most frequent (and favorite) opponent, and certainly the guy I had the best matches with, induct me. I couldn't have made a better choice.

EPILOGUE

I KNOW A LOT OF WRESTLERS FROM MY GENERATION ARE BITTER about how things turned out for them, but I am nothing but grateful for my 30-plus years in wrestling. It's because of wrestling and knowing Jay Youngblood that I met Debra, the love of my life, and wrestling has allowed me to make a good living for my family.

There is a segment of fans, a few folks who really get into it and read newsletters and watch videos from all over the world, and to some of them, my style's not something they appreciate. No hard feelings—different strokes for different folks. Besides, trust me, none of those folks are harder on me than I am. I can't even watch my own matches or interviews, because I'm my own worst critic. I'll sit there and go, "I can't believe I did that! Aw, that was horrible! Geez!"

But I also know that a lot of people have gotten a lot of excitement, and maybe even joy, from watching me do my thing, and that's all I ever wanted. And nothing makes my day like hearing from fans at an independent show that I made them feel better, or how something I was involved with in the ring helped give them courage to deal with something in their own life.

In 2010, my friend Howard Finkel, himself a WWE Hall of Famer and maybe the best ring announcer of all time, sent me a video of my 1980 WWWF debut, as "Big" Jim Duggan. In a way, it was painful to watch, because I was pretty bad. But it was also fun to see, because I thought about all the things I'd learned since then, and all those experiences along the way.

Could I have made some better decisions? Sure. Do I think promoters failed to use me to my fullest potential at times? You bet. How does that song go? "Regrets, I have a few..."

But I made a very good living for myself and my family, saw the world (damn near the *entire* world), made a few lifetime friends, and got to entertain millions of people. I couldn't ask for anything more.

So, to all of you "Hacksaw" fans who made it possible for me to stay on this wild ride, I can only say thank you. To everyone who bought a ticket or a pay-per-view to see me, thank you. To everyone who bought this book, thank you.

I hope I gave you your money's worth; if you had even one-tenth as much fun as I did, then it was worth it. And now, one last time, let's all do it together:

"HO-OH!"

Growing up in Glens Falls, New York, I was a straight-arrow kid who was in love with the game of football.

Big kid that I was, I knew that playing offensive line might help me get a college scholarship...

...and being a double threat in wrestling didn't hurt, either. I eventually enrolled at Southern Methodist University.

Some of the fan magazines and newsletters of the day didn't always appreciate my wrestling style, but Bill Watts and Vince McMahon put me on my fair share of covers over the years.

Here I am with the legendary Dick Murdoch. Dick was my opponent in my first match in Mid-South back in 1982.

Steve "Dr. Death" Williams was a great friend of mine and one of the toughest guys in the history of the business.

"King" Duggan, actor Randy Quaid, and The Rockers, aka Marty Jannetty and Shawn Michaels. Shawn would go on to become one of wrestling's all-time greatest performers.

I had more than a few gimmicks over the years, including "Wildman" Duggan (top), a member of Team Canada (middle), and the janitor of WCW.

My father, James Edward Duggan Sr., was a police officer for 44 years and I would not be the man I am today if it wasn't for him. Here we are with another major figure in my life, Vince McMahon.

Here I am with my dad and my sisters, Sheila, Angel, and Mary Ann.

I am so lucky to share my life with three wonderful ladies: my daughters, Rebecca and Celia, and my wife, Debra.

One of the proudest moments in my wrestling career: the night I was inducted into the WWE's Hall of Fame in 2011.

Growing up in Glens Falls, New York, I was a straight-arrow kid who was in love with the game of football.

Big kid that I was, I knew that playing offensive line might help me get a college scholarship...

...and being a double threat in wrestling didn't hurt, either. I eventually enrolled at Southern Methodist University.

Some of the fan magazines and newsletters of the day didn't always appreciate my wrestling style, but Bill Watts and Vince McMahon put me on my fair share of covers over the years.

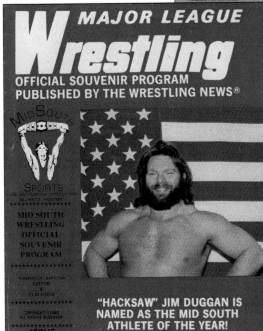

Here I am with the legendary Dick Murdoch. Dick was my opponent in my first match in Mid-South back in 1982.

Steve "Dr. Death" Williams was a great friend of mine and one of the toughest guys in the history of the business.

"King" Duggan, actor Randy Quaid, and The Rockers, aka Marty Jannetty and Shawn Michaels. Shawn would go on to become one of wrestling's all-time greatest performers.

I had more than a few gimmicks over the years, including "Wildman" Duggan (top), a member of Team Canada (middle), and the janitor of WCW.

My father, James Edward Duggan Sr., was a police officer for 44 years and I would not be the man I am today if it wasn't for him. Here we are with another major figure in my life, Vince McMahon.

Here I am with my dad and my sisters, Sheila, Angel, and Mary Ann.

I am so lucky to share my life with three wonderful ladies: my daughters, Rebecca and Celia, and my wife, Debra.

One of the proudest moments in my wrestling career: the night I was inducted into the WWE's Hall of Fame in 2011.